CW01648668

Looking for Marshall McLuhan in Afghanistan

Text and iPhone Hipstamatic Photography by Rita Leistner

intellect Bristol, UK / Chicago, USA

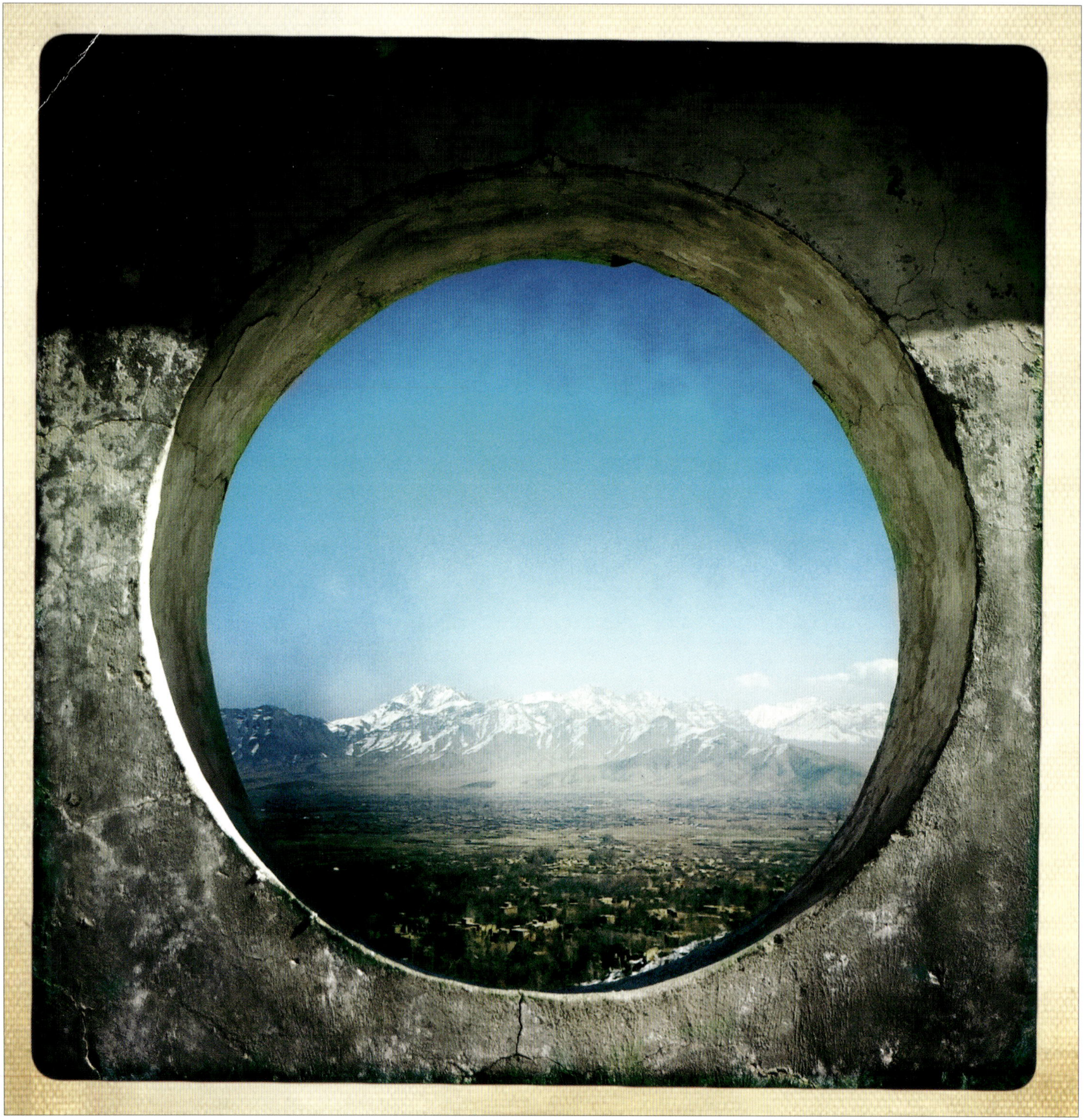

To my dad

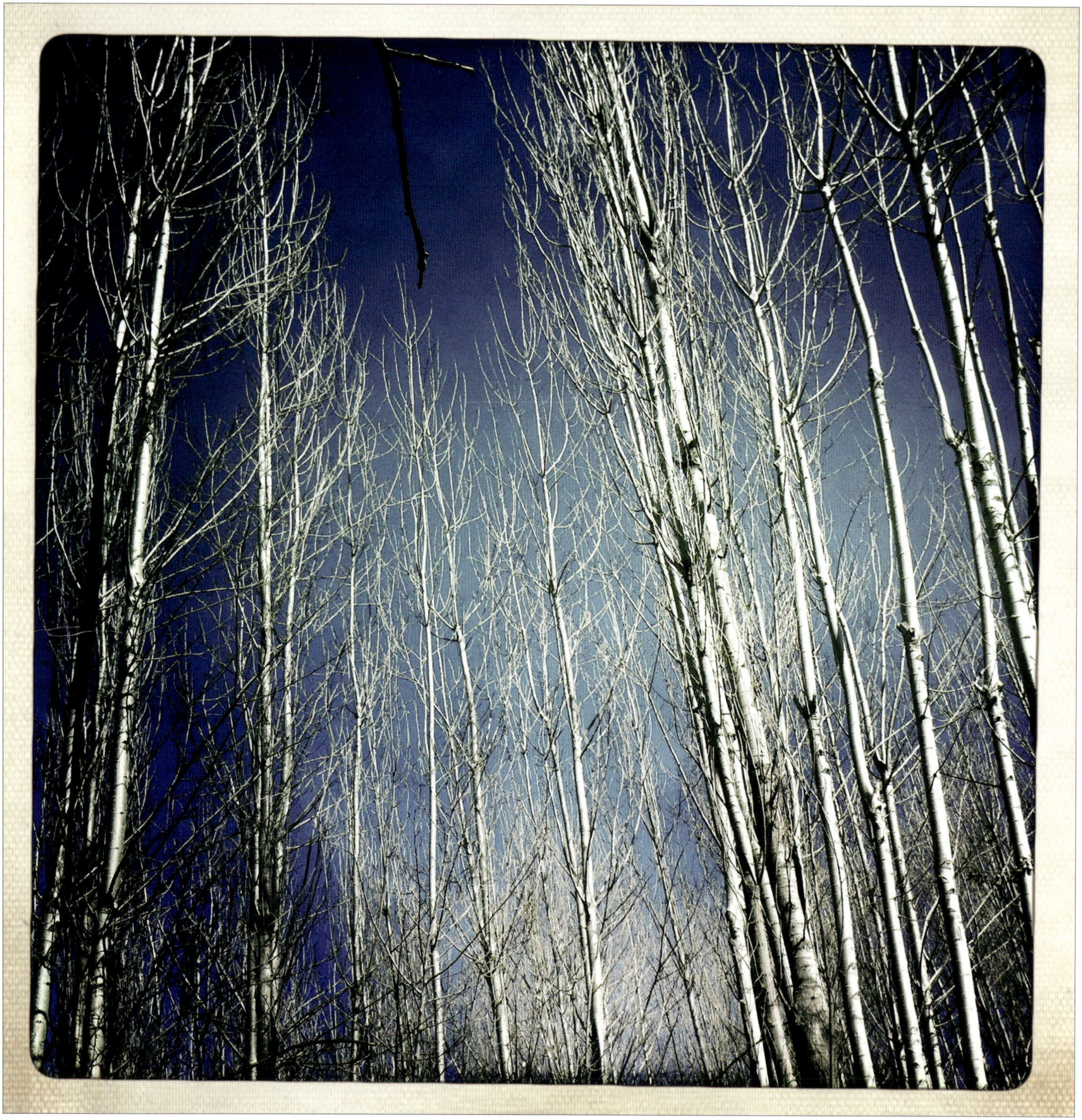

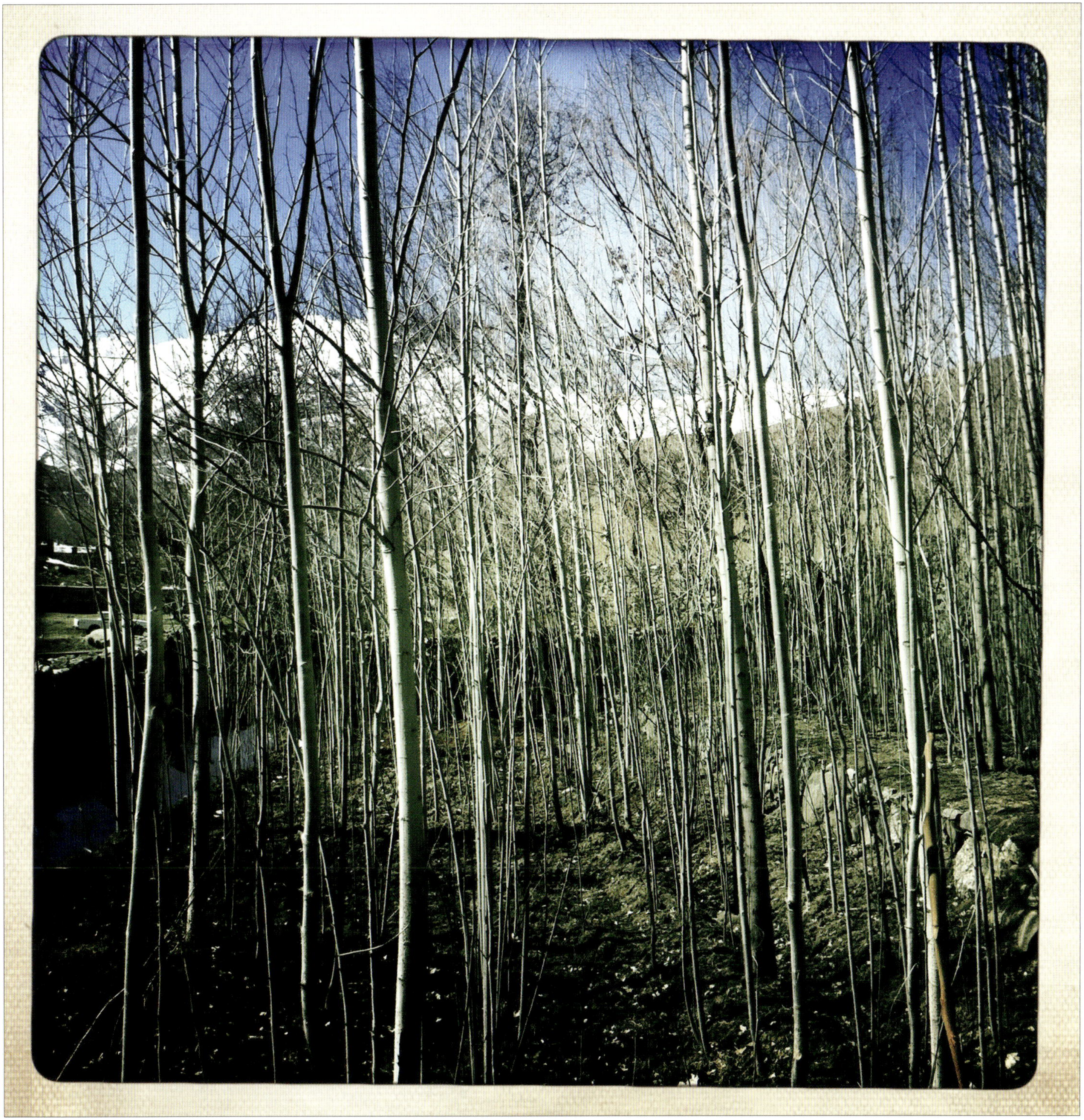

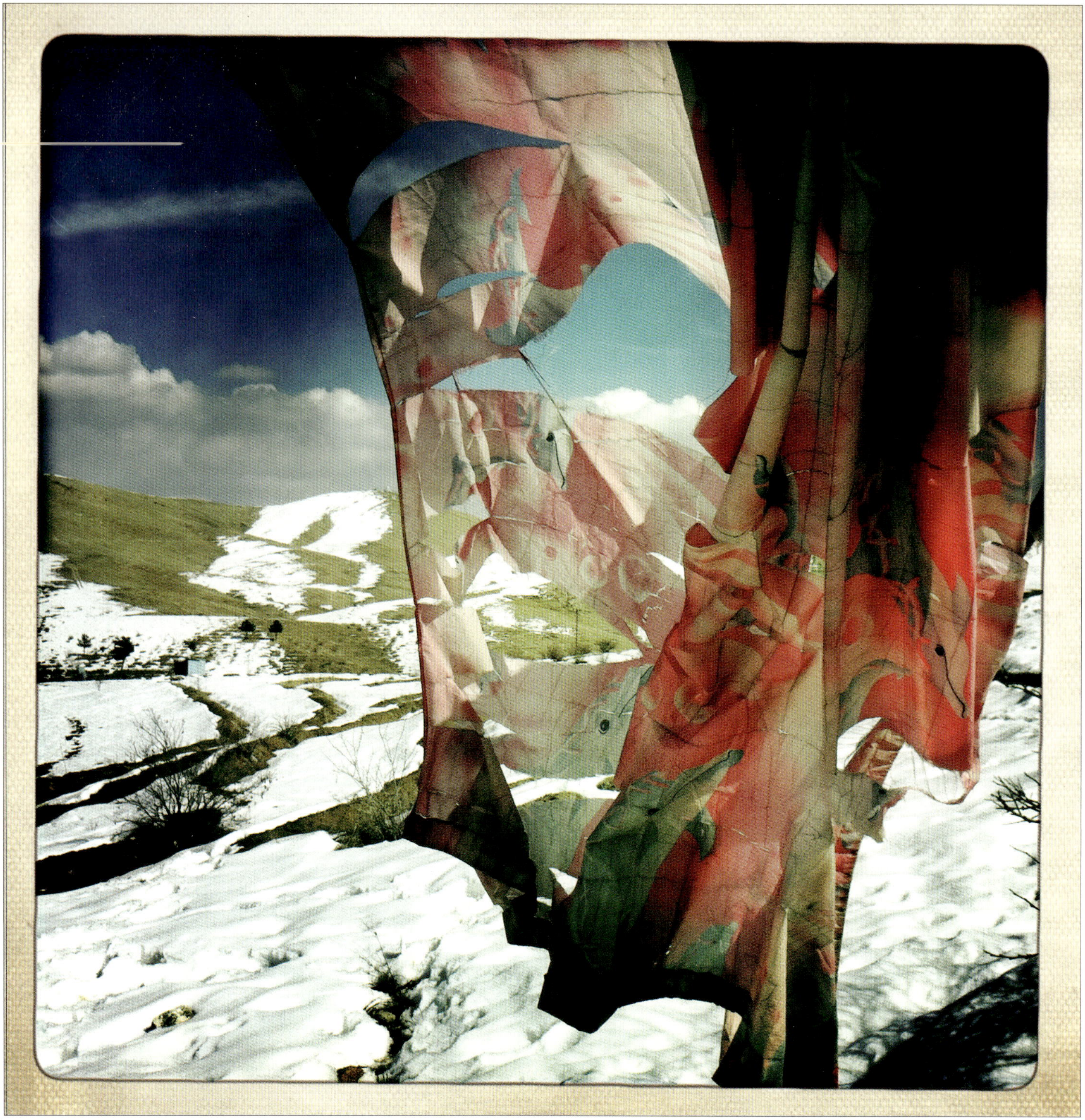

Foreword:
Hipstamatic Blues
by Julian Stallabrass

Designed by
Jenny Armour
and Rita Leistner

With drawings by
Jason Logan

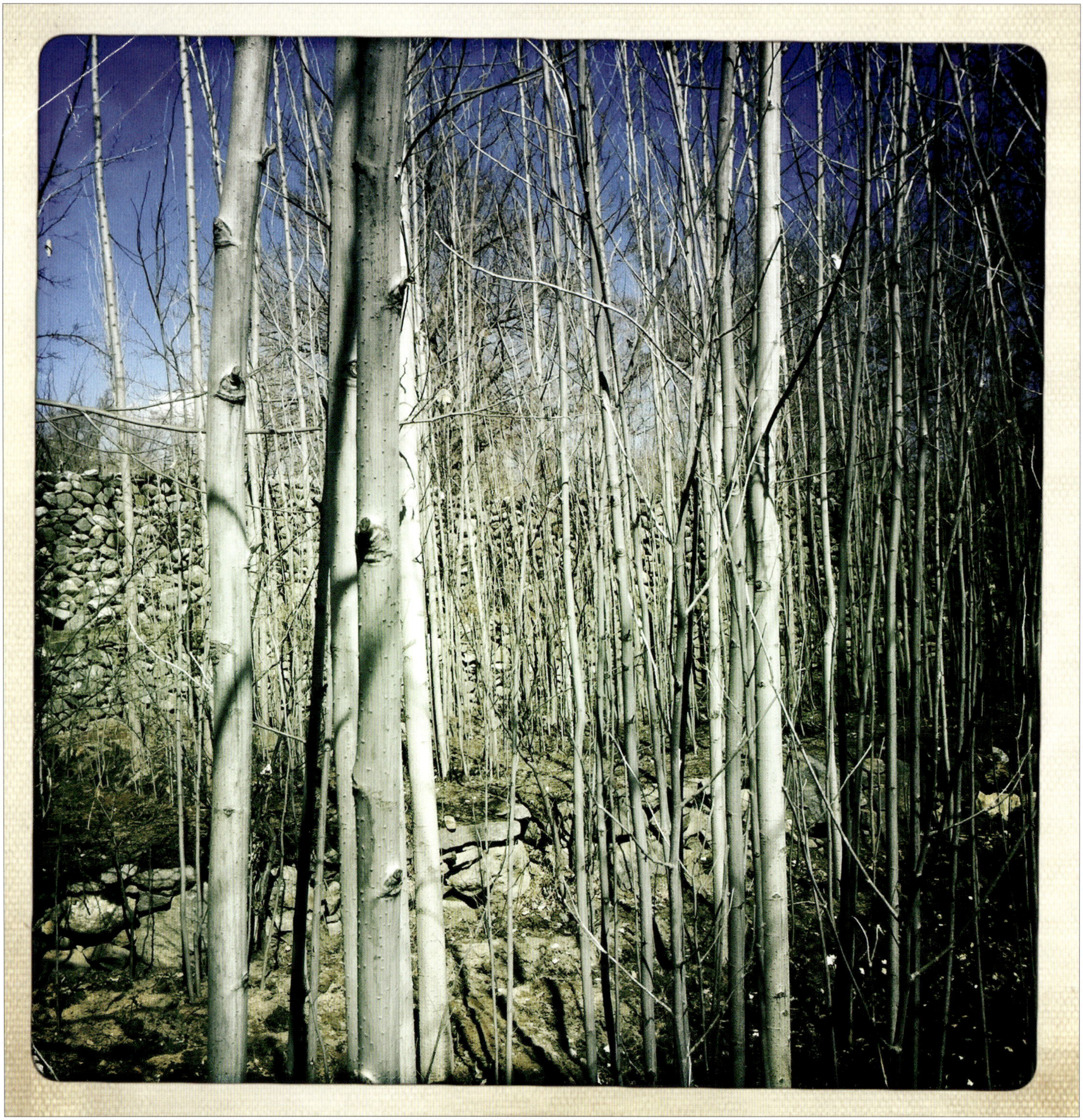

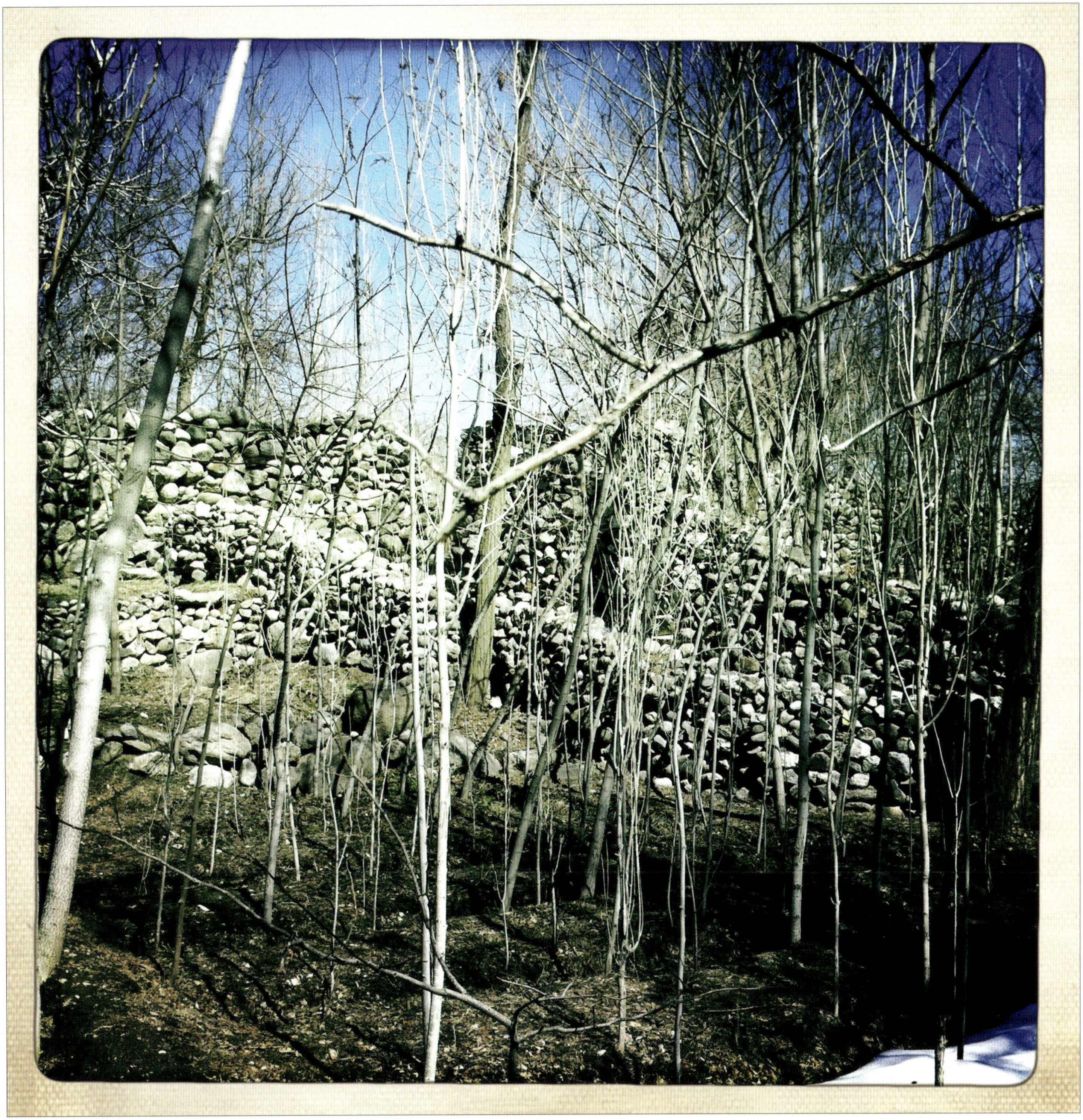

First published in the UK in 2013 by
Intellect, The Mill, Parnall Road, Fishponds, Bristol, BS16 3JG, UK

First published in the USA in 2013 by
Intellect, The University of Chicago Press, 1427 E. 60th Street,
Chicago, IL 60637, USA

A catalogue record for this book is available from the British Library.

Design: Jenny Armour and Rita Leistner
Art Direction: Rita Leistner
Copy-editors: Diana Kuprel, Alastair Cheng, Lin Stranberg and Emma Rhys
Production Manager: May Yao

Print ISBN: 978-1-78320-030-6
ePDF ISBN: 978-1-78320-073-3
ePub ISBN: 978-1-78320-074-0

Printed and bound by Gwasg Gomer Cyf / Gomer Press Ltd, UK

Table of Contents

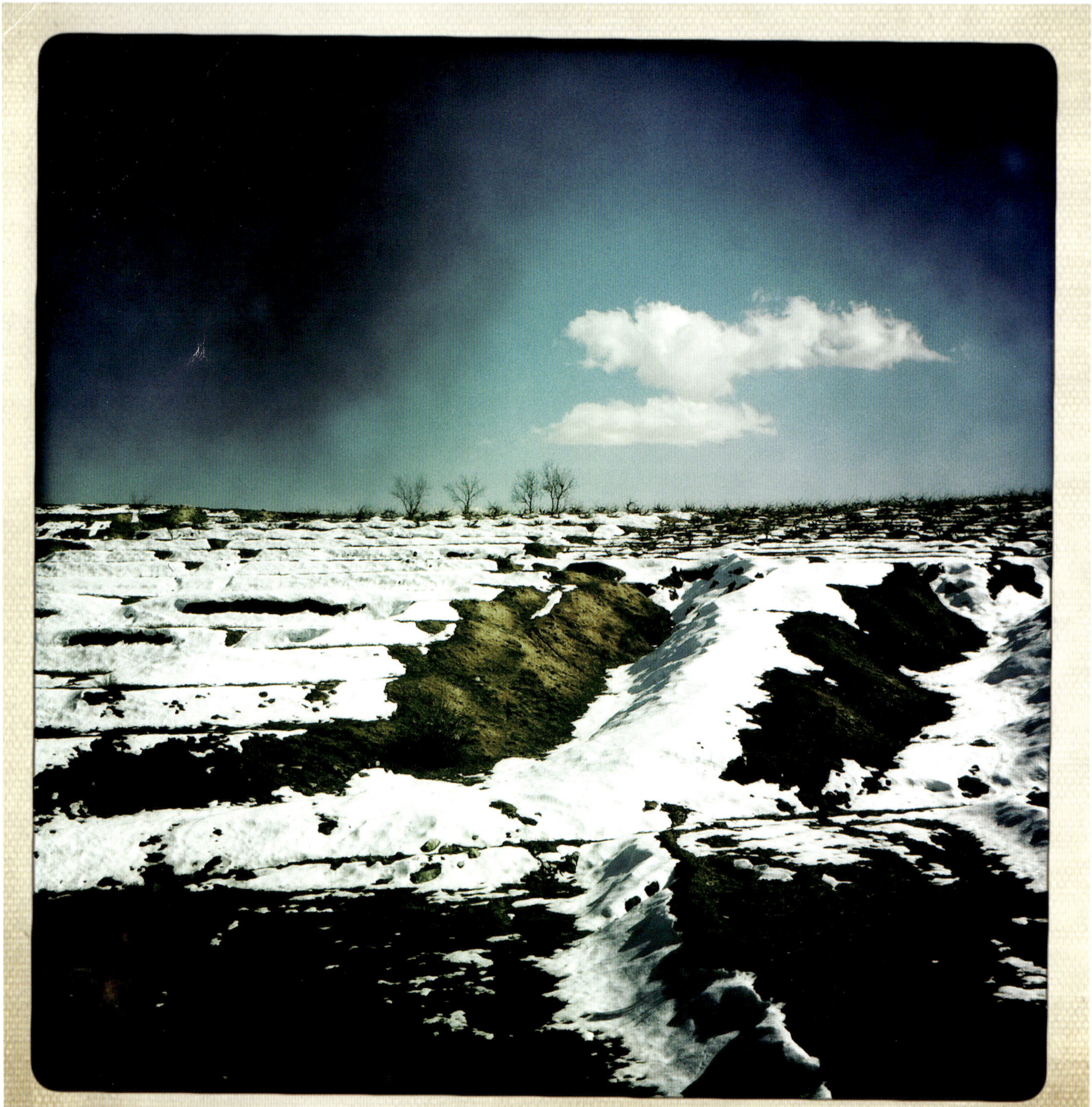

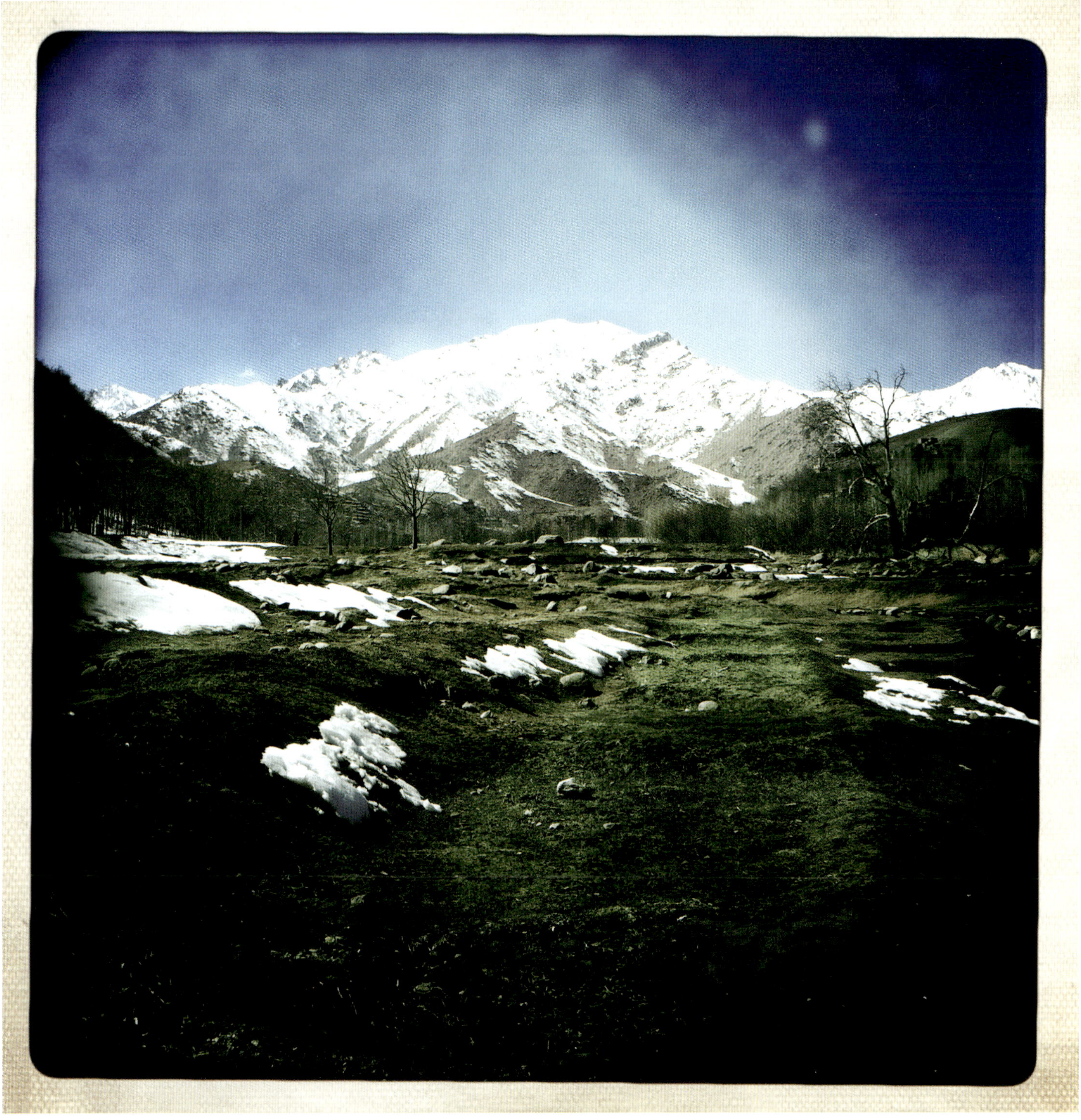

Foreword_Hipstamatic Blues by Julian Stallabrass

McLuhanite books are usually hard to read—and this one is no exception. Rather than let regimented ranks of type parade down the page, every attempt is made to seize readers, stop their conventional thought in its tracks, and insist: attend to the medium! Look at the font, the paper, the gaps between the words! Then, hopefully, the book will engage more than just sight and its dreary consort, linear thought, and open readers to a richer, synaesthesia experience, and to the organic, integral mental processes of the pre-literate. Or, given that this remains a book, at least a little. Perhaps, like monks reading illuminated manuscripts (in McLuhan's imagination), as you turn the pages, you should mutter the words.

Should McLuhanite photographs also be hard to read? You would think so. The same bias against the supremacy of vision should also bite here, and McLuhan does claim that photographs turn people into things.[1] Yet, on the face of it, Rita Leistner's photographs are highly recognizable, displaying a series of eerie familiarities. Taken on the iPhone using the Hipstamatic app, they seem at once old and new. The app provides a caricatured simulation of the (retrospectively) charming faults of analogue photography, particularly of the way film and prints age. It, too, says: attend to the medium, though it adds: here is the post-medium universal simulator, pretending to be an antique and particular analogue medium. Now that every option is available to you, express yourself by choosing your limitation from a menu.

In 2010, Simon Norfolk took a view camera to Afghanistan and worked in the footsteps of photographer John Burke making current versions of his imperial topography and anthropological portraits. This temporal span, of the new as old, encompassed a history in which the British Army, once again in Afghanistan, 130 years on, still attempt to impose order on its (largely pre-literate) people, to enduring geopolitical purpose. Norfolk's old and new media pointed to the long constancy of imperial domination.

Leistner's pictures do not appear to be quite that old, despite the distance she often takes from her subjects, which suggest the formality and shallow depth-of-field of the view camera. With their square format, simulated lens faults, mottling and rounded edges with borders, they evoke 1960s and 1970s Polaroid; snapshots made perhaps by U.S. soldiers in Vietnam. In a McLuhanite fantasy realized, Hipstamatic effects can be applied arbitrarily to any subject matter. Refugees in the shanty towns of Kabul taken with a rosy 'Susie' lens and 'Dylan' film (described as being 'left out in the sun too long')? Nothing to stop you ... But this is not what Leistner does. Instead, here are the Marines again, in their fortified bases, posing with guns, exercising, training, resting. As in Vietnam, they are the 'front line' in a war without fronts; the fragile, fleshy skin of a massive, networked, remote-controlled war machine; disposable men acting as a lure designed to draw the enemy into the sights of the gunships and the bombers. The photographs that they take, these occupying forces amid a largely hostile population—of themselves, of the camps, of tourist sites, of corpses, of torture and mutilation (very useful, Polaroid, for keeping such things from outsiders), have not changed much.

Leistner departs from these genres by dwelling on apparently mundane aspects of the military environment, and the surroundings that it affects, which point to the structural roots of the conflict. The use of sandbags, large and small, as temporary fortifications; the way in which fuel is stored and distributed; the home-made IED; the view from behind the bulletproof screen; and the landscape itself, as if created with resistance in mind. Her text also points to the many factors of the conflict that she cannot photograph: the opposition, the role of drug trafficking and drone warfare.

Why, in these circumstances, revive that closet God-botherer, McLuhan, with his belief that new media would deliver humanity to a realm of village-like, synaesthetic, universal bliss?[2] The very presence of the Marines in Afghanistan, an extreme and violent culture clash, would seem to refute him. It is often said of McLuhan that he anticipated global networked culture, and it is partly on those grounds that his work has attracted renewed attention.[3] There is something deeply comforting in the idea that networked culture will produce, in and of itself, a universal humanism. You might even point to the many recent revolts against authority, particularly against dictatorial powers, and the way activists have communicated and shared tactics, as a symptom of evolving global humanism.

Yet Leistner's book also points to the obstacles, both trivial and grave, to the realization of such a vision: the project for which she worked, meant to connect troops to their families through social media, ran into the micro-management mentality of the military bureaucracy, and was eventually cancelled. Drones—invisible from the ground, and avoiding the usual circuits through which the news media operate—launch missiles to blow up people who have no access to social media. It is hard to imagine the U.S. government exploding a bomb in a mall in Bristol or Vancouver because they suspected that terrorists were shopping there. But if the communities are exclusively of poor, brown-skinned people without access to cameras or phones, then slaughtering anyone in the vicinity of the suspects is just fine. The victims of remote warfare may not be the products of networked society, but the operators surely are. Raised from birth within the networked environment, they guide the drones and launch the Hellfire missiles; and of those, and the vast number of computer-literate armed forces operatives and private contractors who can see the murderous extent of the 'war on terror', very few have acted on conscience.

Since knowledge is power and wealth, the ideal of the global, digital, universally available library has been replaced with the reality of a massively spied-upon and data-mined individually tailored commercial environment, in which secrets and proprietary information abound. Certainly, one should pay attention to its materiality, its combination of media and its sensory and psychological effects; yet action, purpose and subject matter cannot be downplayed as mere side-effects of media. It matters whether social media are used to fake enthusiasm for a brand (with the use of click farms) or to foment rebellion against arbitrary and violent power.

1. MARSHALL MCLUHAN, *UNDERSTANDING MEDIA: THE EXTENSIONS OF MAN*, LONDON: ROUTLEDGE & KEGAN PAUL, 1964, P. 189.

2. ON MCLUHAN'S CATHOLICISM AND THE WAY IT GUIDED HIS THINKING, SEE JONATHAN MILLER, *MCLUHAN*, LONDON: FONTANA PRESS, 1971.

3. SEE, FOR EXAMPLE, PAUL LEVINSON, *DIGITAL MCLUHAN: A GUIDE TO THE INFORMATION MILLENNIUM*, LONDON: ROUTLEDGE, 1999.

All new technologies bring on the cultural blues, just as the old ones evoke phantom pain after they have disappeared.

(MARSHALL MCLUHAN AND QUENTIN FIORE, *WAR AND PEACE IN THE GLOBAL VILLAGE*) [1]

This book is an artefact of a period in history **when smartphones were coming into contact with war for the first time.**

I arrived home from Afghanistan in March 2011—after being embedded for three weeks as a photojournalist with the United States Marine Corps, 1st Battalion, 8th Marines (1–8), in the remote southern province of Helmand—with an iPhone full of photographs and a bad case of the blues. Walking through the streets of Toronto, I would burst into spontaneous tears. I was happy to be back in the safety and familiarity of the place where I was born,

but my trip to Afghanistan had left me with an **unsettled feeling,** verging on depression.

It had been nearly ten years since the American-led coalition had invaded Afghanistan in October 2001, and the best I'd heard anyone say was that things had not gotten worse. As the first Canadian General in Afghanistan, Lieutenant General (Retired) Andrew Leslie put it at a lecture I attended in Toronto:

"Though it may not offer much solace to the families of the fallen,
we didn't lose.
Sometimes in Afghanistan
you've got to take a
'we didn't lose'
[as being] as good enough
as a 'win.'" (sic)

(CANADIAN LIEUTENANT GENERAL (RETIRED) ANDREW LESLIE
AT A PUBLIC LECTURE HELD BY *THE LIERARY REVIEW OF CANADA*,
DECEMBER 3RD, 2012 IN TORONTO) [2]

And if the Afghans were happy when the Americans (and their coalition) first arrived, the welcome didn't last long. As Kathy Gannon, who has written one of the best books on Afghanistan, noted, "within a year of the Taliban's defeat, the U.S. army, once welcomed as a liberator, was feared by ordinary Afghans." (Kathy Gannon, *I is for Infidel . . . J is for Jihad, K is for Kalashnikov*) [3]

Despite all their superior technology, the Americans and their allies **were not winning over hearts and minds and were not winning the war in Afghanistan.**

Marshall McLuhan
b.1911 in Alberta, Canada

2011 was, incidentally, also the 100th anniversary of the birth of Marshall McLuhan, the charismatic and controversial media theorist, best known for saying,

"THEME
THEME

DIUMIS
SSAGE"

But he also said a lot of other provocative things such as,

"The favourite stance
of literary [western] man
has long been
'to view with alarm'
or 'to point with pride,'
while scrupulously
ignoring what's going on."

(MARSHALL MCLUHAN, *UNDERSTANDING MEDIA: THE EXTENSIONS OF MAN*) [4]

and

**"Every
new technology
necessitates
a new
war."**

(MARSHALL MCLUHAN AND QUENTIN FIORE, *WAR AND PEACE IN THE GLOBAL VILLAGE*) [5]

It was because of the 100th anniversary and its associated cultural events that, one May afternoon in Toronto, I went to see my friend Professor Peter Nesselroth give a talk on McLuhan's applications of the gestalt concepts of Figure and Ground and how they were playing out in the context of the Arab Spring. Peter had been my professor at the Centre for Comparative Literature during my graduate school days in the 1980s at the University of Toronto where, in 1963 (a year before I was born), McLuhan had set up the Centre for Culture and Technology in an old coach house behind St. Michael's College. Today, McLuhan's old office is surrounded by a parking lot off Queen's Park Crescent and I now work around the corner, at U of T's Victoria University teaching courses on the history of photojournalism and documentary photography.

This confluence of events—
the invention of the smartphone,
the war in Afghanistan,
the 100th anniversary of the birth
of Marshall McLuhan

and my participation in a social media embed experiment in Afghanistan called Basetrack, combined with my training in semiotics—laid the groundwork for the *McLuhanesque* probes that follow. To borrow from the title of an essay by one of the world's most renowned semiologists, Umberto Eco,

this book
is an act of
Semiological Guerrilla Warfare.[6]

I went to Afghanistan to embed with United States Marines Corpsand work for

an American **Military-approved** social media experiment called Basetrack

—an international collaboration of designers, writers, researchers and photographers

spearheaded by Teru Kuwayama and funded by the Knight Foundation in the United States.[7]

In keeping with social media conventions, most of the team shot on iPhones. **Basetrack** used the new social media to bring the Marines closer to their people back home. It comprised a live website featuring daily posts of stories and images taken by our iPhone cameras within the perimeters of a U.S. Marines Battalion during its seven-month deployment. There was also (and as of this day continues to be) a Facebook page where the Basetrack Team, families back home and anyone who wanted to join the Facebook page could post comments.

It was a great opportunity for me to go to Afghanistan, and to be part of a cool project that was pushing social media technologies to new extremes.

Before embarking on the trip,
I'd never owned an iPhone;
I'd never even taken a photograph
on a mobile phone;
I'd never used Twitter; and only
reluctantly participated in Facebook

(Facebook still pretty much gives me the creeps, even though I own some stocks in it). I'd be the first to admit I was and still am not well suited to the Fast Art of Social Media.

**In fact,
the very idea
of sending
a tweet
puts a
sick feeling
in my stomach
and makes
me want to
retreat into
a long novel,
say
*War and
Peace*.**

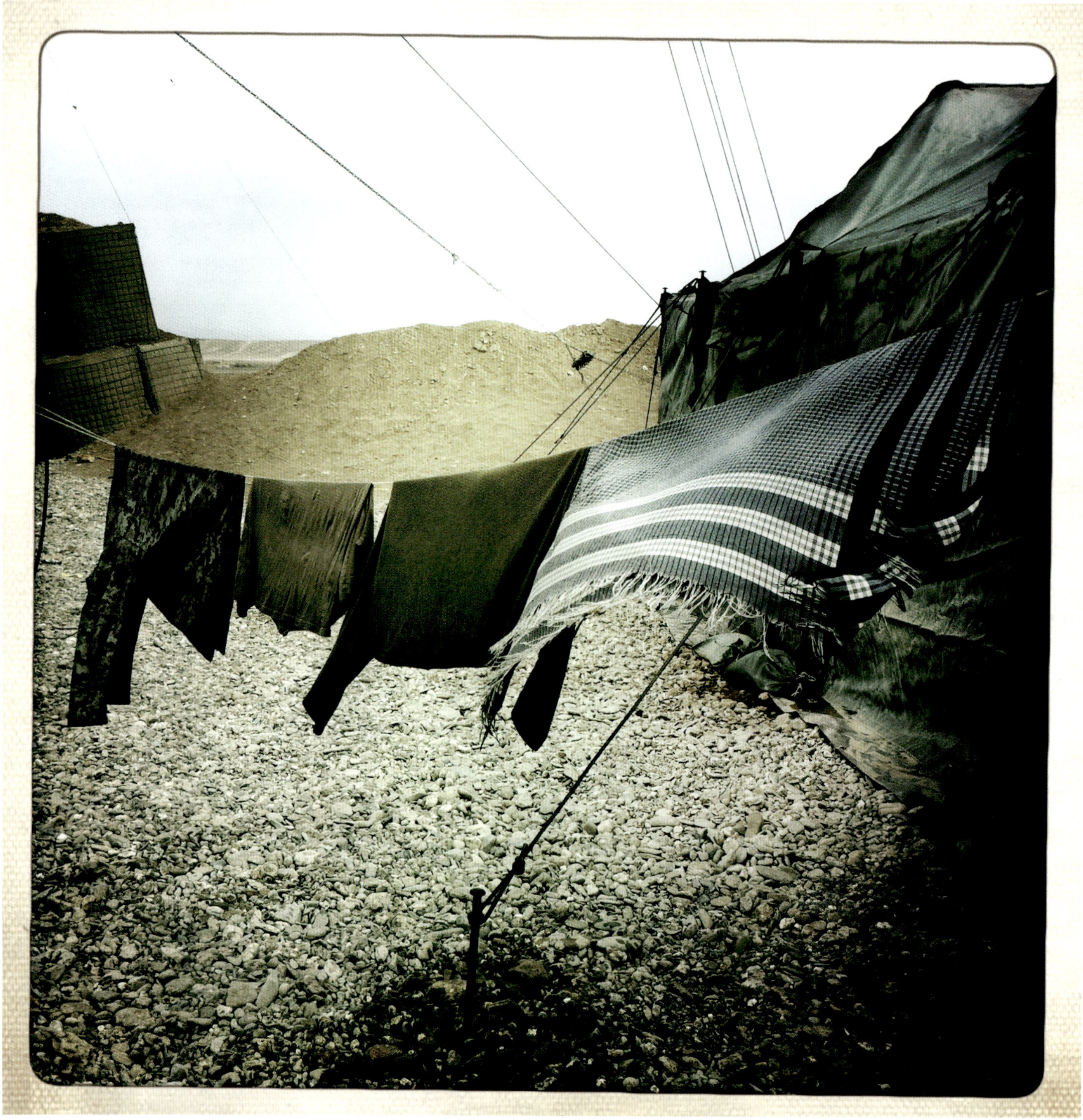

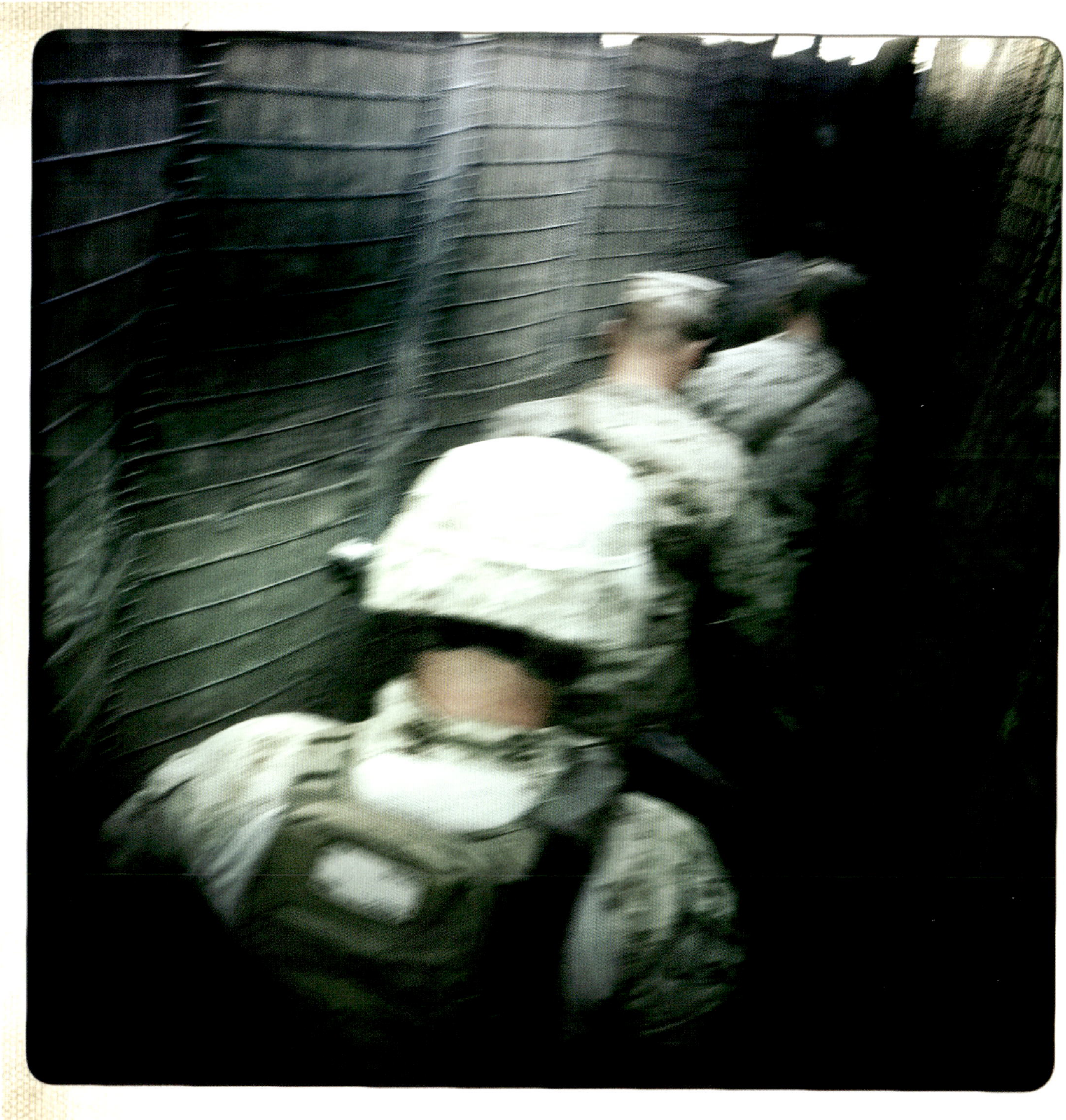

"Metaphor is our rational power to translate each of our senses into the others."

(MARSHALL MCLUHAN AND ERIC MCLUHAN, *LAWS OF MEDIA: THE NEW SCIENCE*) [8]

Semiotics is the interpretation of signs, symbols and metaphors—starting with language, but also applicable to all things that stand for something other than themselves. When McLuhan says that

"each of man's artefacts is in fact a kind of word, a metaphor that translates experience from one form into another," [9]

he is saying that artefacts are "signs," that they represent things other than themselves—he is looking at the world semiologically.

Artefacts are

"signs."

Figure + Ground

Figure + Ground is a way of talking about how our perception shifts when we open our minds to the relationships between subjects and contexts, foregrounds and backgrounds, media and content, hardware and software. In this formula, McLuhan's theories and the iPhone applications are Figures, and Afghanistan is the Ground (the context). Epiphanies can take place when one is willing to experience both Figure and Ground simultaneously, in what McLuhan describes as "resonating intervals."

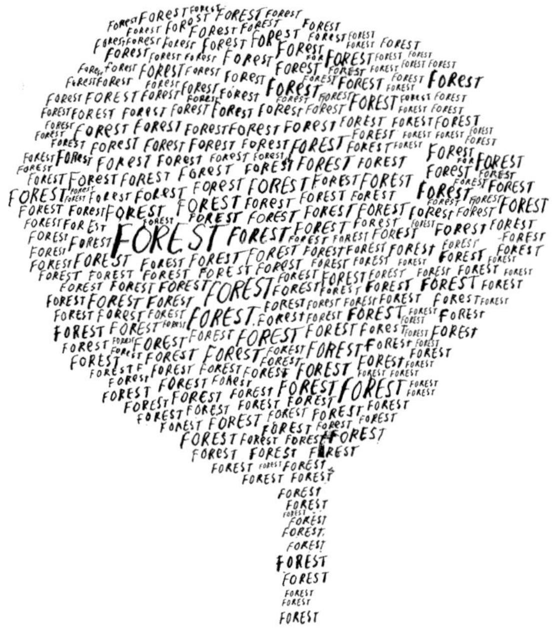

McLuhan said:

> "Study the modes of the media, in order to hoick all assumptions out of the subliminal, non-verbal realm for scrutiny and for prediction and control of human purposes."

(MCLUHAN, SUMMARIZING HIS FAMOUSLY LABELLED "SUGGESTIONS" IN *REPORT ON PROJECT IN UNDERSTANDING THE NEW MEDIA*, 1960).[10]

The "non-verbal realm" for McLuhan is something like the "not obvious." The verbal is what is on top, what we see first, like the words on the page. We don't see the words that have been left out, or the white paper without which the type would be invisible. This "subliminal" is also what McLuhan calls "Ground," borrowing a term from Gestalt Therapy. In resonating relationship to Ground is Figure. In typography, type is Figure; page is Ground. In weaving, weft is Figure; warp is Ground.[11]

Hoick
all assumptions out of the subliminal, non-verbal realm.

Another way of looking at it is:

The whole is more than the sum of its parts

or

You can't see the forest for the trees.

This book is an example in itself of Figure + Ground:

Looking and Finding are in resonating relationships to each other. Through the process of looking, I hope to shed some light on Marshall McLuhan as well as on a new technology a failed war, and some of the things that connect us as humans.

McLuhan's books are not easy to navigate. **They often frustrate.**

They are full of quotations from the myriad sources McLuhan seemed able to keep in his head and mind-bending aphorisms that provoke more questions than they answer, or simply give this author/reader a headache—

"The imagined stasis and continuity of abstract space permits its infinitesimal divisibility."[12]

His books are fragmented and disjointed; they challenge linear narrative and logic (as much as is possible in a book). Perhaps this is part of McLuhan's popularity today:

The modes of production made available with smartphones, the Internet, social media—the free-flowing form of Tumblr is a good example—were not just predicted by McLuhan's ideas, but by the discontinuous form of his books and his thoughts themselves (the medium is the message).

the
dis
con
tinu
ous
form

of
his
books

and
his thoughts
themselves

aphorisms and sententiae

This style is deliberate, and echoes the oratorical styles of teaching and expression he describes in *The Gutenberg Galaxy: The Making of Typographic Man,* where "memories are furnished with a large repertory of aphorisms and *sententiae*" in contrast to the "method of explicit spelling out of information in the form of continuous prose" more suitable to literary cultures.[13] The printing press and the spread of the written word to the masses after the invention of moveable type led to a bias of written culture over the oral. McLuhan quotes the influential linguist Walter J. Ong: "The change in human sensibility resulting from the rise of typography [showed] how

the use of printing moved the word away from its original association with sound and treated it more as a 'thing' in space."[14]

(Of course photography did the same thing to the visual world, and as I shall explain in my chapter on the iPhone camera and the Hipstamatic app,

digital technologies accentuate the "thingness" of things by making all the eye can see reducible to an algorithm.)

McLuhan urges us to beware of the controlling linearity of writing and the seeming immutability that print imposes on it. Here is an example of the relish with which he considers the "oral prose" of Elizabethan poet Thomas Nashe (1567–1601): "The oral polyphony of the prose of Nashe offends against lineal and literary decorum. . . . This sensuous relish for the complex interplay of qualities persists in the sixteenth century even in language intended for the printed page."[15]

Near the end of *The Gutenberg Galaxy*, his treatise on typographical man and the invention of moveable type—where he lays out the theories he will spend the rest of his life expanding and elaborating—McLuhan declares the whole book "a gloss of a single text of Harold Innis." [16] (See iProbe_02 Phone Texting.) "Gloss" is a term that comes up a lot in the McLuhan canon. It comes from the Latin word glossa, which comes from the Greek word for language, γλωσσα (*glóssa*), and refers to marginal notes that expand on or add to existing texts (which, etymologically speaking, is what language does). It's safe to say that

everything that has to do with Marshall McLuhan begins with language

(language: from the French word "langue" for "tongue").

This book, too, is a gloss of things I read in McLuhan, things I'd read before I'd read McLuhan, and things I read because I'd read McLuhan. It's an "essay" in the literal sense of the word, as in an effort with no claims to completion—a work in perpetual progress.

glóssa

glossa

"gloss"

Musa Qala

Helmand province is located on the border with Pakistan. Around Musa Qala, where 1–8 operations were centred, it is mostly barren and stony desert highlands, sparsely populated with adobe villages, mosques and minarets. A few people owned motorbikes or rusty old cars. Electricity was a luxury. There was no running water. A handful of gas pumps serviced the region (see iProbe_07, Fuel Dispensers).

In her brilliantly researched book ***Seeds of Terror: How Drugs, Thugs, and Crime are Reshaping the Afghan War***, **Gretchen Peters,**

who spent over a decade working as a journalist in Afghanistan and Pakistan, gives us some insights into what Musa Qala was like only a few years before I was there:

"The district of Musa Qala, which has shifted between Taliban and coalition control in recent years, is emblematic of the type of unending violence ordinary villagers have endured. It also provided a rare window into life under the Taliban."[17]

"When Afghan and international troops retook Musa Qala in December 2007, they found the Taliban had hung alleged spies in the town square and oversaw heroin production and more than fifty heroin labs."[18]

"Taliban commanders will literally cart off 10 percent of a farmer's gross input. One Afghan intelligence officer based near Musa Qala described opium storehouses where

Taliban commanders could deposit and later withdraw quantities of poppy as if using an ATM machine."

GRETCHEN PETERS, *SEEDS OF TERROR: HOW DRUGS, THUGS, AND CRIME ARE RESHAPING THE AFGHAN WAR.*[19]

By the time I arrived in Musa Qala in February 2011, the Afghan National Army (ANA) and the International Security Assistance Forces in Afghanistan (ISAF) had been back "in control" for three years. On Fridays, a market (of men only) bustled outside the gates of the main operations base. The Americans, alongside the ANA, had set up camp in the same building complex the British ISAF troops had been living in during the Battle of Musa Qala in November–December 2007. The base had seen a series of occupiers, and graffiti from Taliban coexisted with that of the Americans and the British.

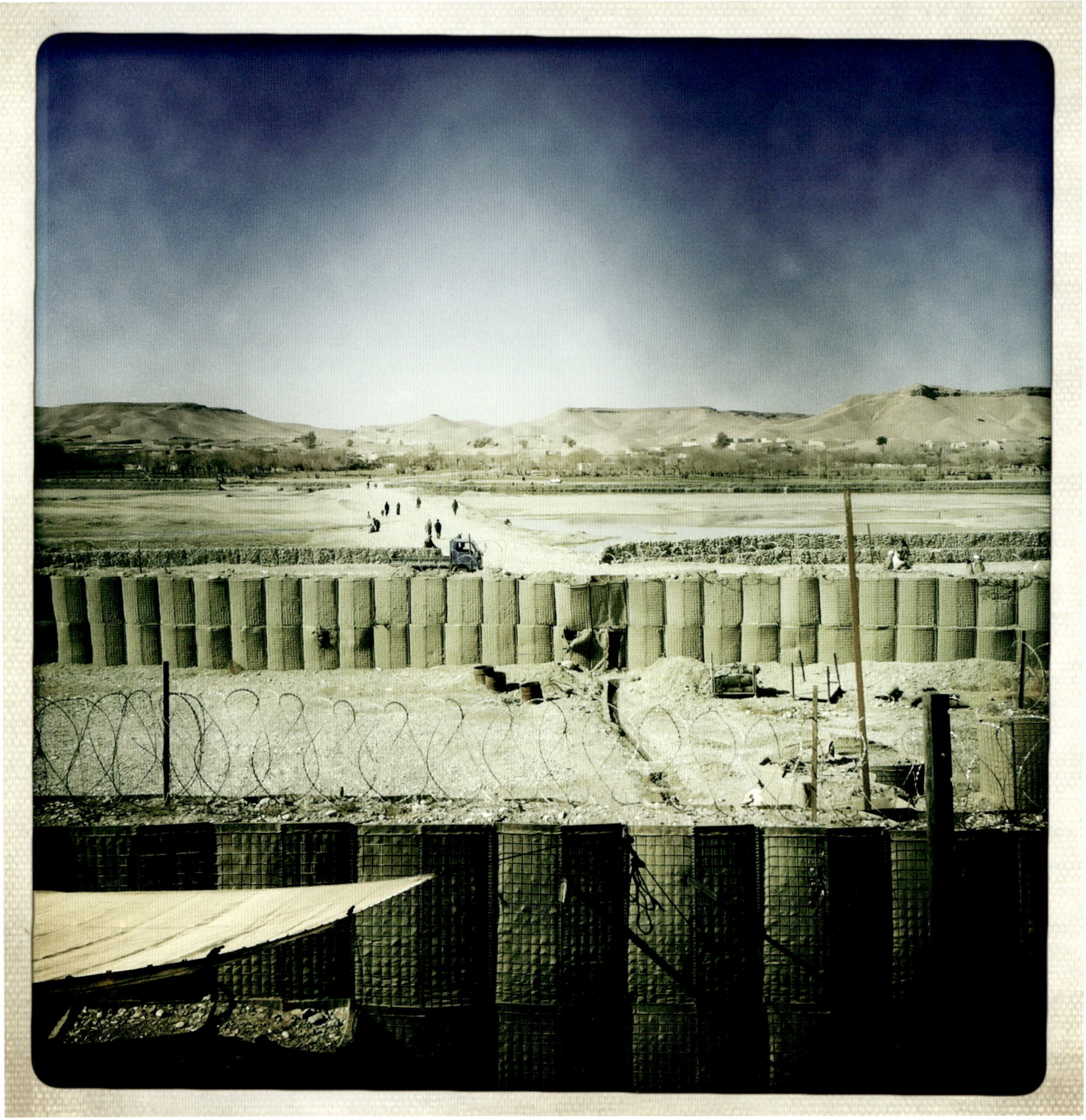

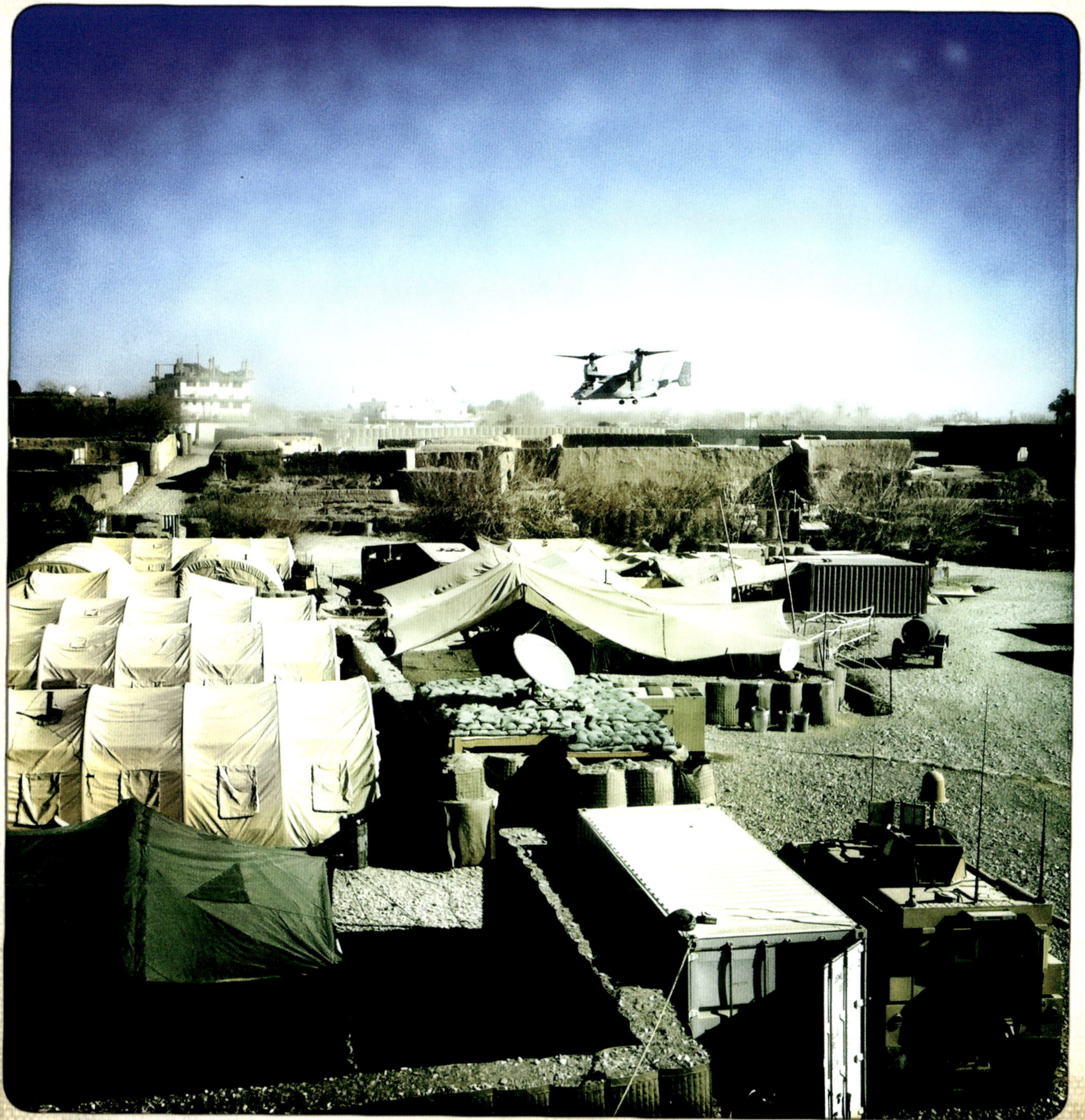

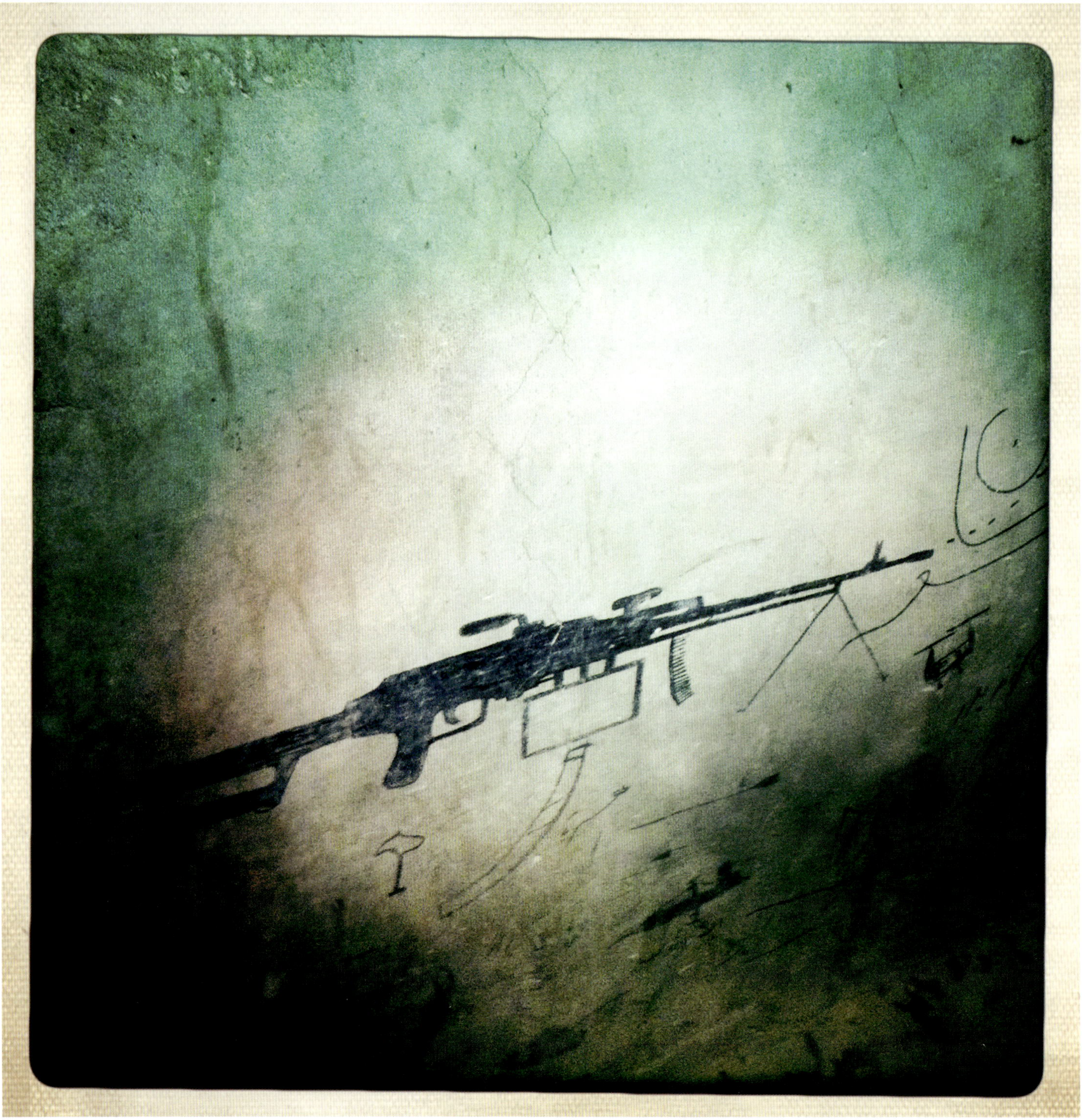

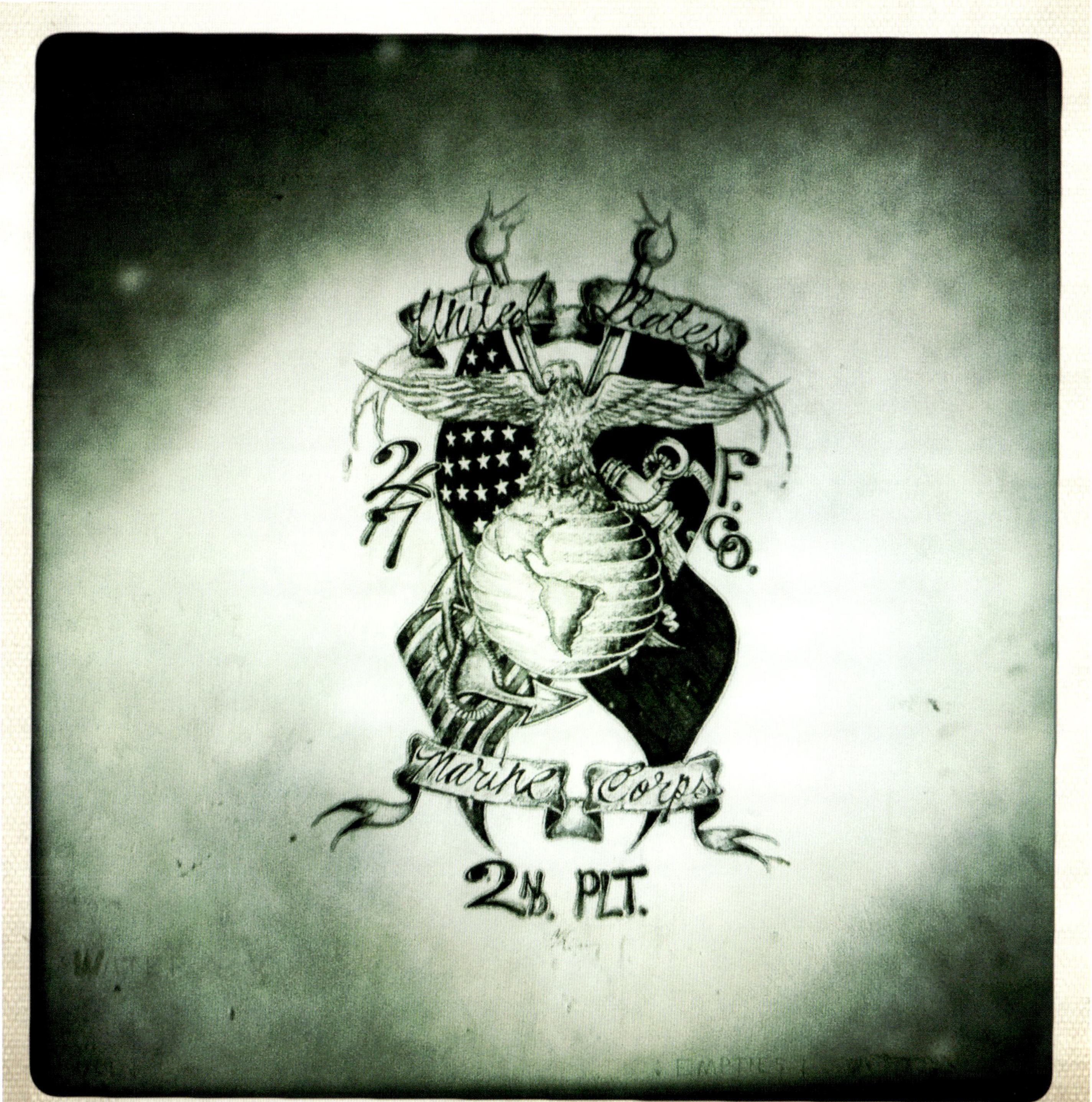
United States
2/7
F. Co.
Marine Corps
2nd. PLT.

From Musa Qala, a four-hour convoy south brought us to the hamlet of Shir Ghazay. In my ten days there, I met only one woman—a midwife at the local clinic—and saw only a few others from a distance, before they deked out of view. There was no school, other than the one the Female Engagement Team attached to 1–8 tried to open, but its future seemed doubtful. On the first day of school, about a dozen excited children arrived as paper, pencils and brand-new knapsacks were handed out. A courageous (male of course) teacher began the lessons, pointing to the letters of the alphabet on a blackboard as the children recited along. At first the girls were in the classroom with the boys. Some of the students' fathers arrived, polite words were exchanged, and the girls were put in a separate room. An older boy, perhaps eleven or twelve, helped the girls to write the first letters of the alphabet.

Obviously, some of the parents wanted their girls to attend the school. But some of the parents did not want that. Soon, the girls were made to leave. Our photo op now seemed tainted.

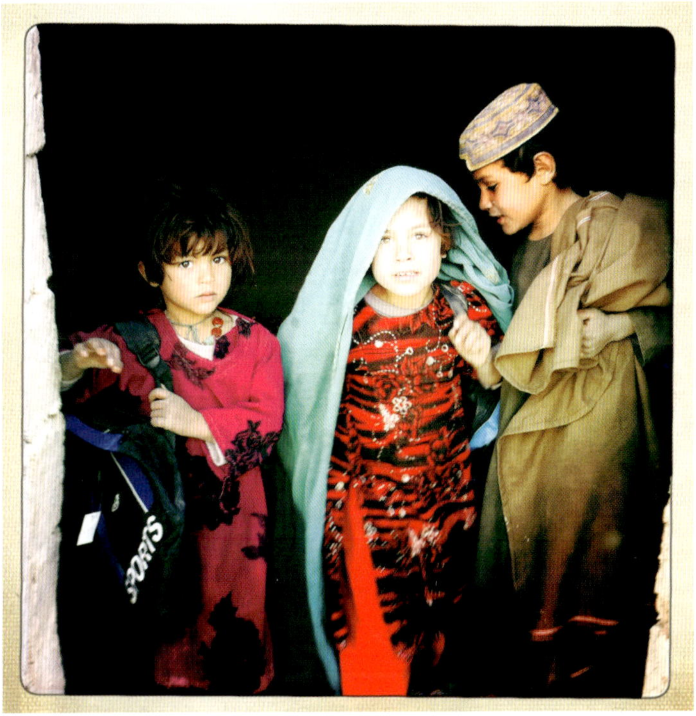
SPORTS

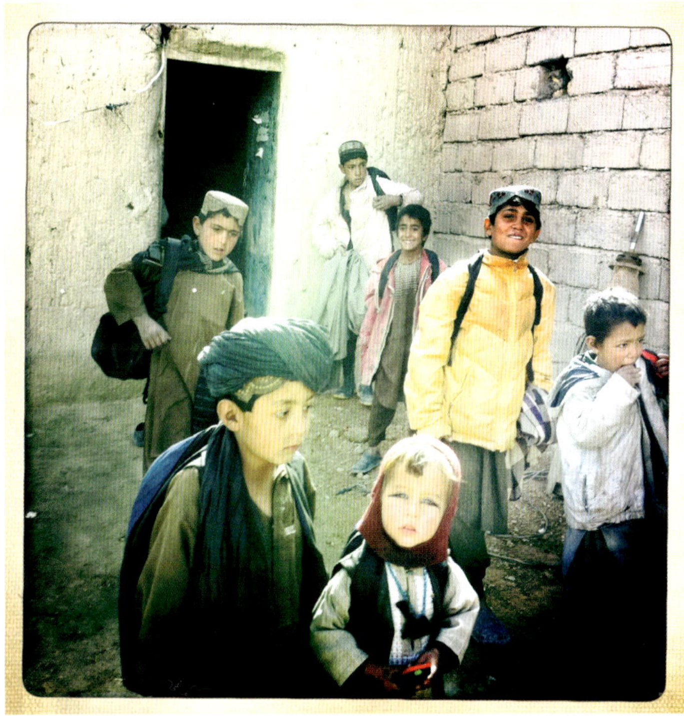

The figures of the heavily armed and armoured Marines patrolling across the Afghan desert seemed out of place and surreal.

"I feel like I'm on the set of a Star Wars movie," I said one day.

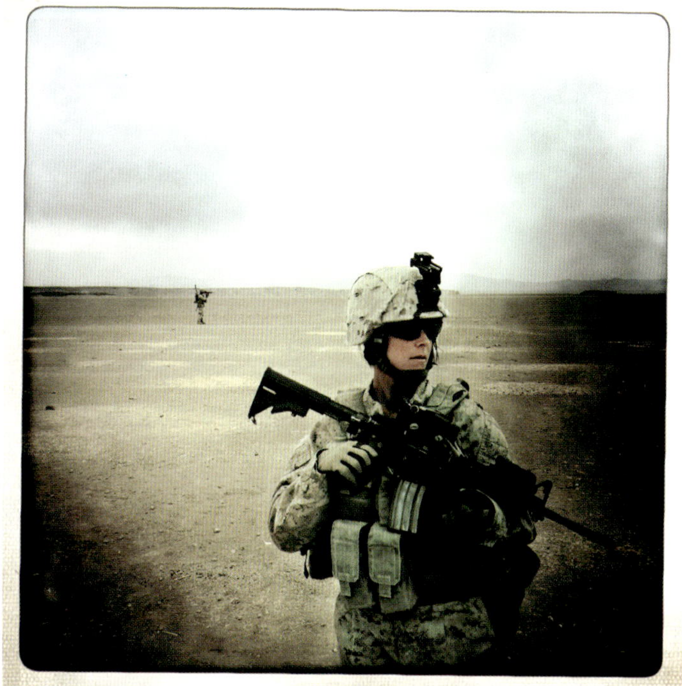

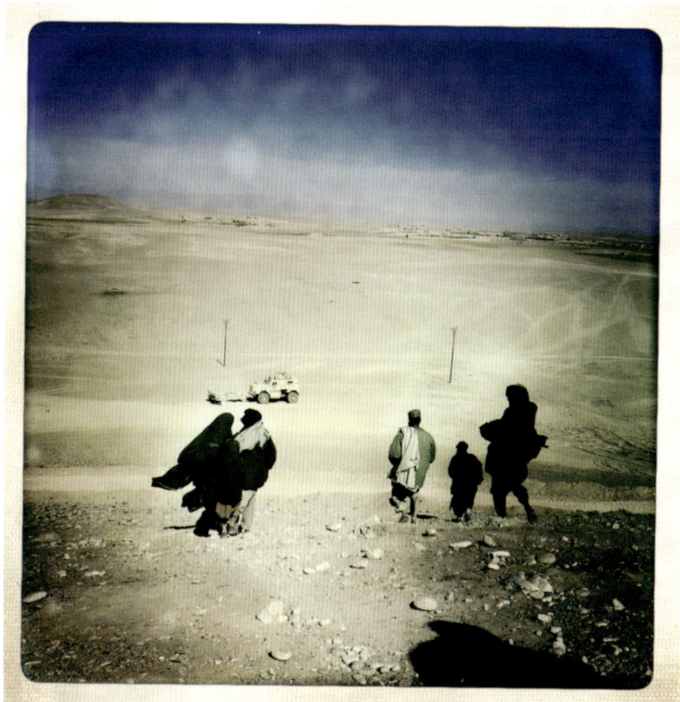

The Battalion Commanders were already in a foul mood before I arrived.

The Battalion had lost a lot of men—but that is not unique in front-line units, and it didn't explain why they were so on edge.

They certainly did not hide how unhappy they were to have us and our social media accoutrements, including our battery of iPhone cameras, in their midst.

Still, they honoured the Basetrack embed, to which they'd agreed long before, and which was already in its sixth month of the Battalion's seven-month deployment—the longest continual embed in Afghanistan by a media organization with a single military unit.

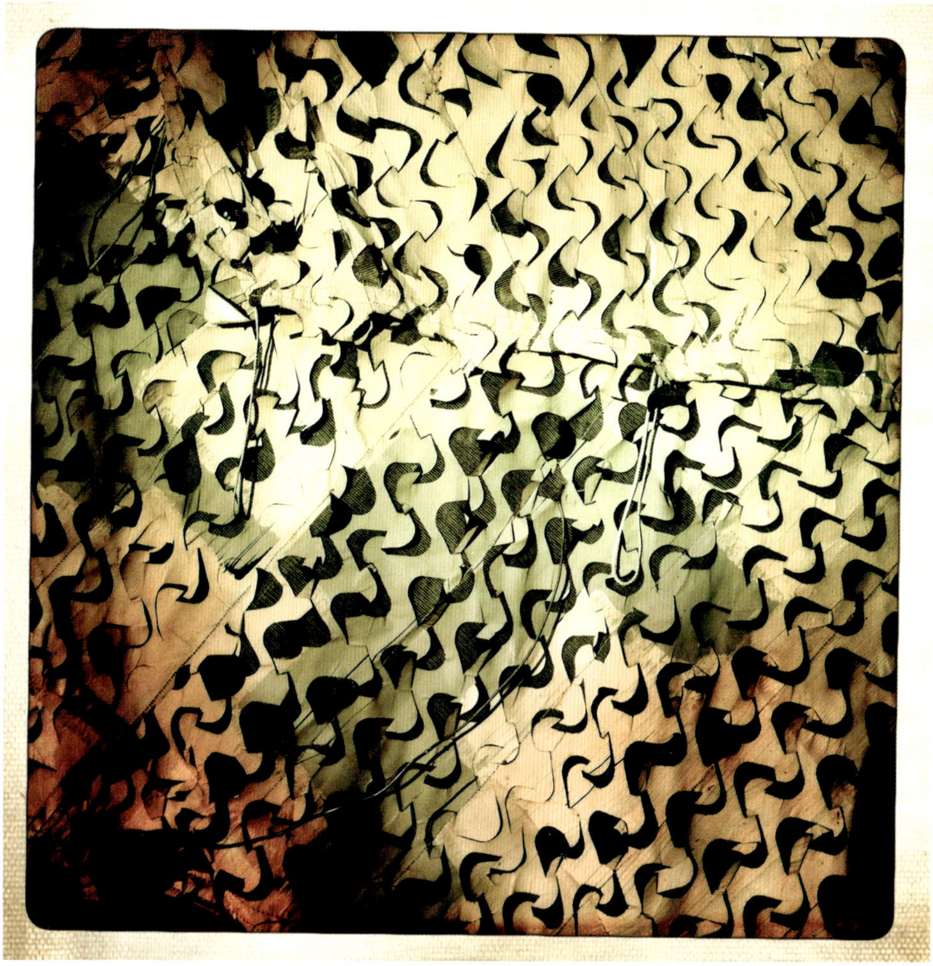

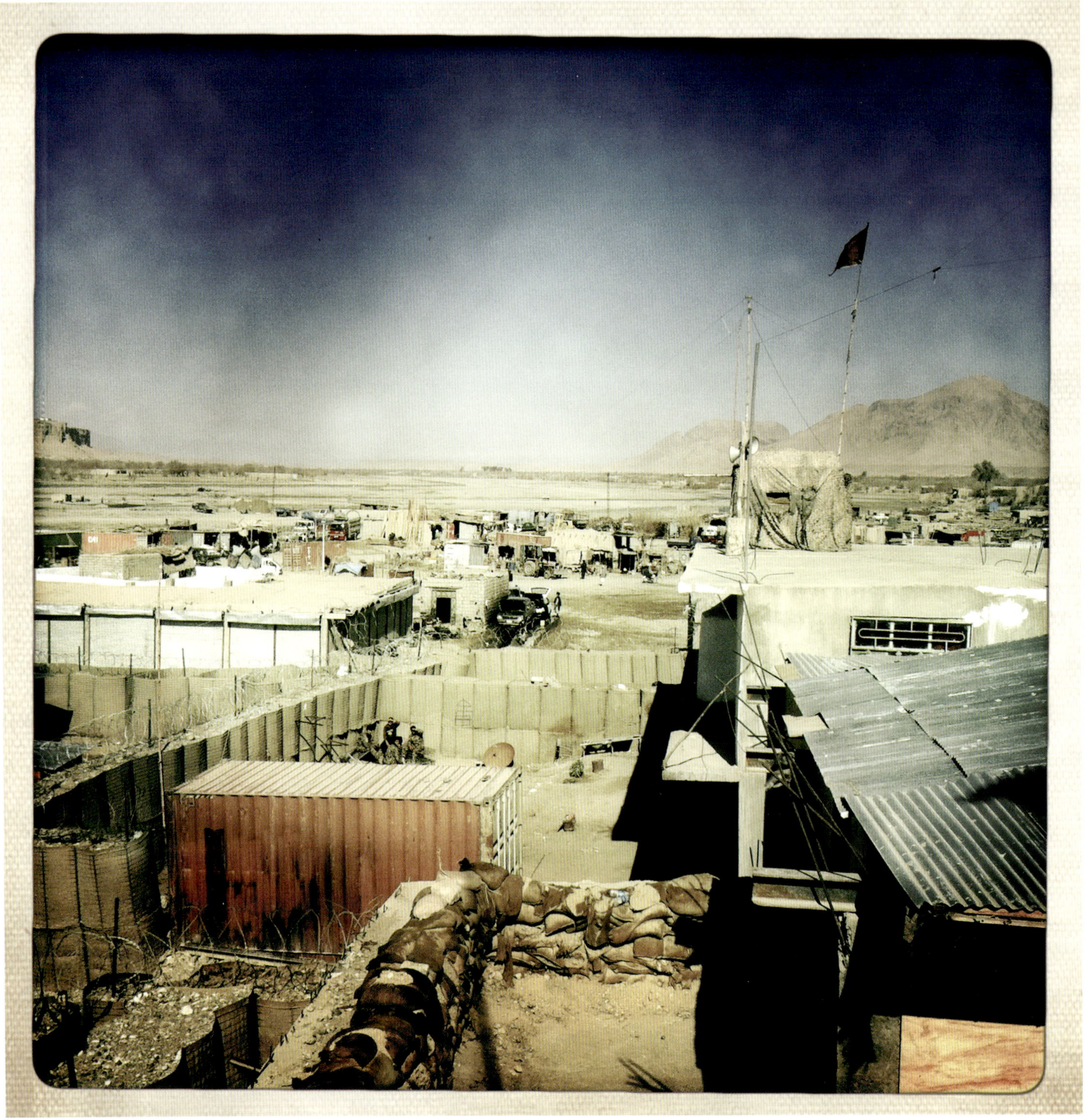

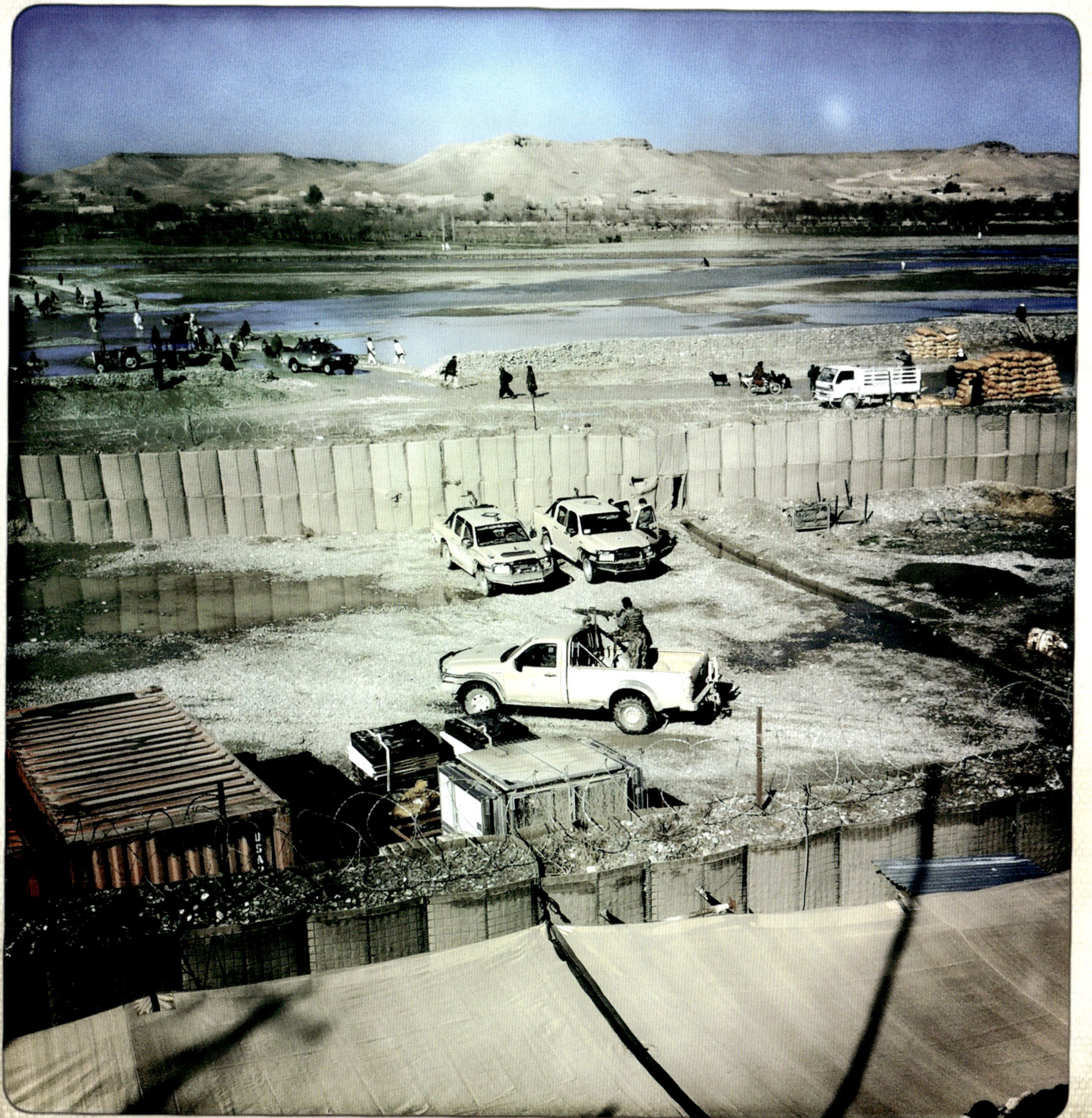

The social media

The reason for the Battalion Commanders' foul mood, I came to suspect, had to do with a general sense of powerlessness over the situation in Afghanistan, despite the Americans' obvious military and technological supremacy. Basetrack, which went further than anyone previously had in integrating military coverage with social media, was a symbol of this loss of control over technology, and Facebook (and to some extent, we) became the scapegoat. The people back home did not always post things the Battalion Commanders wanted to see. When Facebook proved impossible to fully censor, the Commanding Officer (CO) and his Executive Officer and second in command (XO) asked that the Basetrack Facebook group be shut down. The Basetrack team leader, Teru Kuwayama, a ten-year veteran of covering the war in Afghanistan, whose Knight Foundation-funded media initiative was always openly interactive with Marine families back home, was within reason to refuse.

"Sure, we'll just call Mark Zuckerberg and tell him Facebook is over," we joked.

If the Basetrack site were in any way threatening the mission or the safety of the Marines, I would have understood. But it was absurd to say it was. The Facebook site was mostly wives and mothers sending words of encouragement to their boys. There was some criticism of the war. Yes. But we couldn't ethically censor that (by omitting or deleting posts critical of the war). And certainly it was nothing one couldn't read elsewhere all over the web—in fact these posts were mostly links to articles in other media. If anything, the Basetrack website, which was redacted (censored) by the XO, was pro-military. The vast majority of the images, due to censorship requirements and the intention to provide comfort to families, were straightforward, flattering portraits of the daily life of the Marines. Those of us who embedded[20] had extensive experience on military embeds and front-line warfare; we had moreover faced the even greater dangers of unilateral (or unembedded) coverage of conflict zones. All of us had covered much tougher imagery over the years, and we were doing this, by and large, to give something back to the Marines and their families back home. See, for instance, the posts and the photographs on the Basetrack.org site during the embed period (October 2010–February 2011).[21]

While the

co

and

xo

scolded us for taking photographs of Marines out of uniform (which would look bad to people back home), we were being accused by other journalists of toeing the military line and creating propaganda.

Given the number of Marines, soldiers and Afghan civilians getting their limbs and heads blown off in Afghanistan, the emphasis placed on how we represented their haircuts seemed absurd. Yet we complied.

Before long, families back home started getting warnings from their Marines that if their mothers, brothers, girlfriends, wives, etc., didn't boycott the Basetrack Facebook page, there would be consequences for their boys on deployment. "You have to understand," the XO told me, "that if wives back home got together over Facebook, the next thing you know, they'll be going to bars and cheating on their husbands. Marriages could be ruined." And besides, he said, "The CO's wife doesn't like Facebook." I tried to explain to the CO that I wasn't a big fan of Facebook myself—the Internet, by competing with print media for advertising money and giving rise to a new force of citizen journalism had, after all, forced the closings of many newspapers and put a lot of journalists out of work; blogging and Facebook were all a part of that—but it was unstoppable, and the whole point of this experiment was to figure out how the military, and we, were going to operate in this new media world.

Shirts Off / Shirts On

After taking a photograph of Marines lifting weights with their shirts off, I asked them to put their shirts on for a second frame so we could post it on the website for families back home to see.

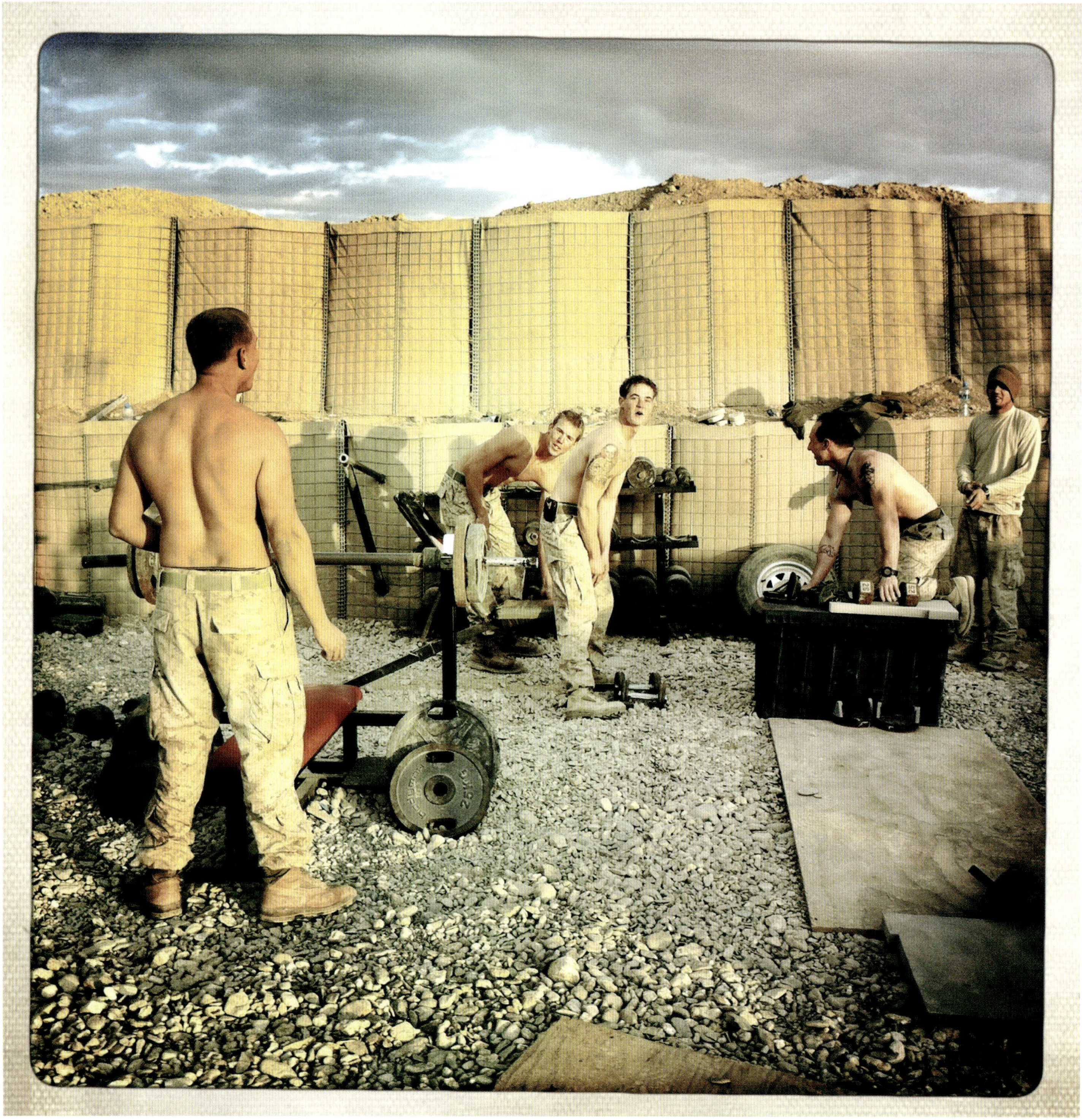

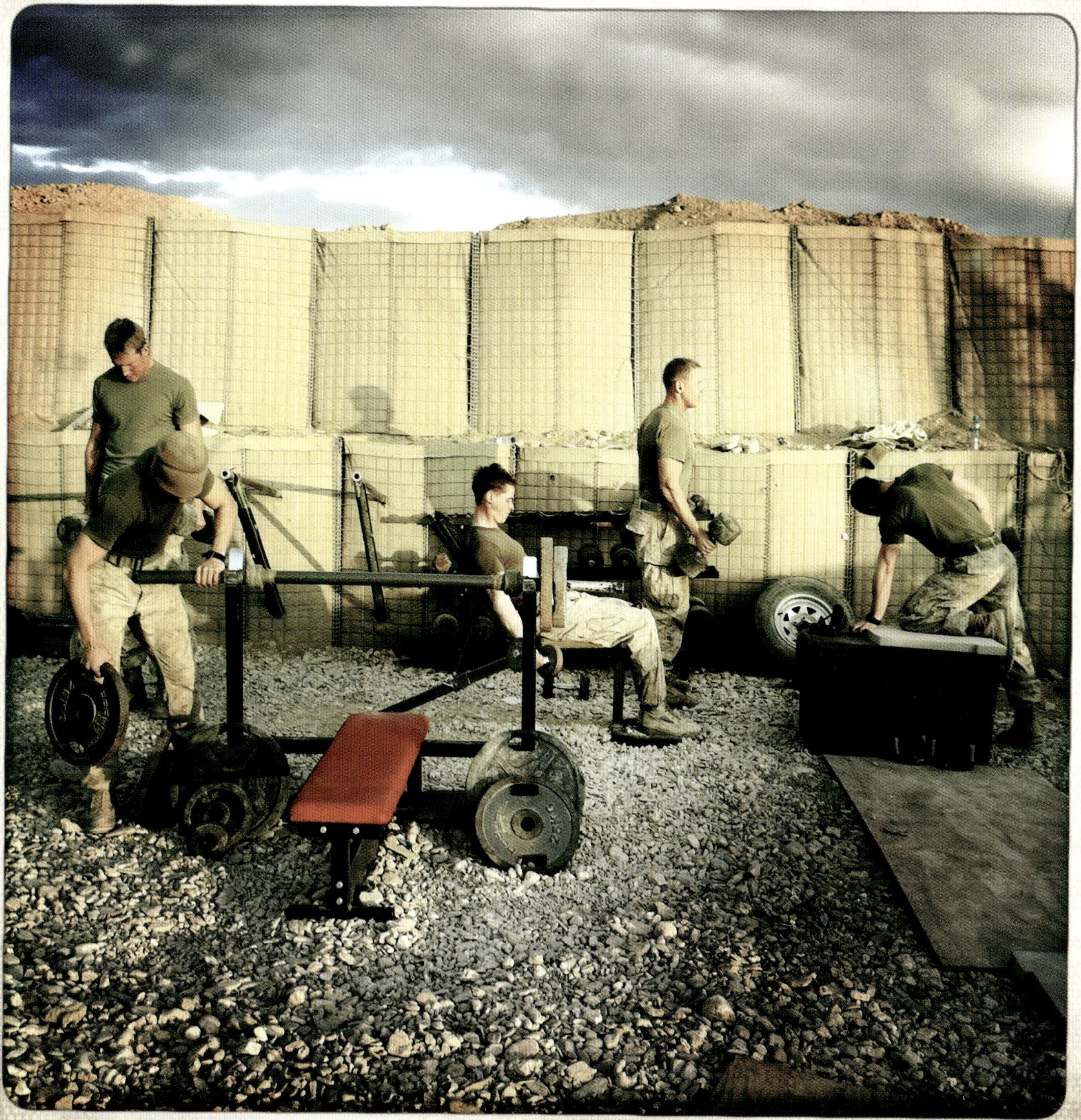

In the end, the Basetrack team embed was terminated just one month before the Battalion would be heading home.

In his probes on the telegraph (in the 1950s and 1960s), Marshall McLuhan explained how instant messaging threatens any organization:

"There is a col

lapse

of delegated authority and a dissolution of the pyramid and management structures."

(MARSHALL MCLUHAN, *UNDERSTANDING MEDIA: THE EXTENSIONS OF MAN*) [22]

Technologies are fine as long as they are in the hands of the right people.

But making technology accessible to the masses (and to soldiers!) poses a threat to those in charge. McLuhan recounts in *Understanding Media* that the advent of

"the easier, phonetic alphabet, and the cheap transportable papyrus together effected the transfer of power from the priestly to the military class." [23]

This is a dilemma that is much bigger than the Basetrack project. What happens when the citizenry, or worse, your enemies, get hold of the same technology?

It was amazing, really, that the Marines were allowed to use the Internet at all.

It's supposed to be good for morale, but as it turns out, it might have the opposite effect.

River City

The military thought they could at least monitor what goes on over the Internet, and they could shut it down at will.

They did shut down communications, for instance, when the camp was

“in River City.”

When a Marine is injured or killed in action, local bases restrict all out-going communications in order to prevent pre-emptive news from leaking to families, to the media or to the public.

When this happens, communications are said to be in “River City.” If the base has communications services for the Marines, like computers or telephones, they are locked up or put away.

Musa Qala camp was on River City the day my Basetrack colleague Monica Campbell and I returned from Shir Ghazay and were told on arrival that the Basetrack embed was over, and we would be getting on a helicopter to leave that night.

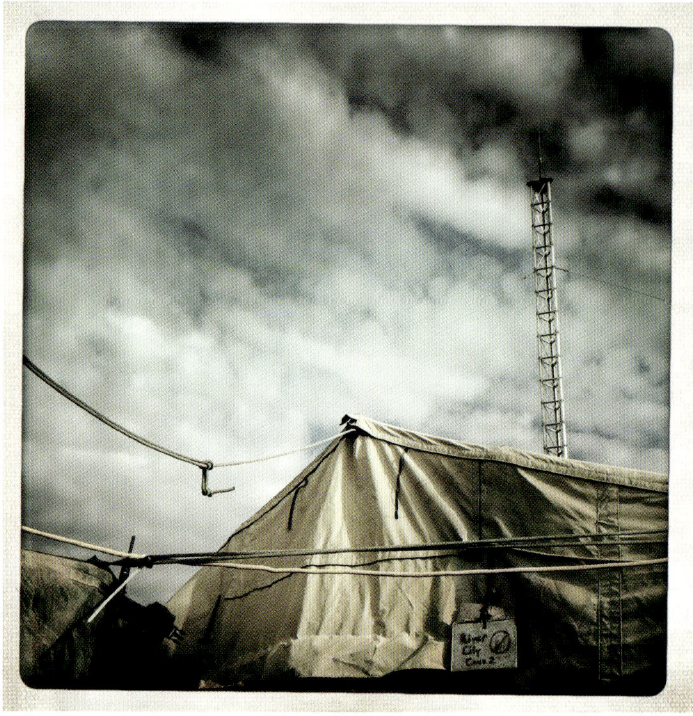

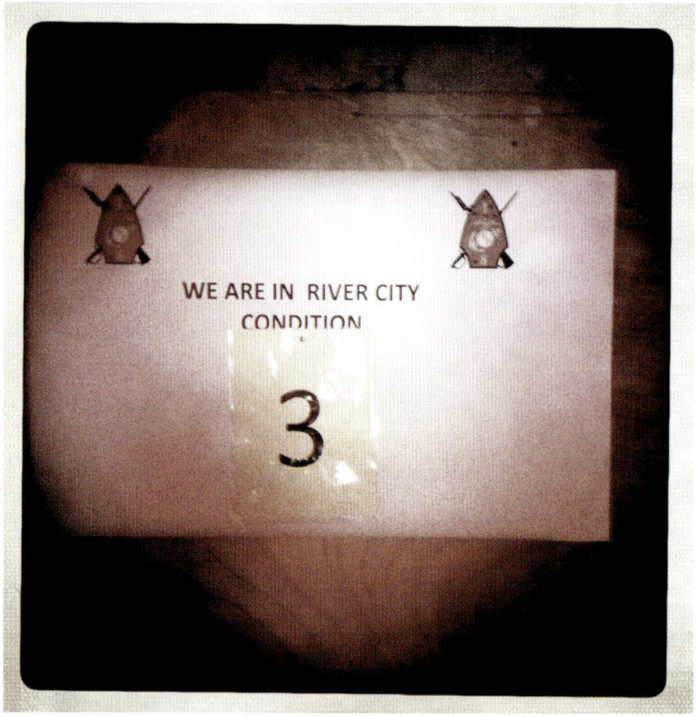

Mobile phones were another thing altogether and were not permitted for the Marines, although the Afghan National Army soldiers had mobile phones that they could use to call home and to bank their military pay.

One of the Marines on base in charge of military-sourced media, aka "Combat Camera Guy," told me that he thought the military would be better off with no media access at all. He was right, of course. But the truth is, while the media gets a great deal of access to the military, embedding journalists is still the best way for the military to control media reporting.

In Afghanistan, as in Iraq, embeds are by far the safest, most feasible way for journalists to cover the conflicts. Media outlets know this, and so they have to placate the military just enough to hold on to

"good" embeds

(i.e., front lines, not out-of-the-way outposts doing little more than handing out candy to children). As we witnessed this unravelling of their sense of control over the Internet and Facebook, it occurred to me that it might seem to the military that they were being betrayed by the very technologies that were meant to empower and protect them.

Facebook was just one more technology that wasn't doing as it was told.

Em bed ding

journalists

is still the best way for the military to control media reporting.

control media

reporting.control
media reporting.
control media
reporting.control
media reporting.
control media
reporting.control
media reporting.

iPhone + the Hipstamatic app

A big part of what had unsettled me about my experience in Afghanistan was working with the iPhone camera instead of a "real camera," and even more so, the iPhone Hipstamatic app

(a set of algorithm presets—akin to Photoshop Actions—that create heavily affected images meant to look "retro" right in the device for you)

(see iProbe 01_The iPhone Camera + the Hipstamatic app). We weren't the first journalists to use iPhone cameras in war, but it was still new enough that blogs filled up with opinions of how the technology would affect people's relationships to war through photography. A common criticism was that it rendered war nostalgic. And yet for professional photographers who had spent most of their lives working with film and printing their own photographs in darkrooms,

there is nothing nostalgic about the Hipstamatic. On the contrary, its obvious and aggressive referencing of traditional photography served only to highlight

the digitalness of the device

and its distance from mechanical cameras and traditional wet **darkrooms.**

The iPhone camera and the Hipstamatic app made me feel removed from the process of taking and making the photographs, and this contributed to my difficulty in coming to terms with the very experiences I'd photographed.

Surrounded
by all the
dehumanizing
technologies
of war,
I felt
myself
being
erased
as an
artist
by the
very
technology
I was using.

Months later, when I heard Professor Nesselroth talking about Figure and Ground, it helped me to frame the Hipstamatic images differently. Rather than feeling alienated by them and by my lack of control over them, I tried allowing myself to enter into the resonating intervals of meaning between digital and mechanical, virtual and tangible, that might be discovered inside them.

McLuhan notes that

"all wars have been fought by the latest technology available in any culture."

(MARSHALL MCLUHAN, *UNDERSTANDING MEDIA: THE EXTENSIONS OF MAN*) [24]

Photographers do the same thing with new technologies, always upgrading to compete with each other. But because we are artists as well, as McLuhan also notes, we are supposed to

"exult in the novelties of perception afforded by innovation."[25]

"The artist is the person who invents the means to bridge between biological inheritance and the environments created by technological innovation."

(MARSHALL MCLUHAN AND ERIC MCLUHAN, *LAWS OF MEDIA: THE NEW SCIENCE*)[26]

Besides, 172 years of traditional photography doesn't seem to have done much to bring an end to war,

so it made sense to me to try the new technology and the latest social media.

It wasn't a requirement of the Basetrack project to shoot with iPhones, but when I first saw the curious and often compelling images my colleagues were making, it was an easy decision to buy myself an iPhone and see what I would do with it.

The instantaneity and artificiality of the Hipstamatic images seemed to accentuate the "thingness" of everything.

And so it was that bit by bit, I started to look at my images again and all I could see were

artefacts and technology:

armoured vehicles and body armour and weapons and radio towers; loudspeakers and improvised explosive devices; fuel dispensers and mobile phones; sandbags and HESCO barriers; the occasional flag. I realized that part of what had unsettled me so deeply was the conspicuous absence of humanity in it all. The Americans dehumanized the Afghans and the technology dehumanized the Americans—it was infectious. That is the job of war: you have to dehumanize someone, after all, in order to kill or torture them with a clean conscience.

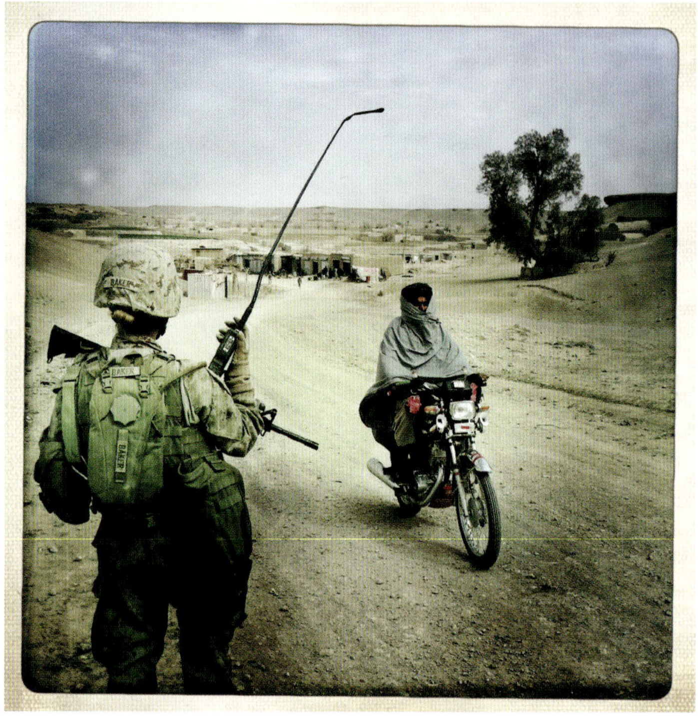

McLuhan says,

"all media are extensions of some human faculty—psychic or physical."

(MARSHALL MCLUHAN AND QUENTIN FIORE, *THE MEDIUM IS THE MASSAGE: AN INVENTORY OF EFFECTS*) [27]

"The etymology of all human
technologies is to be found
in the human body itself:
they are, as it were, prosthetic
devices, mutations, metaphors
of the body or its parts."

(MARSHALL MCLUHAN AND ERIC MCLUHAN, *LAWS OF MEDIA:THE NEW SCIENCE*) [28]

The iProbes

Once you start looking for Marshall McLuhan, it's impossible not to see traces of him everywhere.

Everything becomes an artefact you can unpack and un-layer like a phyllo pastry.

What follows is a series of probes of images and artifacts stripped to the bones.

They look at the digital captures of the iPhone Hipstamatic app in the context of a military embed and probe military technology, as well as the technology of the iPhone itself.

I've used the word iProbe, as a portmanteau of iPhone and Probe—

Marshall McLuhan's linguistic and semiological investigations into culture, technology and artifacts—after being encouraged by my friend and editor **Diana Kuprel**, who also gets credit for coining the term iProbe.

A probe looks at artefacts metaphorically, with the understanding that every object has the capacity to stand for something other than what is obvious or on the surface. It goes mining for meaning—something I was determined to find in my iPhone full of photographs as a way of making sense of and giving meaning to my experience.

Taking a photograph is only part of the process of photographic storytelling. In the case of this story, it began with an opportunity given me by Teru Kuwayama (an email message in December 2010: "What are you doing? Do you want to come to Afghanistan and work with us on Basetrack.org and shoot on an iPhone?") (This is a paraphrase of a series of e-mails.)

McLuhan says,

"with man his knowledge and the process of obtaining knowledge are of equal magnitude." [29]

But what happens when our tools start putting greater and greater distances between what we see and what we get, or when so much of the process is over the moment we take the photograph,

"when the action and the reaction occur at the same time"?

(MARSHALL MCLUHAN, *UNDERSTANDING MEDIA: THE EXTENSIONS OF MAN*) [30]

My friend Dr. Anthony Feinstein, who has written several books on the psychological effects of covering war, once told me that

a journalist's coping mechanism is in part tied up in the work itself—because we are confronting what we are seeing at the moment of recording it, and later in the acts of editing and publishing—so, our "talk-therapy" is built into the process.

These iProbes are also a kind of prophylactive therapy—

a proactive coping strategy, a way for me to find relief for the sick feeling of unresolvedness I'd been left with after my embed with the 1–8 Marines.

I have tried in previous work to show the human face of war. With the tools of Marshall McLuhan in hand, this is an attempt to do something different and see what can be revealed by looking at

The Face of War through the Extensions of Man.

"The human body is the magazine of inventions,

the patent office

where are the models from which every hint was taken. All the tools and engines on earth are only extensions of its limbs and senses. One definition of man is 'an intelligence served by organs.'"

(RALPH WALDO EMERSON IN 1888, QUOTED BY MARSHALL MCLUHAN AND ERIC MCLUHAN IN *LAWS OF MEDIA: THE NEW SCIENCE*) [31]

“Today man has developed extensions for practically everything he used to do with this body. The evolution of weapons begins with the teeth and the fist and ends with the atomic bomb.

Clothes and houses are extensions of man’s biological temperature-control mechanisms. Furniture takes the place of squatting and sitting on the ground. Power tools, glasses, tv, telephones, and books which carry the voices across both time and space are examples of material extensions. Money is a way of extending and storing labor. Our transportation networks now do what we used to do with our feet and backs.

In fact, all man-made material things can be treated as extensions of what man once did with his body or some specialized part of his body.”

(EDWARD T. HALL, *THE SILENT LANGUAGE*, QUOTED BY MARSHALL MCLUHAN AND ERIC MCLUHAN IN *LAWS OF MEDIA: THE NEW SCIENCE*) [32]

Camera obscura

"If there is sunshine outside and a pinhole in one wall, then the images of the outer world will appear on the wall opposite."
(MARSHALL MCLUHAN, *UNDERSTANDING MEDIA: THE EXTENSIONS OF MAN*) [33]

"The box, still thought of as a small room, was called a 'dark room,' or 'camera obscura.' This camera could be aimed at a landscape, street, garden party. A group of people looking in amazement at the moving images in the box may well have resembled a group watching a television."
(ERIK BARNOUW, QUOTED BY MARSHALL MCLUHAN IN *THE GUTENBERG GALAXY*) [34]

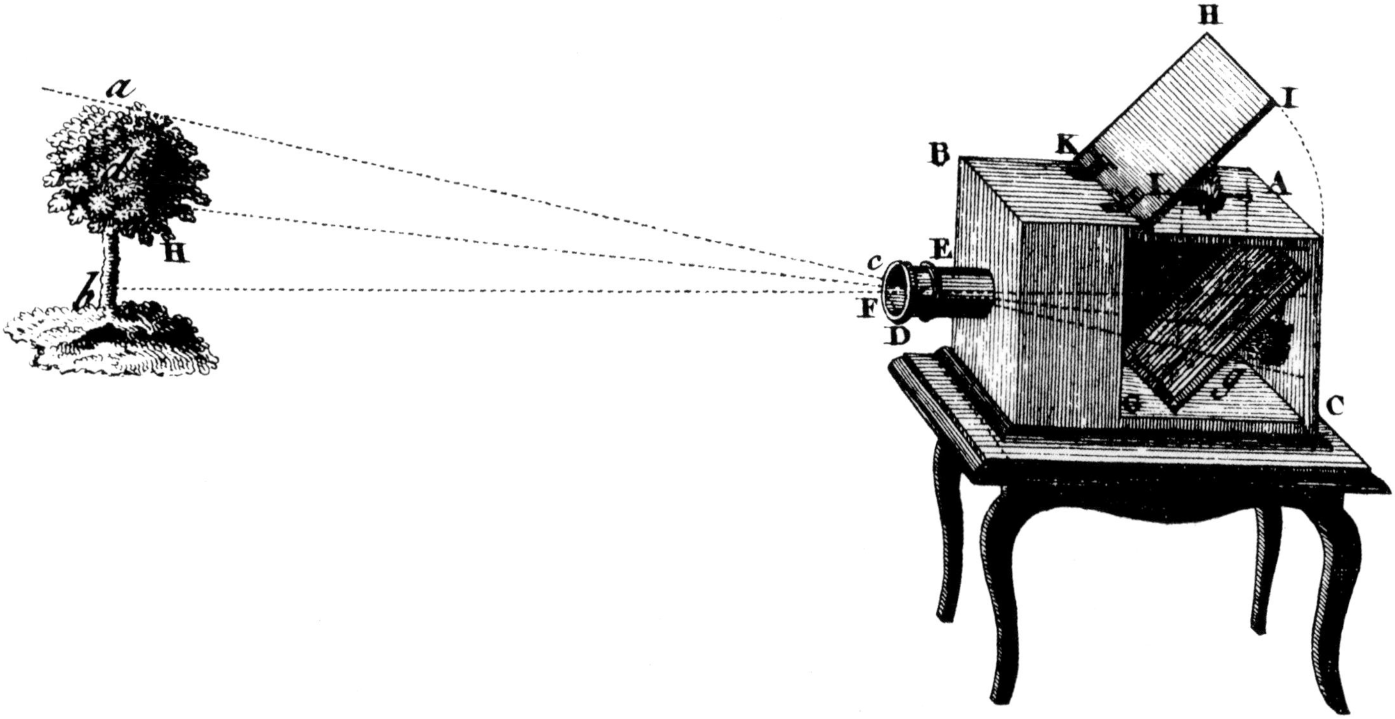

DRAWING BY MATHURIN-JACQUES BRISSON,
DICTIONNAIRE RAISONNÉ DE PHYSIQUE, 1781

Electric light

"Whether the light is being used for brain surgery or night baseball is a matter of indifference. It could be argued that these activities are in some way the 'content' of the electric light. This fact merely underlines the point that 'the medium is the message' because it is the medium that shapes and controls the scale and form of human association and action."

(MARSHALL MCLUHAN, *UNDERSTANDING MEDIA: THE EXTENSIONS OF MAN*) [35]

T. A. EDISON.
Electric-Lamp.

No. 223,898. **Patented Jan. 27, 1880.**

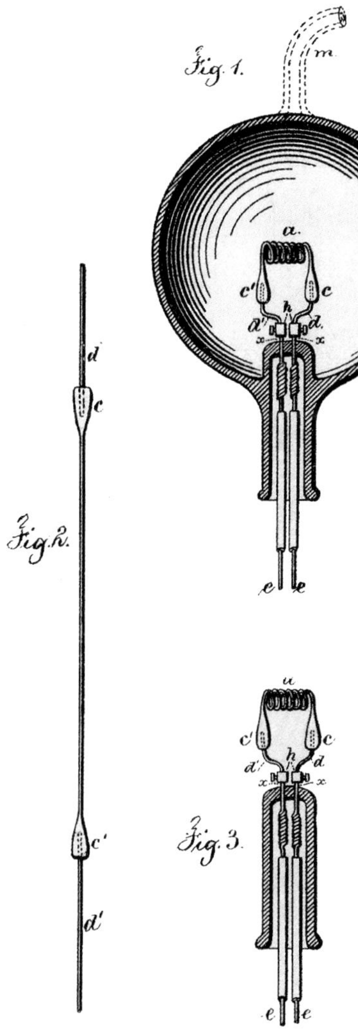

Inventor
Thomas A. Edison

Witnesses
Chas H. Smith
Geo T Pinckney

per Lemuel W. Serrell
att'y

Typewriter

"An army needs more typewriters than medium and light artillery pieces, even in the field, suggesting that the typewriter now fuses the functions of the pen and sword." [36]

"As expediter, the typewriter brought writing and speech and publication into close association." [37]

"The typewriter and the telephone are most unidentical twins that have taken over the revamping of the American girl with technological ruthlessness and thoroughness." [38]

(MARSHALL MCLUHAN, *UNDERSTANDING MEDIA: THE EXTENSIONS OF MAN*)

3 Sheets—Sheet 2.

C. L. SHOLES.

Type-Writing Machine.

No. 207,559. Patented Aug. 27, 1878.

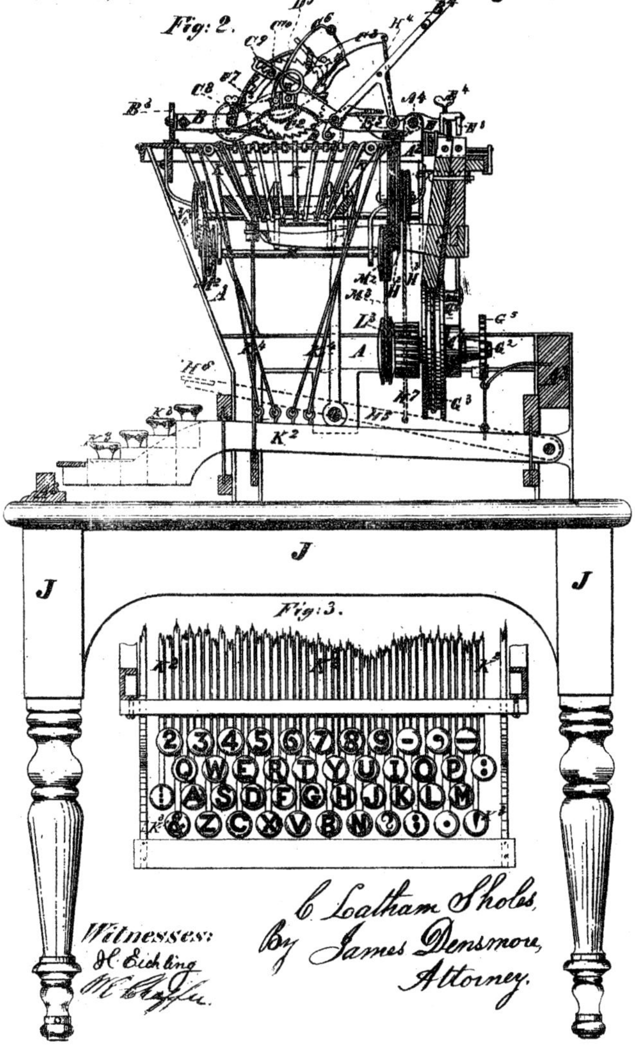

Telephone

"Phony implies that a thing so qualified has no more substance than a telephone talk with a supposititious friend." [39]

"The telephone demands complete participation, unlike the written word and printed page." [40]

"Why should the phone create an intense feeling of loneliness?" [41]

"Why does a phone ringing on a stage create instant tension?" [42]

"Like the typewriter, the telephone fuses functions, enabling the call-girl, for example, to be her own procurer and madam." [43]

(MARSHALL MCLUHAN, *UNDERSTANDING MEDIA: THE EXTENSIONS OF MAN*)

A. G. BELL.

SPEAKING TELEPHONE.

No. 250,704. Patented Dec. 13, 1881.

Fig. 2.

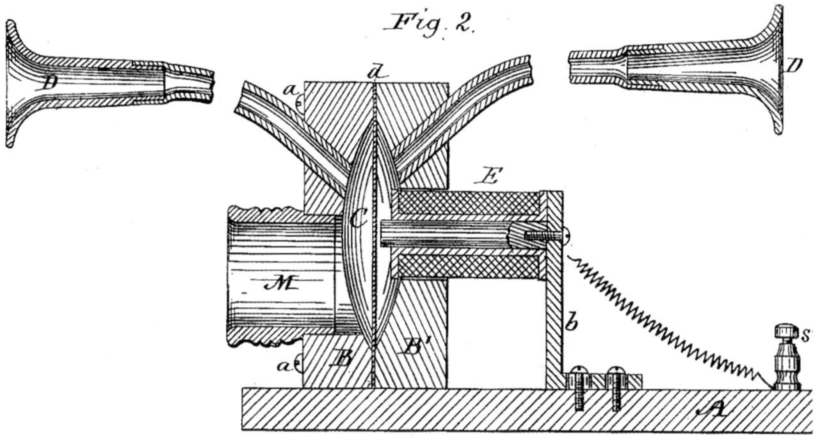

Fig. 1.

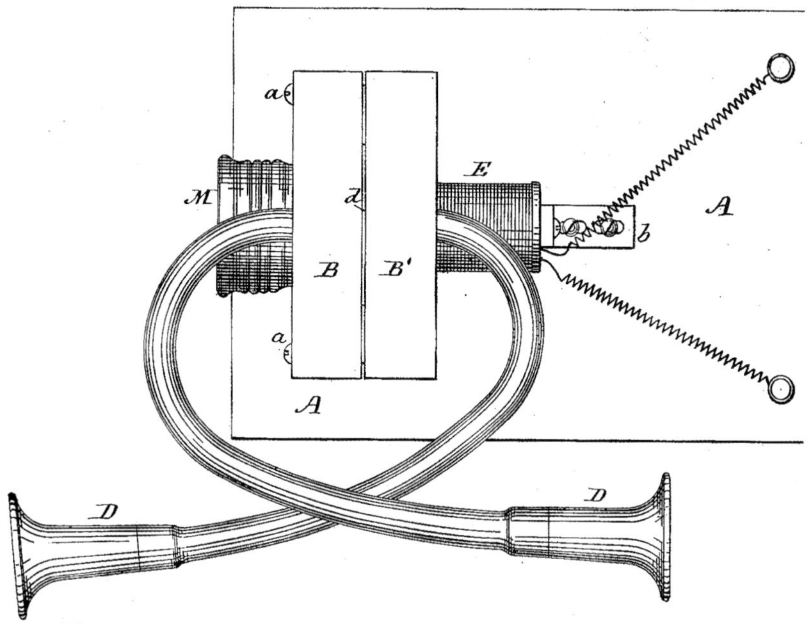

Witnesses:

C. J. Hedrick.

Philip Mauro

Inventor.

Alexander Graham.

by A Pollok

his atty

Phonograph

"Edison was delayed in his approach to the solution of [the phonograph]'s problems by considering it at first as a 'telephone repeater'; that is, a store-house of data from the telephone, enabling the telephone to 'provide invaluable records, instead of being the recipient of momentary and fleeting communication.'"

(THOMAS EDISON IN 1878, QUOTED BY MARSHALL MCLUHAN, *UNDERSTANDING MEDIA: THE EXTENSIONS OF MAN*) [44]

T A. EDISON.
Phonograph or Speaking Machine.

No. 200,521. Patented Feb. 19, 1878.

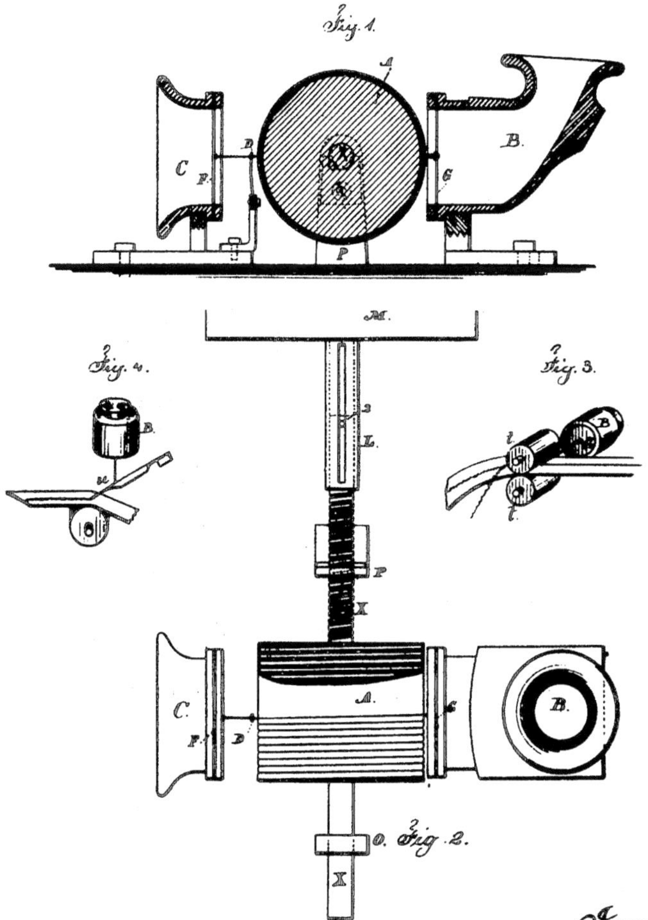

Witnesses
Chas H. Smith
Harold Serrell

Inventor
Thomas A. Edison.
per Lemuel W. Serrell
atty.

Smartphone

"**Man the tool-making animal,** [as McLuhan calls us],

whether in speech or in writing or in radio, has long been engaged in extending one or another of his sense organs in such a manner as to disturb all of his other senses and faculties."[45]

But **never before** have so many of Man's Media-Making Tools been found in a single device. With the smartphone,

we are no longer just looking at and writing about photography and written information on the same devices, we are making photography and writing on the same devices.

Today, the camera, the typewriter, the telephone, the phonograph, the radio … now all live in the body of a smart phone.

How can this not have profound implications—technological and psychological?

"**The psychic and social changes resulting from these forms have altered the whole of our lives.**"

(MARSHALL MCLUHAN, *UNDERSTANDING MEDIA: THE EXTENSIONS OF MAN*) [46]

The following anecdote from Kathy Gannon's *I is for Infidel . . . J is for Jihad, K is for Kalashnikov*—one of the best books on Afghanistan—highlights the evolution of technology in a short decade:

"[In 2001], the Taliban didn't allow photography or videotaping. But Amir Shah [Gannon's Afghan colleague and friend who remained when foreign journalists were kicked out in the early weeks of the war] was brilliant, brave, and uncanny, and he managed to do both. He had a handheld video camera, and one day when he was filming, a couple of Taliban soldiers surprised him. He thought fast. With one quick motion he put the camera to his ear, pretended it was a radio, and said: 'Brothers, it's the BBC.' They had seen so few cameras that they believed him."[47]

Today, phonecams are indistinguishable from phones and radios, and even the Taliban use social media and smartphones. What seemed technologically absurd in 2001 would become the norm by 2010.

your smartphone's HIDDEN LAYERS

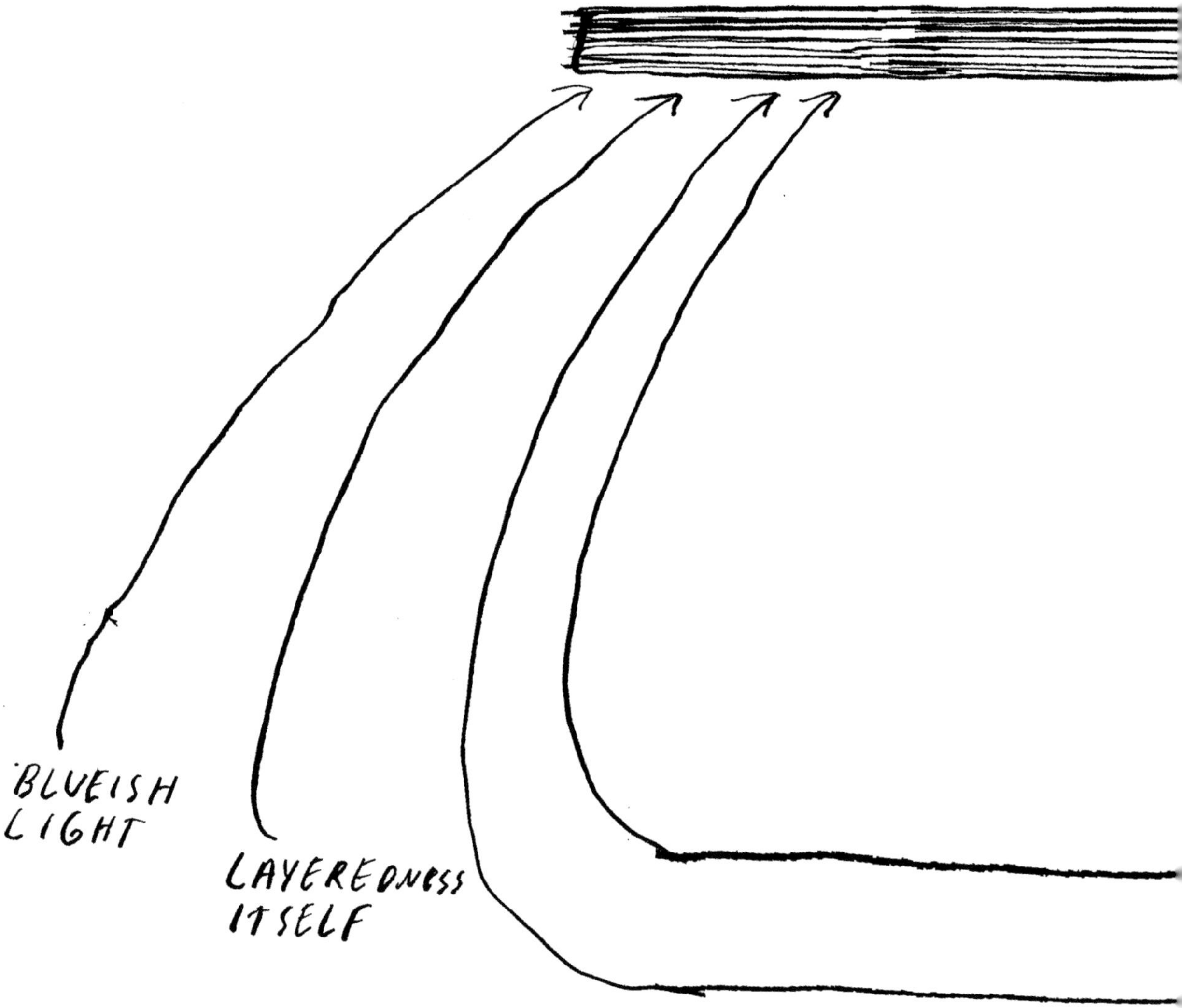

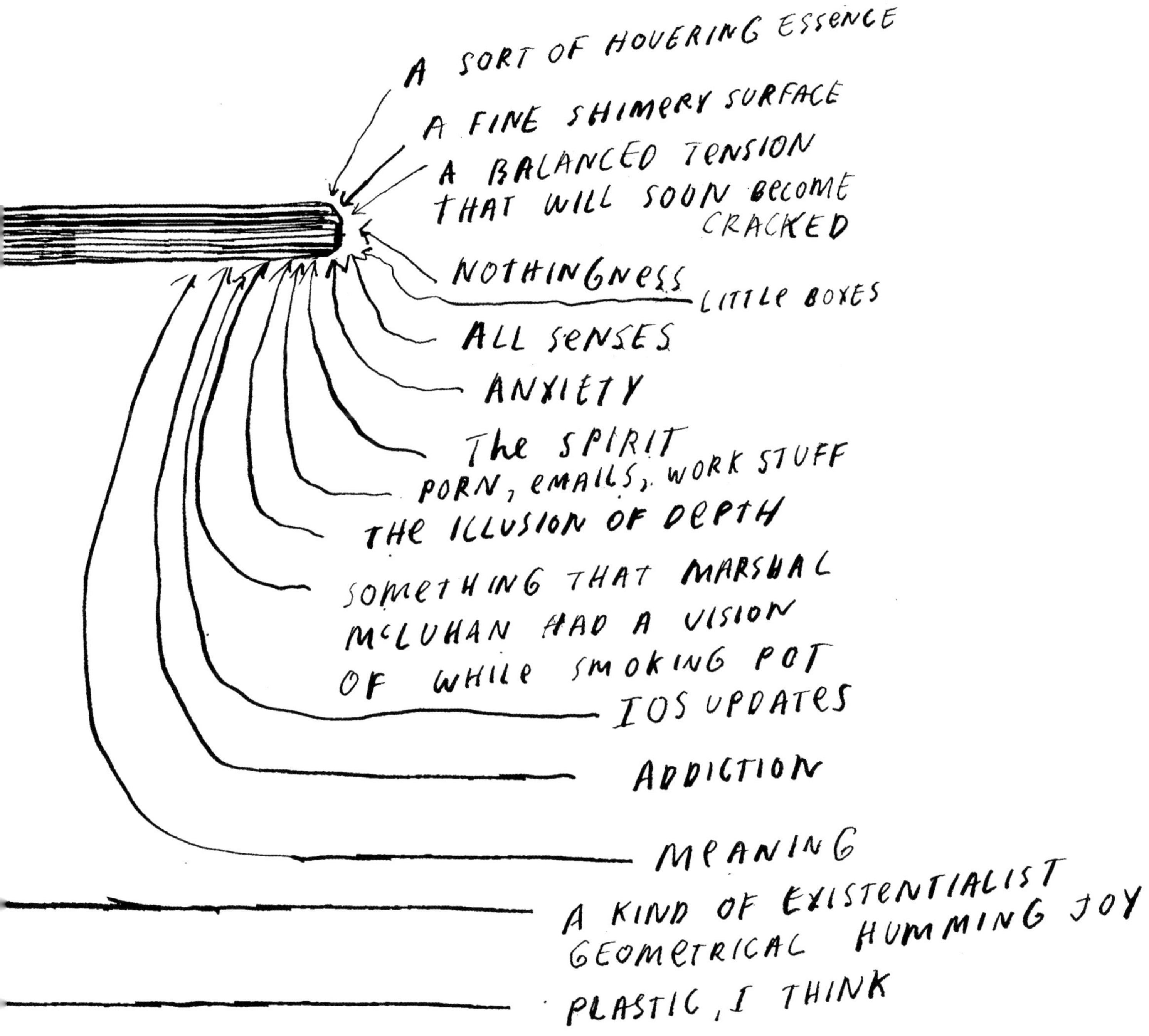
A SORT OF HOVERING ESSENCE
A FINE SHIMERY SURFACE
A BALANCED TENSION THAT WILL SOON BECOME CRACKED
NOTHINGNESS
LITTLE BOXES
ALL SENSES
ANXIETY
THE SPIRIT
PORN, EMAILS, WORK STUFF
THE ILLUSION OF DEPTH
SOMETHING THAT MARSHAL MCLUHAN HAD A VISION OF WHILE SMOKING POT
IOS UPDATES
ADDICTION
MEANING
A KIND OF EXISTENTIALIST GEOMETRICAL HUMMING JOY
PLASTIC, I THINK

form = content
medium = message

"Having noticed nothing about the *form*, they could discern nothing of the *contents* either."

(MARSHALL MCLUHAN, *UNDERSTANDING MEDIA: THE EXTENSIONS OF MAN*) [48]

It felt subversive to take images shot on an iPhone and hoick them out of the safety of their little black device (the digital womb) into the outside world to be printed with ink on paper.

They were born, after all, to flow freely from phone to phone or across social media networks, to be taken and looked at and perhaps never looked at again—almost as ephemeral and transient at the light images cast by the camera obscura, as impermanent as reflections in a mirror.

But I wanted to make this book while books were still being made as material objects and I wanted to pay homage to McLuhan's collaborations with graphic designer Quentin Fiore and journalist Jerome Agel—

The Medium is the Massage: An Inventory of Effects
and
***War and Peace in the Global Village*,**

where the dictum "the medium is the message" is played out in the collaboration and coexistence of form and content.

Creating visual text layouts that drew attention to "the thingness" of the writing was a way to accentuate the collusion between words and images that today takes place inside the very devices we use to gather information (that is, inside the smartphone).

I had to honour the special role of typography in the Figure and Ground relationship—here eloquently described by Carl Dair, a Canadian contemporary of McLuhan's, in his 1952 landmark book, *Design with Type*:

"The page which you are now scanning is a white sheet of paper with a multitude of black characters on it. For you to see it, there must first of all be light; the light must fall on the paper and be reflected back to the eye from the white portions and absorbed by the dark.

"When we read, what we really see, then, is not the printed type, but the paper itself. The type has only a negative value; we are aware of it only because it represents an area of the sheet from which no light is reflected; we do not really 'see' it." [49]

(The digital womb.)

Light falls

"The theme of the letter and the spirit, a dichotomy deriving from writing, was frequently alluded to by Our Lord in his 'It is written, but I say unto you.' The prophets had usually been at war with the scribes in Israel. This theme enters into the very texture of medieval thought and sensibility, as in the technique of the 'gloss' to release the light from within the text, the technique of illumination as light *through* not *on*."

(MARSHALL MCLUHAN, *THE GUTENBERG GALAXY: THE MAKING OF TYPOGRAPHIC MAN*) [50]

When text and images are viewed on iPhones or computer monitors, the light does not fall on but emits from. They are like the stained-glass windows of Gothic architecture that McLuhan compared to Scribal (pre-typographic) culture. Similar to the images on an iPhone monitor, the light shines through the windows of cathedrals (and appears to emanate from).

Figuratively, "the light" refers to the light of The Spirit as well as the physical light, and to the divine origin of "the word." This priestly domain of the word was threatened by typography that let writing fall into the hands of the lower classes. Smartphone monitors go a step further: today, the light of the spirit is in the hands of the masses.

Unplugged

A key feature of a book—whether for reading from or writing in—is that it doesn't require electric or battery power, or connection to the Internet. It's unplugged. You can read it by ambient light (the sun, a candle, an electric lamp) without wondering how long your batteries will last. It's timeless. The only thing you can't do is read it in the dark. You can write in it all alone and no one ever needs to know. There is something ineffable about the experience of the book off the grid.

Off the grid.

Portability

"Typography tended to alter language from a means of perception and exploration to a portable commodity."

(MARSHALL MCLUHAN, *THE GUTENBERG GALAXY: THE MAKING OF TYPOGRAPHIC MAN*) [51]

Typography gave rise to the mass-produced book which in turn gave people more autonomy over their intellectual and cultural lives—**knowledge could be "carried with."**

Like cameras, typewriters, phonographs and stone cuneiform tablets, a book is heavier than an iPhone.

As a photographer who has spent much of the last three decades lugging camera and lighting equipment and computers around the world, through airports and customs, across mountain ranges and deserts, embedded and unembedded, and almost never with an assistant or anyone to help me carry my gear, I can attest that there is immense appeal to anything lightweight. I sometimes joke (not so jokingly) that I should have picked "a lighter profession."

It may be that weight, as much as anything else, becomes the deciding factor of how we will make and access information in the future.

In the age of iPhones and social media

the simultaneity and speed of image and information production and transfer creates a **cacophony of instantaneity;**

it's The Global Village on speed.

The great challenge of the future will be archive and data management and

The Lost Art of Slowing Down.

I've said already that I am not so well suited to The Fast Arts, and that by the time the embed and the following weeks spent in Kabul uploading images to the Internet and "feeding the beast" were over, I had a major feeling of unresolvedness.

By focusing on process, I brought myself back to Slow Art Making and found some peace of mind.

I came up with the title for an essay, "Looking for Marshall McLuhan in Afghanistan," which Diana Kuprel and Alastair Cheng edited and published as a twelve-part online series in the *Literary Review of Canada (LRC)* in January 2011. Shortly after the *LRC* piece came out, I approached graphic designer Jenny Armour, a longtime collaborator, about creating a mock-up for a book, even though at the time I didn't have a book publisher. I then showed a "work in progress" version of it in Toronto at Guntar Kravis's photography studio at 401 Richmond. So by the time I was approached by Masoud Yazdani at Intellect,

I already had the framework for a material object—

this book made of paper you can hold in your hands.

The iPhone camera is an extension of the eye and of the finger.

"Nobody can commit photography alone."

(MARSHALL MCLUHAN, *UNDERSTANDING MEDIA: THE EXTENSIONS OF MAN*)[52]

The permanence of the printed image has been exchanged for a transient digital image that most users never intend to preserve on paper. They are meant to be traded and communicated to others, like phone calls:

photograph as transmission of information,
not as material object.

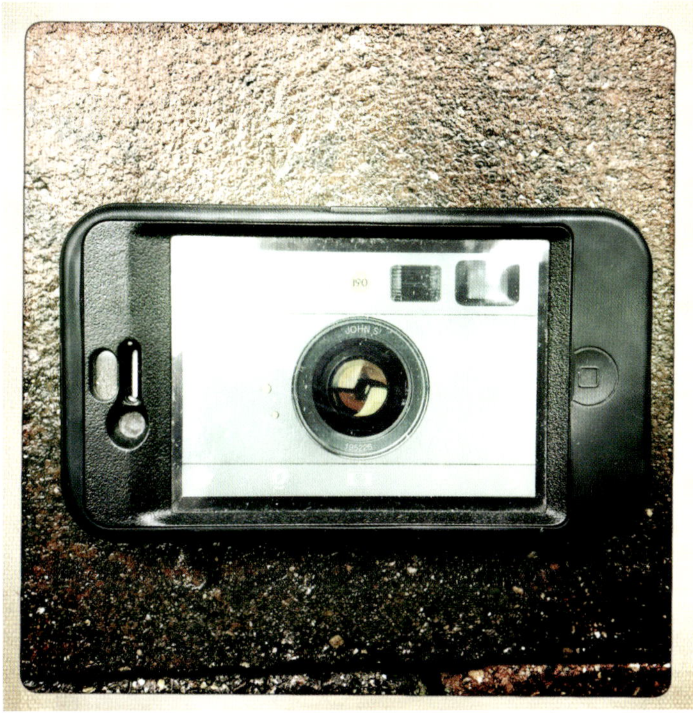

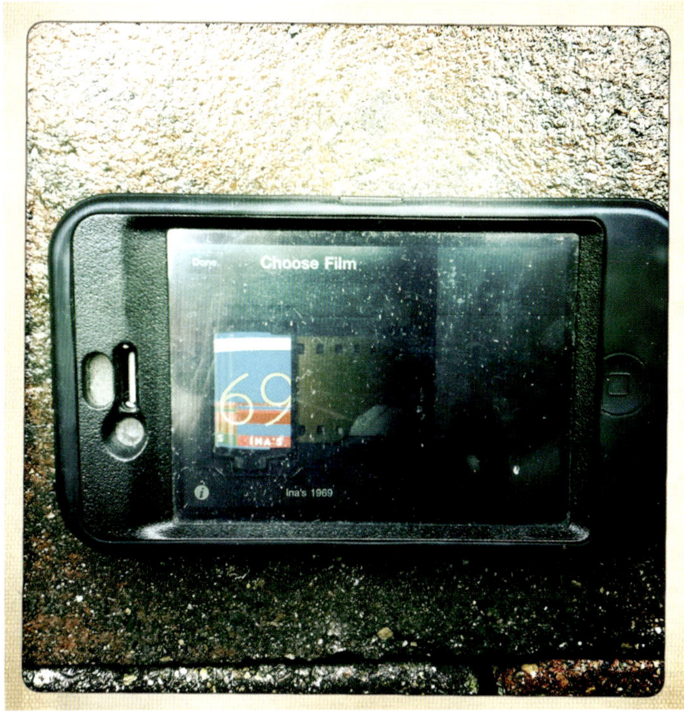
Done
Choose Film
69
INA'S
Ina's 1969

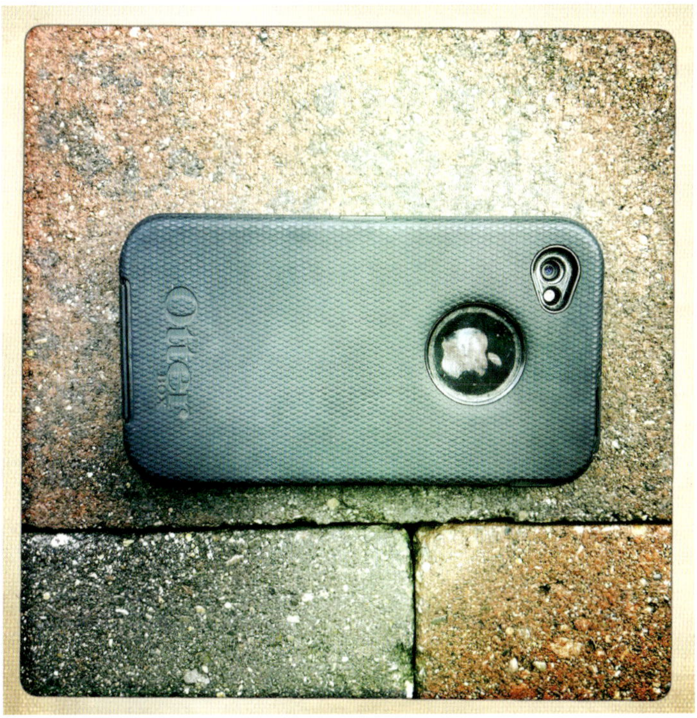
Otter

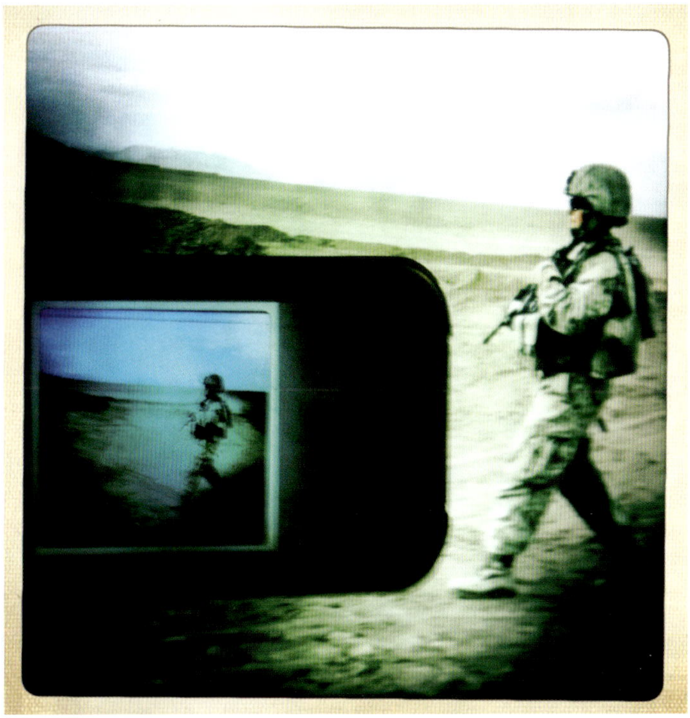

We have come a long way from and back again to the words of William Henry Fox Talbot, one of the fathers of photography, who, nearly 200 years ago, said of the light images projected through the lens of a camera obscura:

> **"How charming it would be if it were possible to cause these natural images to imprint themselves durably, and remain fixed on paper."**
>
> (WILLIAM HENRY FOX TALBOT, C.1820, QUOTED BY MARSHALL MCLUHAN IN *UNDERSTANDING MEDIA: THE EXTENSIONS OF MAN*) [53]

There is something similar but different about the experience of looking at an image of oneself on the back of an iPhone (or any digital device) compared to holding a photograph of oneself in one's hands. The first portrait photography was viewed as a kind of fixed mirror image. It drew analogies to the myth of Narcissus, as described by McLuhan:

“Men at once become fascinated by any extension of themselves in any material other than themselves.”

(MARSHALL MCLUHAN IN *UNDERSTANDING MEDIA: THE EXTENSIONS OF MAN*) [54]

We look at images of ourselves on the backs of digital devices as if looking into mirrors

because the instantaneity of the moment gives over to the feeling of looking at ourselves “as we are.”

This is seen in children who look at pictures of themselves on the backs of cameras with curiosity, with no expectation that the image will ever be more than

the shiny frozen-in-a-second picture that seems to live inside the box.

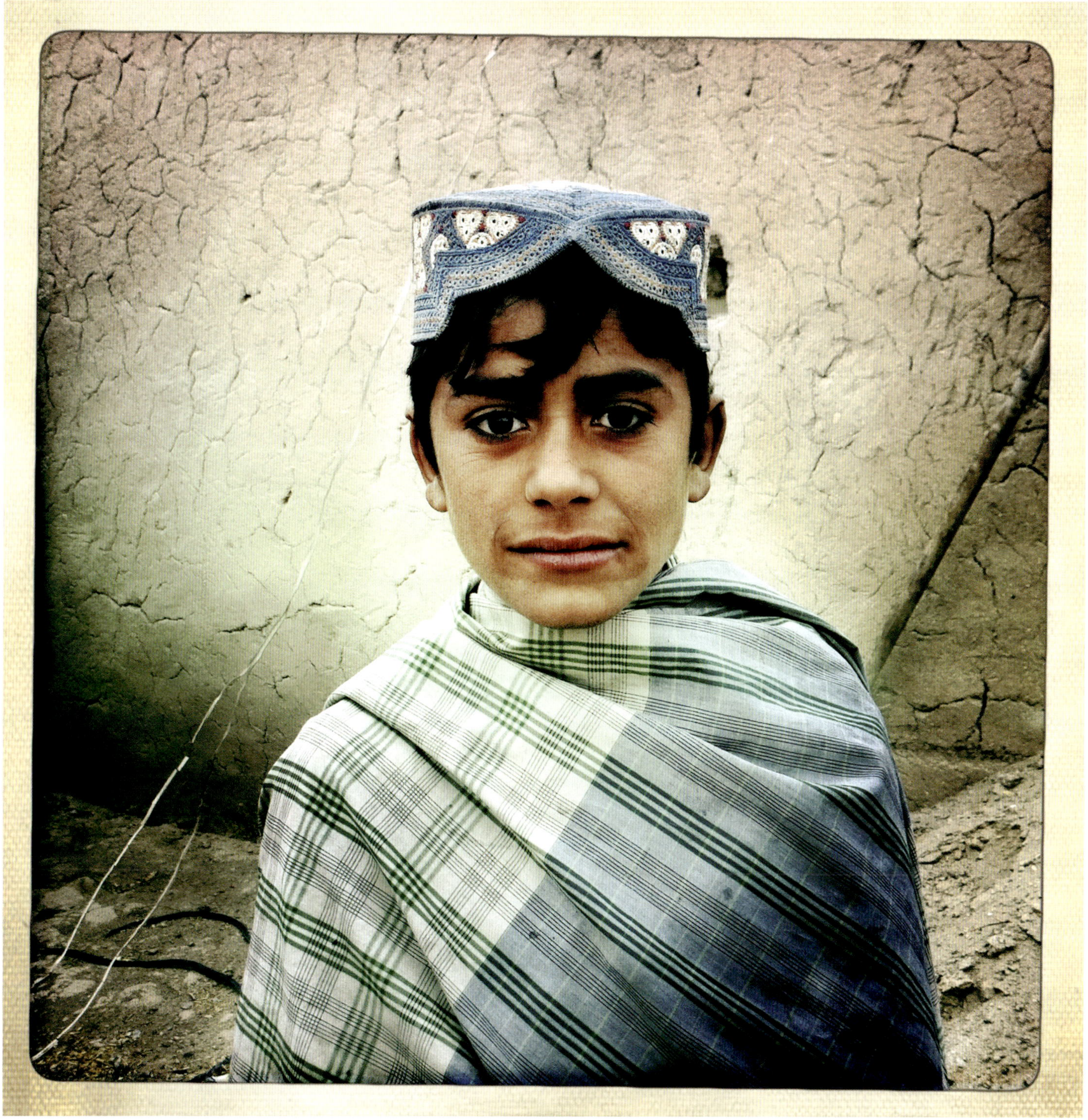

As a professional photographer I own a lot of cameras and lighting equipment, and I'd never imagined I'd ever have a need or desire to use a phonecam. But I'd been intrigued by using this technology in a place that modernity seems on so many levels to have passed by.

Putting aside traditional DSLR photography (single-lens reflex cameras with a digital sensor in place of film) in favour of an admittedly gimmicky iPhone Hipstamatic app was a leap of faith.

I think the Marines were suspicious of our high-tech but low-skill devices. Some said they thought at first it was a joke.

And I believe the Afghans, who recognized we were people of some means, wondered why we weren't using "real cameras." I'm sure it crossed their minds

that it was some sort of trick.

When a Master Gunnery Sergeant (the top military and weapons-tech guy in the Battalion) asked me what it was like to use an iPhone as a camera, I replied:

“Imagine
if one day
all the expensive
equipment you’d
mastered,
all your training,
all your experience
and knowledge,
everything you’d
spent your life
sweating to learn,
became obsolete,
and was replaced
with a
Green Lantern
Power Ring
that anyone
could use.
That’s what using
the iPhone as
a camera
feels like to me.”

Phonecams are mysterious creatures. Unlike DSLRs, which are a kind of Borg-like hybrid, mechanical/digital beast with removable optical lenses and many other recognizable moving parts, camera phones are pure digital Post-Mechanical devices.

The only thing left from their mechanical ancestors is the small optical lens—the extension of the user's eye.

Hipstamatic was founded by Lucas Buick and Ryan Dorshorst and inspired by the Polaroid SX-70 single-lens reflex Land Camera (named after Polaroid founder Edwin Land).

Buick and Dorshorst and the programmers they work with are like the "new chemists" in the equation of the once mechanical-chemical art, names in a lineage that includes William Henry Fox Talbot, Louis Daguerre and Nicéphore Niépce.

But

instead of chemistry, they use algorithms.

The effect of the app is so much a part of the final image, that it makes sense to me to credit the developers in the images' bylines.

The Hipstamatic app is an attempt to reclaim the loss of mechanical photography within the digital medium. The look of the app on the iPhone (with absolutely no functional value) is a virtual-mechanical camera. The "shutter" is represented by an image of a button that you press with your finger—the only "digit" left in digital.

"Digital photography never looked so analog."

(MARKETING TAGLINE FROM THE HIPTAMATIC WEBSITE [HIPTAMATIC.COM])

The Hipstamatic app simulates analog photography by using a set of algorithms to apply exaggerated effects to the image files, mimicking traditional photographic processes and reclaiming some of the artifactual qualities of material objects. It doesn't matter that we know the images are digital. Our eyes and our brains are easy purveyors of semiotics. And so, being affected by the effects of the technology and its near-immediate rendering of a visual experience into a digitally rendered material object,

I began to look at things, in general, more materially.

The extensions of man, all media and technologies, are also removes away from the human hive—like the robotic drones first developed by the Israelis for surveillance purposes.

When I got my iPhone, the first thing I did, as with any new piece of equipment, was look for instructions. But there weren't any. The app has downloadable effects called "film" and "lenses," and I had to figure out what I was going to use in Afghanistan. However, the descriptions of the effects that come with the Hipstamatic app are completely abstract and non-specific—which was frustrating to my

instruction-manual obsessed, literate, linear-thinking habits.

Here's how they described the "Ina's 69" film effect:

"Ina has a bakery today but 40 years ago she was rocking some pretty serious instant film. Peel away the boring with this fine film."

Huh?

In the end I asked my colleagues what they were using based on trial and error: Ina's 69 plus the John S Lens.

In *The Medium is the Massage*, McLuhan declares:

“Printing created the portable book, which men could read in privacy and in isolation from others . . .

The printed book added much to the new cult of individualism.

“The private, fixed point of view became possible and literacy conferred the power of detachment, non-involvement.” [55]

The Hipstamatic app distances itself from this idea of “the book” or the printed word.

It forces users to consult (and conspire) with others as to how it works (face-to-face or on Facebook).

It’s geared toward the Internet and communal sharing and so it deliberately omits instructions or any kind of prescriptive information. It is truly an experiential, involving technology,

like oral culture,
music
or pictographic
languages such
as Chinese:
you can use it
on your own,
but you have to
rely on shared
information from
“the tribe” to
learn how it works.

Texting is an extension of the thumbs and the fingers, and of the eyes.

“The alphabet is an aggressive and militant absorber and transformer of cultures.”

(MARSHALL MCLUHAN, *THE GUTENBERG GALAXY: THE MAKING OF TYPOGRAPHIC MAN*) [56]

"The phonetic alphabet is a unique technology.

There have been many kinds of writing, pictographic and syllabic, but there is only one phonetic alphabet in which semantically meaningless letters are used to correspond to semantically meaningless sounds."

(MARSHALL MCLUHAN, *UNDERSTANDING MEDIA: THE EXTENSIONS OF MAN*) [57]

lkng 4 mrshl m

abjads and alphabets are **the medium;** language is **the message**

abjads and alphabets are **Figure;** language is **Ground**

abjads and alphabets are **visual;** language is **oral and aural**

The Alpha and the Omega

The Roman (Latin) alphabet used by English is a vowel-rich alphabet descended from Ancient Greek. The Greeks had taken the consonantal alphabet of the Egyptians (invented around 2000 bce) and added the vowels AEIOU to it. Texting language flips Latin alphabetic spelling back into the ancestral consonantal systems.

Texting obsolesces speech and ears—and vowels

clhn n ‘fghnstn

W cn rd cnsnts
bt nt vwls
e a ea ooa u o oe[58]

W cn rd
Dnt frgt 2 brng yr pssprt
Bt nt
O oe 2 i ou ao[59]

In the field of computational linguistics, this kind of transliteration is called

collapsed consonant and vowel models

and so the same method that texters use naturally (or **organ**ically, as McLuhan would prefer to say) to transliterate to texting language, is used by computers for translating languages like English to languages like Persian or Arabic and vice versa.[60]

While the Greek alphabet (which was adapted by the Romans into the alphabet today used by English) added vowels to the Canaanite (and later Phoenician) consonantal system, another branch of the alphabet that would become one of the most important in the world, the Arabic alphabet, held on to the consonantal system handed down to them by Aramaic (which is also the grandfather of Hebrew).

Another term for consonantal alphabets is

Abjad

—so-named for the first letters of the Semitic Judeo-Arabic alphabets, such as

Aramaic		**Modern Naskh (Arabic)**		**Hebrew**	
Alaph	א	**A**leph	ا	Aleph	א
Beth	ב	**B**eht	ب	Bet	ב
Gamal	ג	**J**im	ج	Gimel	ג
Dalath	ד	**D**ahl	د	Daled	ד

An example of consonantal spelling of a well-known word is Quran. In Abjad languages, it is spelled with just three consonants

q+r+n (قرن) —

there is no need for vowels to clarify what the letters spell out.

This is a good example of what McLuhan is talking about when he talks about

the reversal of the overheated medium

—technologies, pushed to extremes, revert back to earlier forms of themselves, both causing and being caused by the cross-fertilization of media systems.

(MARSHALL MCLUHAN, CHAPTER 3 "REVERSAL OF THE OVERHEATED MEDIUM," *UNDERSTANDING MEDIA: THE EXTENSIONS OF MAN*) [61]

And so,

some three thousand years later,

two of the great alphabetic writing systems, both stemming from a common North Semitic root

—the Aramaic family branch of Hebrew and Arabic; and the Phoenician Greco-Etruscan family of Latin (used by English and most European languages)—

are joining up again in smartphones.

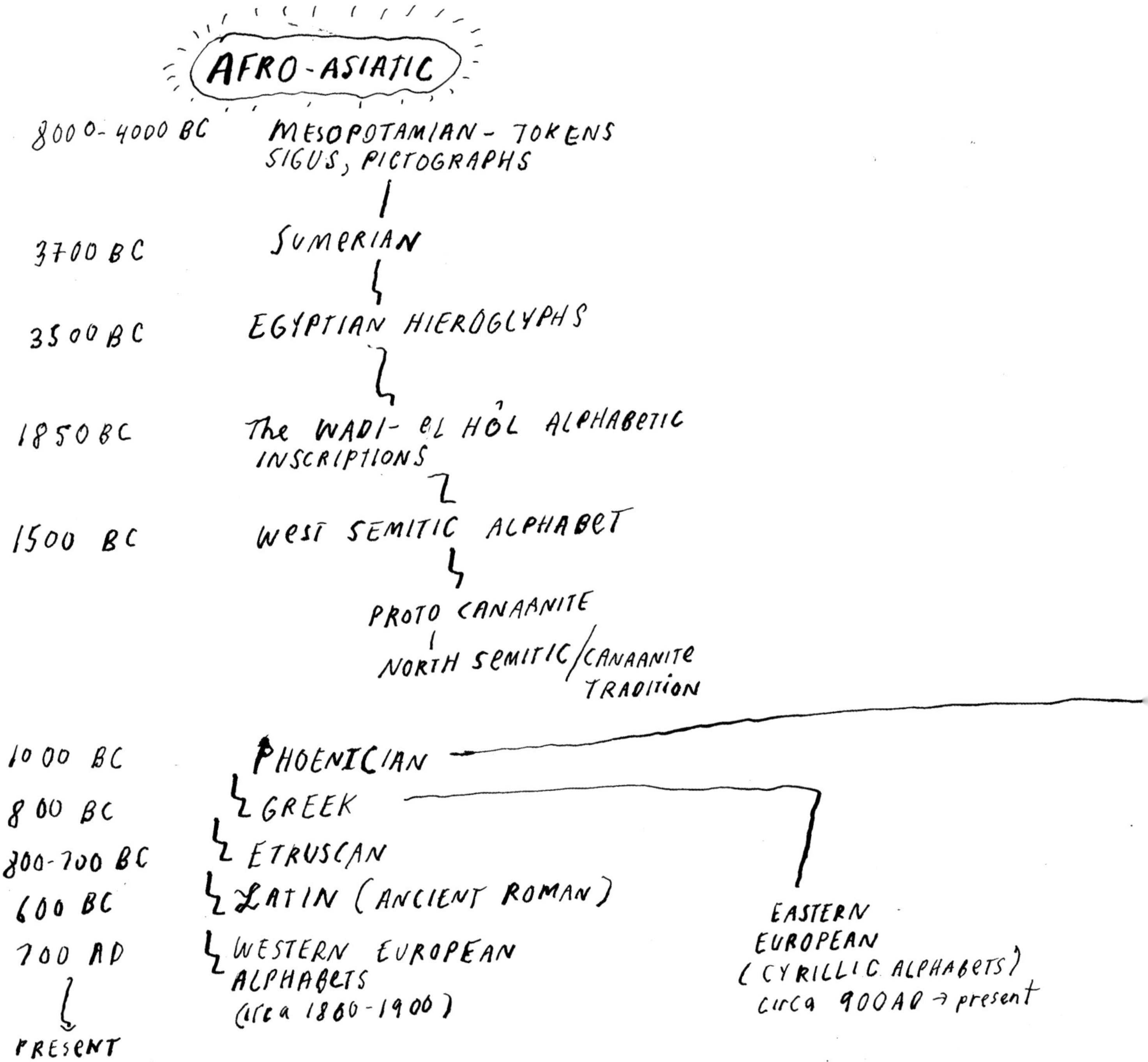
AFRO-ASIATIC
8000-4000 BC
MESOPOTAMIAN - TOKENS SIGNS, PICTOGRAPHS
3700 BC
SUMERIAN
3500 BC
EGYPTIAN HIEROGLYPHS
1850 BC
The WADI-EL HÔL ALPHABETIC INSCRIPTIONS
1500 BC
WEST SEMITIC ALPHABET
PROTO CANAANITE
NORTH SEMITIC/CANAANITE TRADITION
1000 BC
PHOENICIAN
800 BC
GREEK
800-700 BC
ETRUSCAN
600 BC
LATIN (ANCIENT ROMAN)
700 AD
WESTERN EUROPEAN ALPHABETS (circa 1800-1900)
PRESENT
EASTERN EUROPEAN (CYRILLIC ALPHABETS) circa 900AD → present

A Story of ADJADS and Alphabets
(IN A KIND OF TIMELINE FLOW CHART)

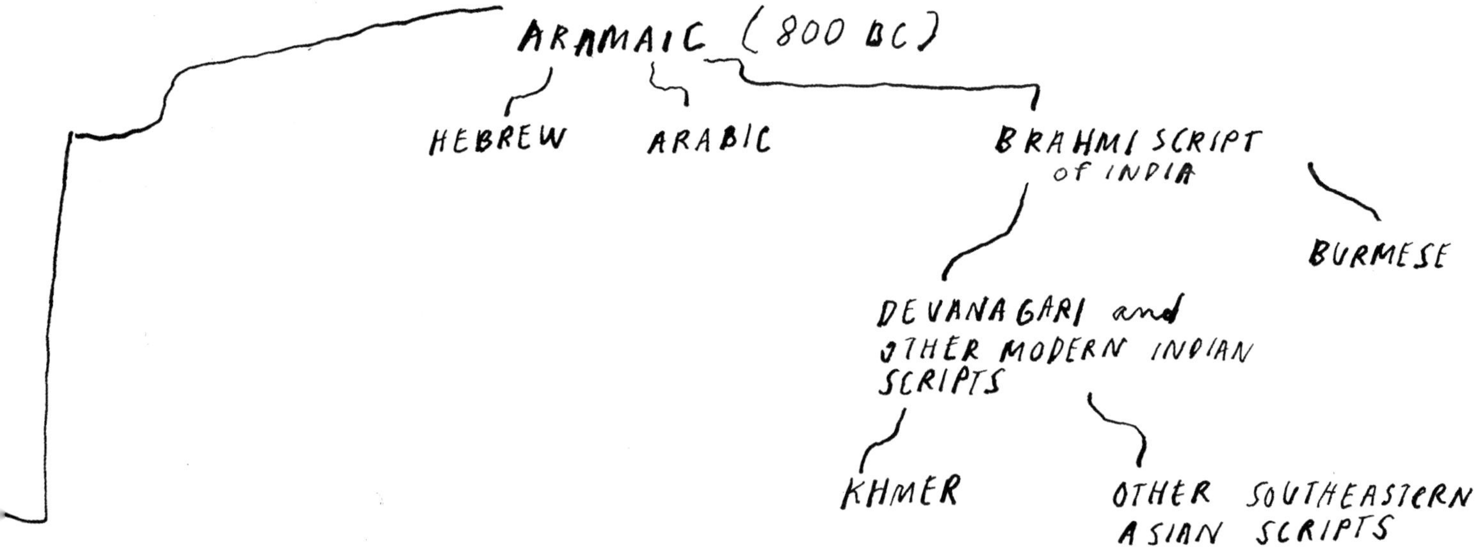

THESE CHARTS ARE SIMPLIFIED VERSIONS OF WHAT IS ALREADY AN INEXACT SCIENCE. ANY ERRORS BELONG TO THE AUTHOR, WHO OWES A DEBT OF GRATITUDE TO THE FOLLOWING SOURCES:

STEVEN ROGER FISCHER, *A HISTORY OF WRITING*, PP. 88-89; DAVID SACKS, *LETTER PERFECT—THE MARVELOUS HISTORY OF OUR ALPHABET FROM A TO Z*, PP. XIV TO XV; AND GORDON J. HAMILTON, *THE ORIGINS OF THE WEST SEMITIC ALPHABET IN EGYPTIAN SCRIPTS*.

SOME PARTS OF THE Story of Languages (IN A CHART FORM)

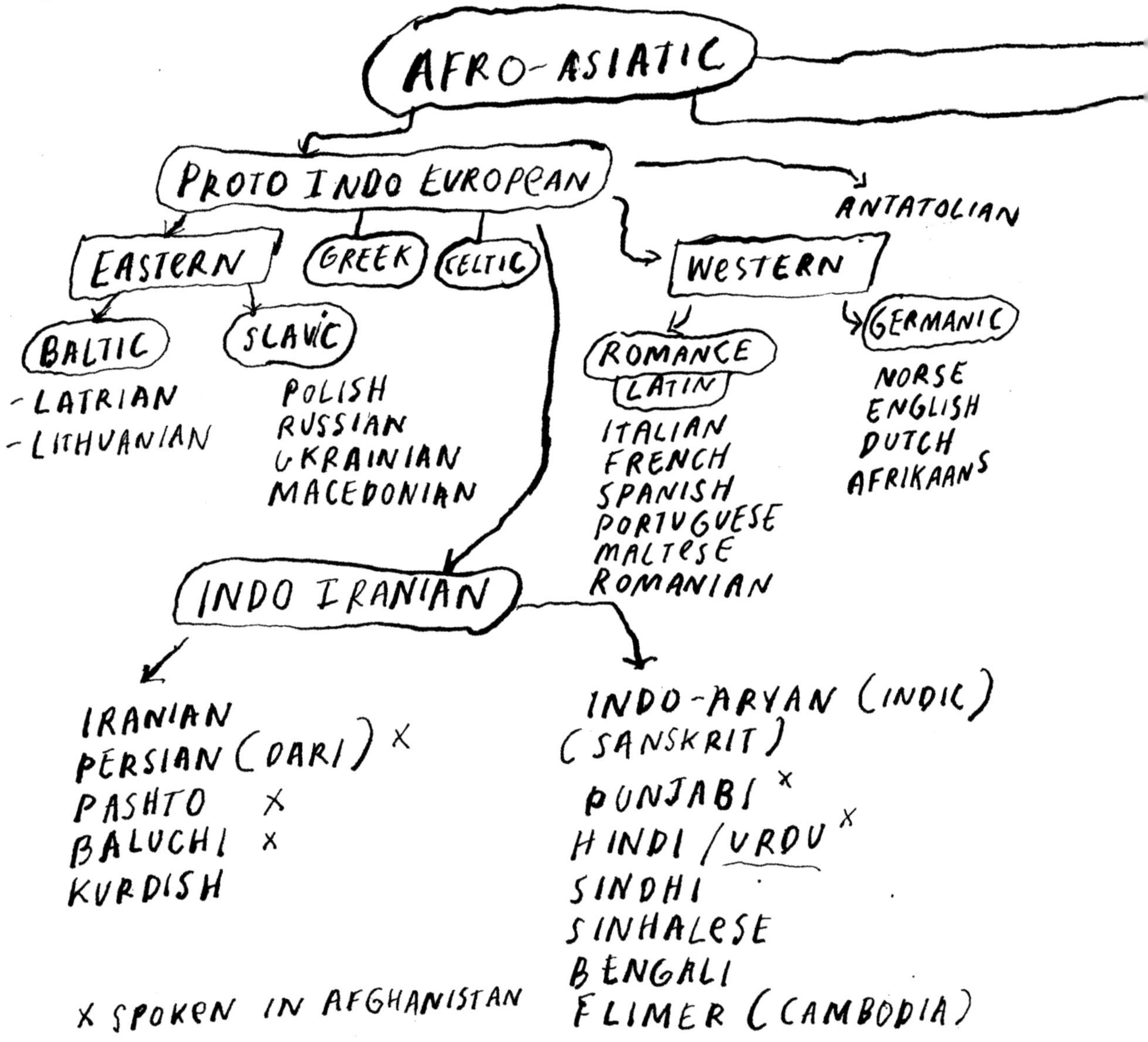

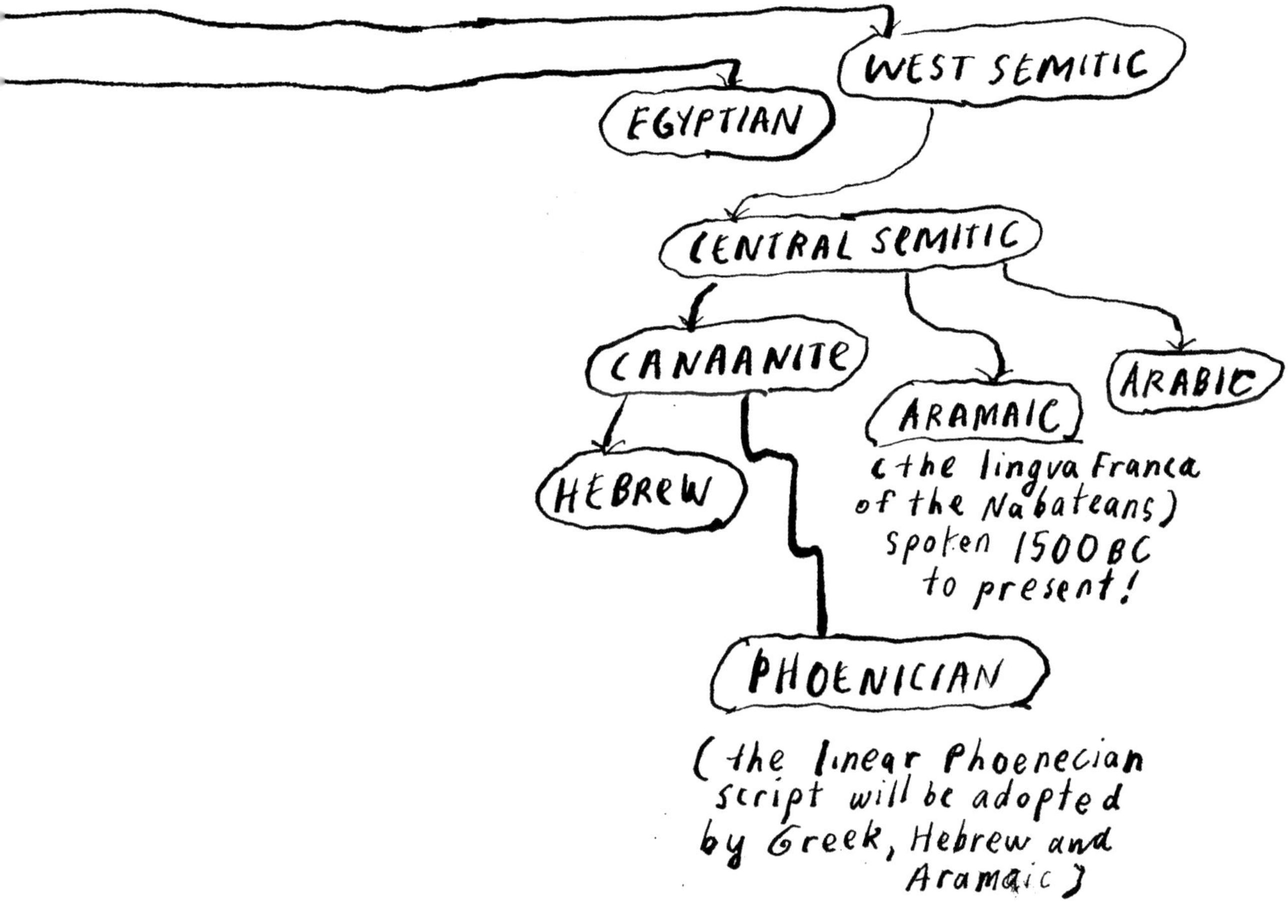

THIS CHART IS A SIMPLIFIED VERSION OF WHAT IS ALREADY AN INEXACT SCIENCE. ANY ERRORS BELONG TO THE AUTHOR, WHO OWES A DEBT OF GRATITUDE TO THE FOLLOWING SOURCES:

FOR THE INDO-EUROPEAN LANGUAGE BRANCH: LOUIS DUPREE, *AFGHANISTAN*, P. 69; STEVEN ROGER FISCHER, *A HISTORY OF LANGUAGE*, PP. 82–83. FOR THE WEST SEMITIC BRANCH: GORDON J. HAMILTON, *THE ORIGINS OF THE WEST SEMITIC ALPHABET IN EGYPTIAN SCRIPTS*; AND ROGER D. WOODARD, (ED.), *THE ANCIENT LANGUAGES OF SYRIA-PALESTINE AND ARABIA*.

Meanwhile, the literary correlatives to the photographic doomsayers who cry out that putting phonecams into the hands of the masses will be the ruin of photography, prophesize about the smartphone's threat to language and about the death of "good writing."

Arabists complain that the merging of English and Arabic alphabets in the hybrid *Arabish* threatens the very existence of the Arabic language, while those who use the Roman alphabet see texting's abbreviations and contractions as a threat to standard spelling and grammar.

But as David Crystal, who has written a lot about texting language in English, points out in his book *Spell it out: The singular story of English spelling*, "it's actually quite tricky to write a heavily abbreviated sentence so that people will be able to read and understand it. And, of course, if it is 'cool' to leave letters out, texters have to know that the letters are there in the first place in order to leave them out. Unsurprisingly, then, the best texters and tweeters turn out to be the best spellers."[63]

Arabish

In the process of transliterating Arabic into Roman texting script—sometimes called *Arabish* or *Arabi el Englizi* or, in regions where French is more used than English, *Arabi el Francia*—Arabic alphabet phonetic letter sounds that are not found in the Roman alphabet are replaced with numbers. **For example, the letter symbol ع that represents the guttural sound "ayn" is represented by the number 3**, so that words like

الشلام عليكم

are written like this:

al salam 3alikum

حبيبي

becomes

7abeebi

عربي

becomes

3arabi

What is surprising is that the

Arabic texting language adds vowels where English texting language removes them.

Of course both of these text languages are evolving.

The two official languages of Afghanistan—Dari and Pashto—are descendants of Indo-Iranian, which also includes Farsi, the language of Iran. All are Persian languages that are written in the Arabic script but have almost nothing in common with the spoken language Arabic (see iProbe 8_Loud Speakers and Sermons from the Mosques and iProbe 10_The Written Word).

In fact, ***F**arsi* is an Arabic alphabet transliteration of the original word for the Iranian Persian language ***P**arsi*, but because there is no ***p*** sound in the Arabic alphabet, it changed to ***F**arsi*.

The smartphone, like the epoch-making invention of the phonetic alphabet, is a huge game changer that is carrying mankind to a new plateau of

mass written and visual literacy.

"Initially, writing had been an instrument of power in the hands of small groups of priests, soothsayers and scribes serving deified monarchs. It was the perfect tool for social ascendency, the expression of a small élite's ideology. With the diffusion of writing following consonantal writing's elaboration in particular, however, writing could no longer remain the monopoly of the rich and powerful. It now served everyone: reading and writing could easily be learnt in a short period of time by many."

(STEPHEN ROGER FISCHER, *A HISTORY OF WRITING*) [64]

The etymologies of the Greco-Roman words for the earliest scripts reflect the elitist, sacred role of writing in history:

Hieroglyph: 'sacred' (Greek *hieros*) inscriptions 'sculptured' (Greek *glypho*) [65]

Hieratic: 'priestly' (Greek *hieraticos*)

(GORDON J. HAMILTON, *THE ORIGINS OF THE WEST SEMITIC ALPHABET IN EGYPTIAN SCRIPTS*) [66]

David Sacks in his accessible and engaging history of the Latin Alphabet, *Letter Perfect: The Marvelous History of Our Alphabet from A to Z,* explains that the inventors of the alphabet were not elite, literate Egyptians, but by and large an illiterate lower social class of "laborers, soldiers, concubines . . . armies, messengers, caravaners, and other land travelers." [67]

Exposed to the complex hieroglyphic writing system used by the Egyptians for whom they worked, these "lower class" people, desiring a simpler way to record their own spoken language, distilled the thousands of pictographic signs into one of the most important technologies man has ever made: the alphabet. **Only the wheel comes close.**

Power to the People

As David Sacks further explains, "aside from the non alphabetic writing systems of China and Japan, almost all major scripts in use today, anywhere in the world, belong to a single 'alphabet family' . . . The family stems entirely from the first Semitic language of 2000 bce [the language of the Canaanites]. This ancestor produced a prime descendant: The Phoenician alphabet (1000 bce), which, from its base in what is now Lebanon, became

the launching pad for a global proliferation."[68]

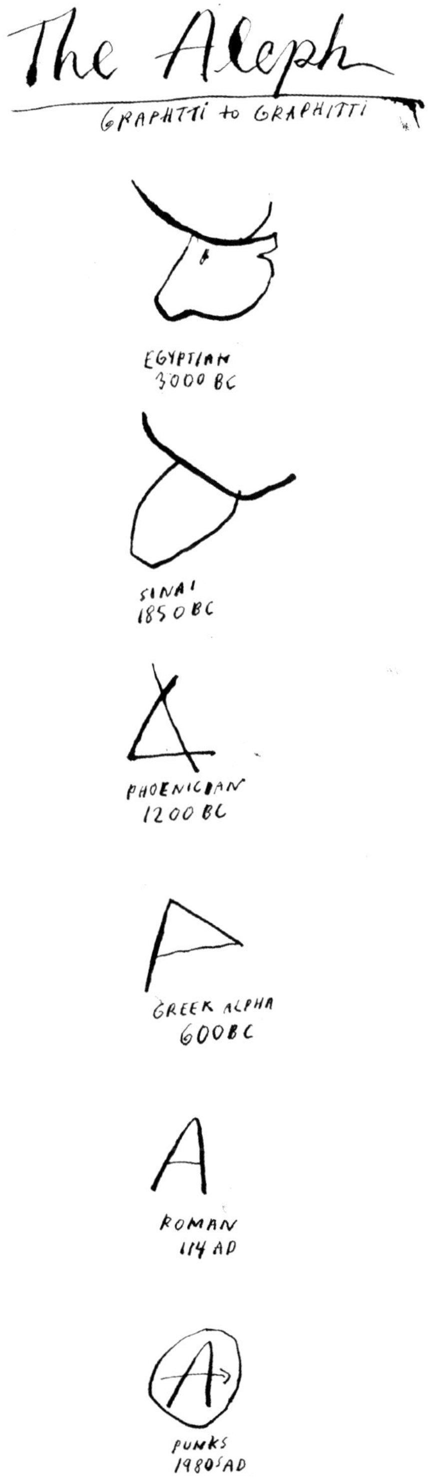

The acrophonic principle

There is some, but little dispute, that the phonetic letters used by all alphabets today were developed from Egyptian pictographic prototypes. Thus, the Egyptian hieroglyph for "head of ox"—pronounced ***alph***—was adopted to represent the single phoneme ***a***. The hieroglyph for "house"—pronounced ***beit***—was adopted to represent the single phoneme ***b***, et cetera. The first alphabets were **acrophonic: a letter's name begins with the letter itself**. Four thousand years later, many of these acrophonic letters are still in use: in both Arabic and Hebrew, for instance, ***beit*** still stands for the letter sound ***b*** and the noun "house."

A modern example of an acrophonic alphabet is the International Radiotelephony Spelling Alphabet used by the military to avoid confusion when spelling out loud. It's the alphabet used for the **acrophonous double entendre** in the title of Ashley Gilbertson's excellent book on the Iraq War, ***Whiskey Tango Foxtrot (*****Chicago: The University of Chicago Press, 2007), which stands for WTF, and also, "What The Fuck?"**

"The computer, developed by a culture using the Latin alphabet, is redefining our modern world in this script; anyone who wishes to share the tool must command its keyboard."

(STEVEN ROGER FISCHER, *A HISTORY OF WRITING*) [70]

Try this experiment:

Switch your computer QWERTY English keyboard to a QWERTY keyboard in Arabic, Hebrew, Cyrillic or Greek (or try all four). The alphabets are similar enough that you will find you can actually type with enough accuracy to make your writing understood phonetically in all languages.

When the typewriter was invented in the 1870s (originally as a prosthetic device for the blind) the QWERTY keyboard (copyright of Christopher Latham Sholes, "father of the typewriter," 1893) became part of the legacy that would take keyboarding into the digital era.

The letters on the QWERTY keyboard were arranged for mechanical reasons (preventing jammed keys), not linguistic ones. Note for instance, that while almost every word in languages using the Roman alphabet of QWERTY has a vowel in it, only the vowel "A" is located on the home row.

The QWERTY keyboard is one the many anachronistic phantoms from earlier technologies that reside in smartphones.

These days when I write in longhand it's mostly because it frees me from a power source and because I still have the habit of making marginal notes in my books with a pen. In fact,

I find it hard to read without a pen in my hand.

But I think people like me are getting fewer and further between. I had a student this year borrow a pen from me to write an in-class exam—"I haven't used a pen in months," he told me.

Spilling ink from the tip of a pen, working by candlelight, electric light or the light of the sun, feels different from typing on a monitor that illuminates the writing from behind. But these are degrees of difference only.

To someone who does not know how to write, writing is full of the mystery of a performance.

Texting is the experience of performance as composition—which is what McLuhan said about typing:

"Seated at the typewriter, the poet, much in the manner of the jazz musician, has the experience of performance as composition."

(MARSHALL MCLUHAN, *UNDERSTANDING MEDIA: THE EXTENSIONS OF MAN*) [71]

All thumbs *fig.* Said of a person who is clumsy or wanting in dexterity.

The old figure of speech "all thumbs" takes on new meaning in the age of thumb texting, where thumb dexterity takes a position in the forefront of human communications for the first time.

Due to a minor motorcycle accident in Cambodia in 1998, I lack fine motor skills in my left thumb. This makes holding a fork in my left hand awkward, and normal "two-thumb texting" impossible. I worry this will render me anachronistic.

Lately, though, it's not just my inability to text fast that makes me feel old. During the course of writing this book on my desktop using a QWERTY keyboard and a mouse, I've noticed a carpal boss forming on my wrist—a bony protrusion caused by repetitive stress injury. But I can't only blame typing. I have no doubt it also has to do with the way I hold my five pound DSLR camera in my right hand, while holding my flash in the left.

The written silent verbal language

Most of us have had the experience of watching someone text to someone who is easily in hearing range of them. Silence is a key feature of texting that isn't often explored. It gives it a kind of telepathic quality. In a way, texting is obsolescing speech. It's the new written silent verbal language.

Steven Roger Fischer predicts that,

"Soon, written language might be more prominent worldwide than spoken language."

(STEVEN ROGER FISCHER, *A HISTORY OF WRITING*) [72]

—Certainly in some circles it already is.

iProbe 03_**Body Armour**

Body armour is an extension of the skin.

A machine gun is an extension of the eye and of the teeth.

(MARSHALL MCLUHAN, *UNDERSTANDING MEDIA: THE EXTENSIONS OF MAN*) [73]

Body armour costs anywhere from $500 to $1,500 for lighter, high-tech ballistic materials.

(2013 PRICES AT WWW.BULLETPROOFME.COM) [74]

Body armour saves lives. It also increases the number of personnel who may survive an attack but suffer grievous injuries, such as amputations.

In World War I, the ratio of injured to killed in battle was 1:1. Today, thanks partly to the availability of high-tech bulletproof materials, the ratio of injured to killed is about 5:1.

When I go into areas at risk, I wear body armour. Obviously, body armour is a good thing. However, while there is a lot of focus on the lives it saves, there is less focus on the injured it inadvertently creates, and governments that publish casualty tolls focus much less on the much higher number of injured.

There are lifelong costs to families, the injured and the government. The level of compensation varies, determined on a 1–5 scale of incapacity: this grading encompasses the physical and the psychiatric, everything from paraplegia (total cord lesion, Grade 1), total blindness (no perception of light, Grade 2) and bilateral, above-elbow amputation (Grade 3) to profound depression requiring constant care in hospital to preserve life (Grade 1) and psychic distress (Grades 4–5). Full details of ratings and compensation are made available on the Veterans Affairs websites in Canada and the United States.[75]

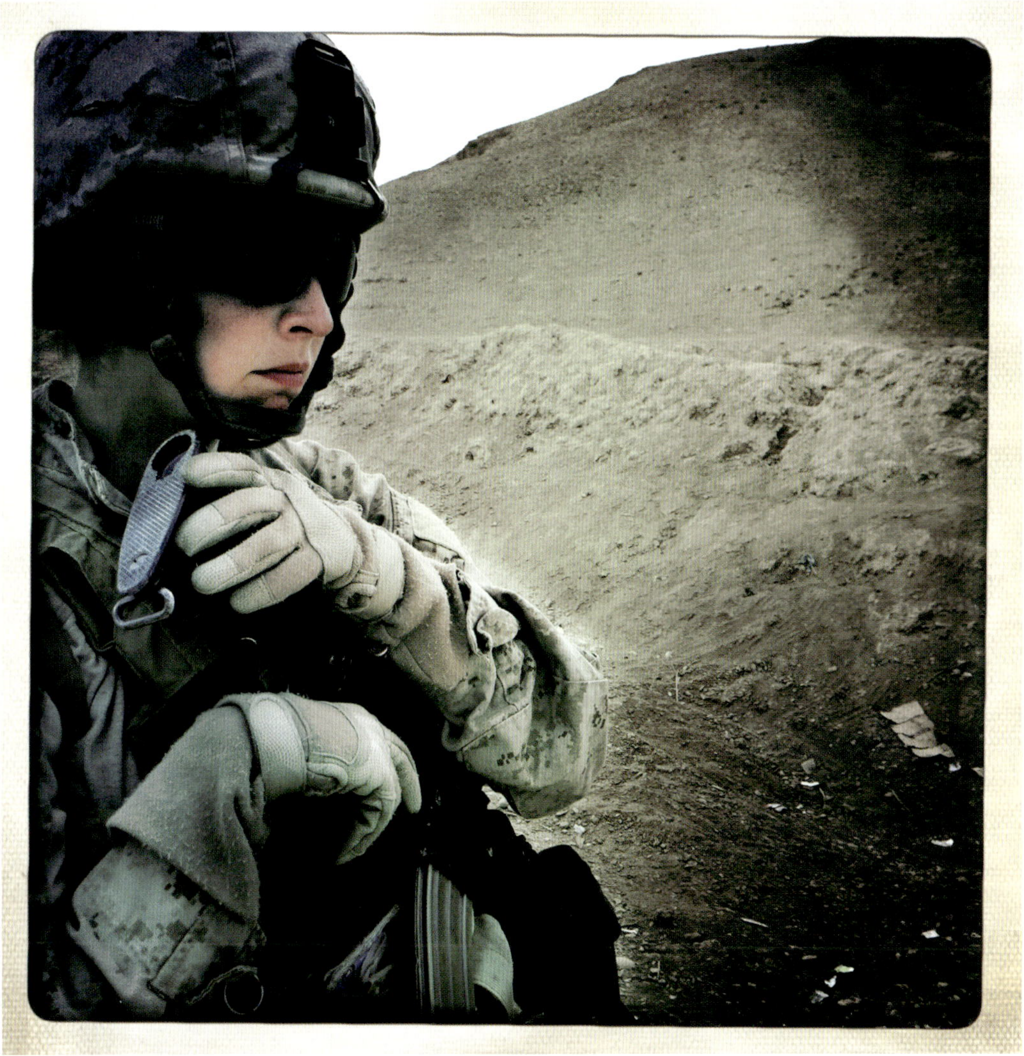

Body armour separates the wearer

from the civilian population.

Civilians don't have body armour. Some journalists refuse out of solidarity to wear ballistic gear when they are amid civilian bystanders or non-military fighters who are not equipped with body armour.

While no one would argue that body armour is not a necessity for military personnel in restive areas like Helmand province, an unavoidable effect is that the

armour renders the wearer intimidating and alien to the civilian population.

Sometimes that effect is desirable, but intimidation is less effective when the mission is to befriend and win-over the local population. As with armoured vehicles—the subject of my next iProbe—it's a damned if you do, damned if you don't scenario.

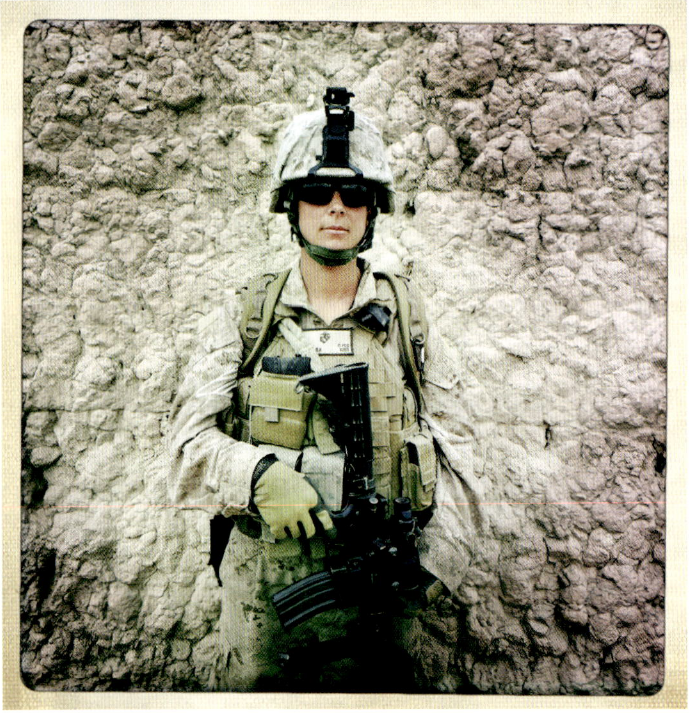

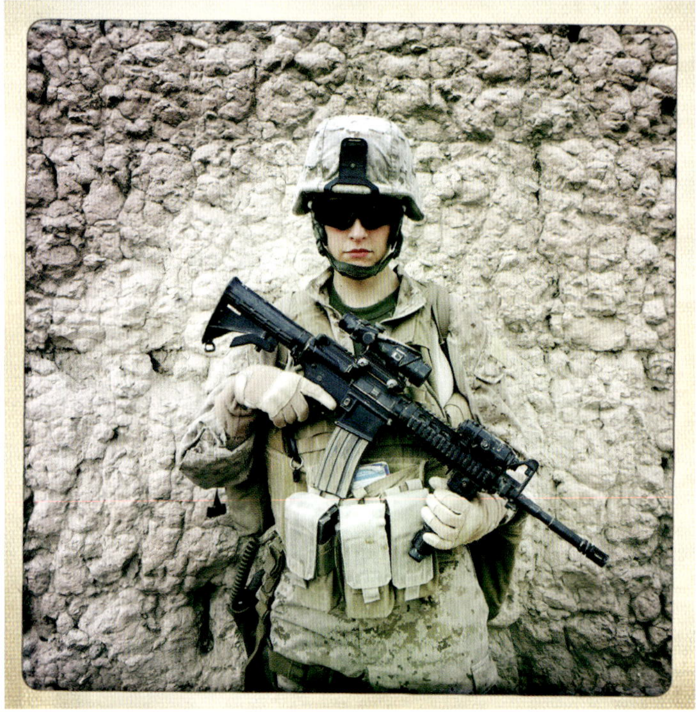

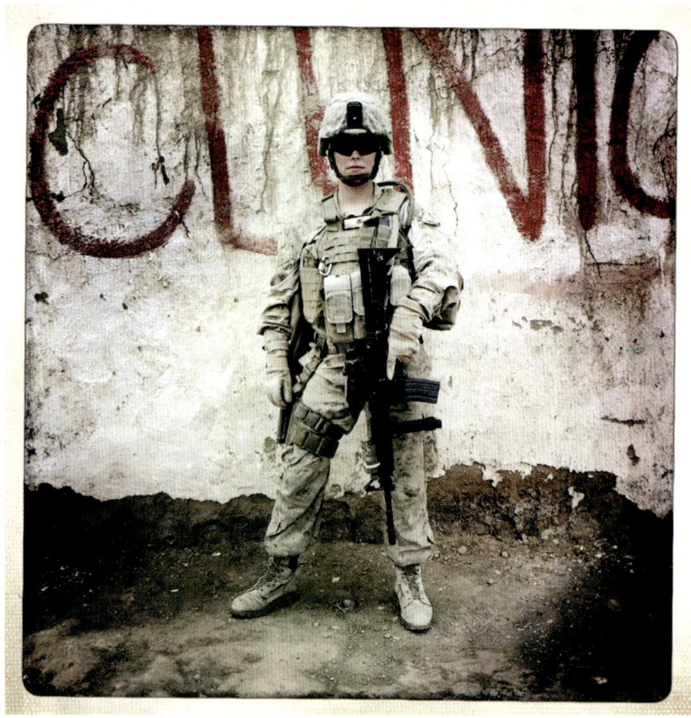
CLINIC

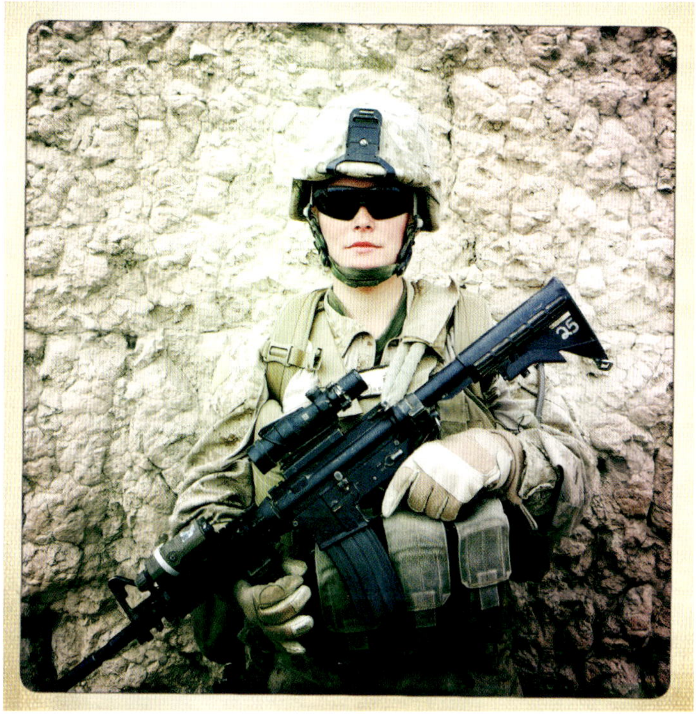
25

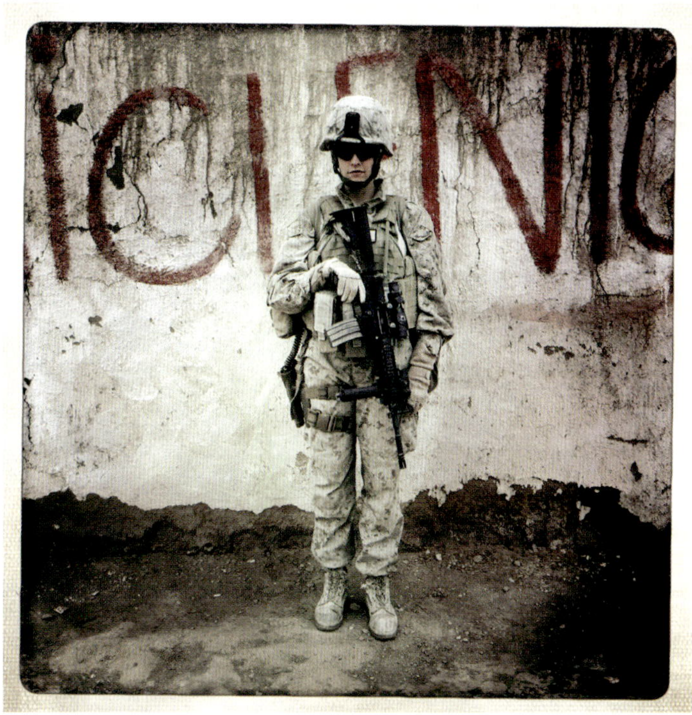

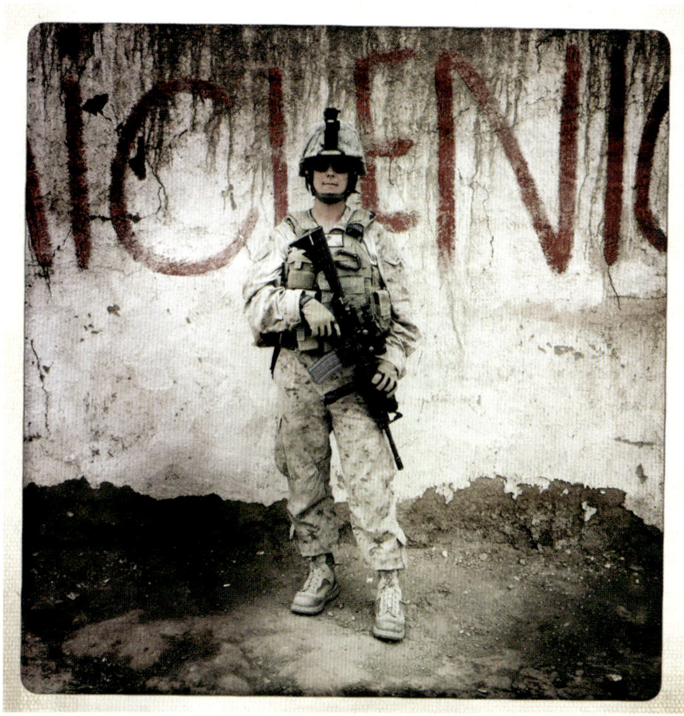

An armoured vehicle is an extension of the skin and of the eyes;

It's an extension of the military personnel inside.

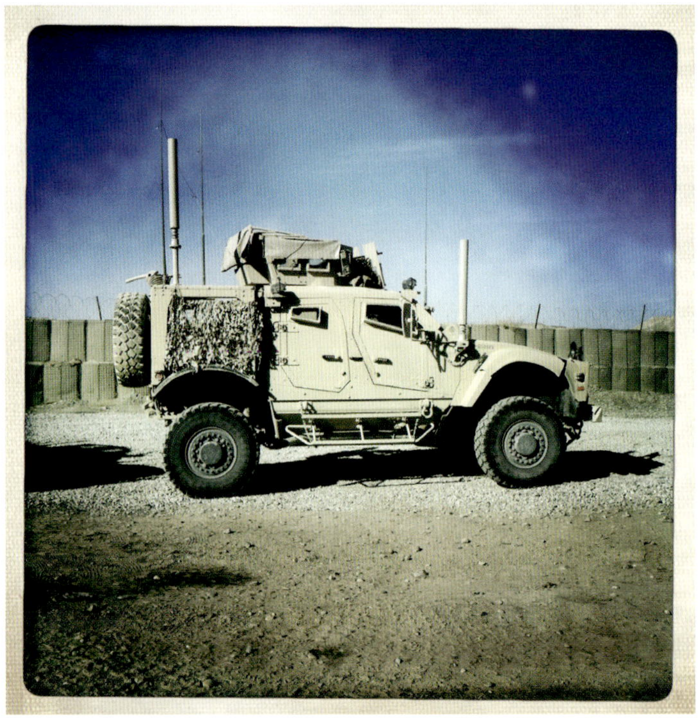

“We had the skin of [an armoured vehicle] wrapped around our lucky asses.”

(CAVALRY SOLDIER, IRAQ, 2003 [TO THE AUTHOR])

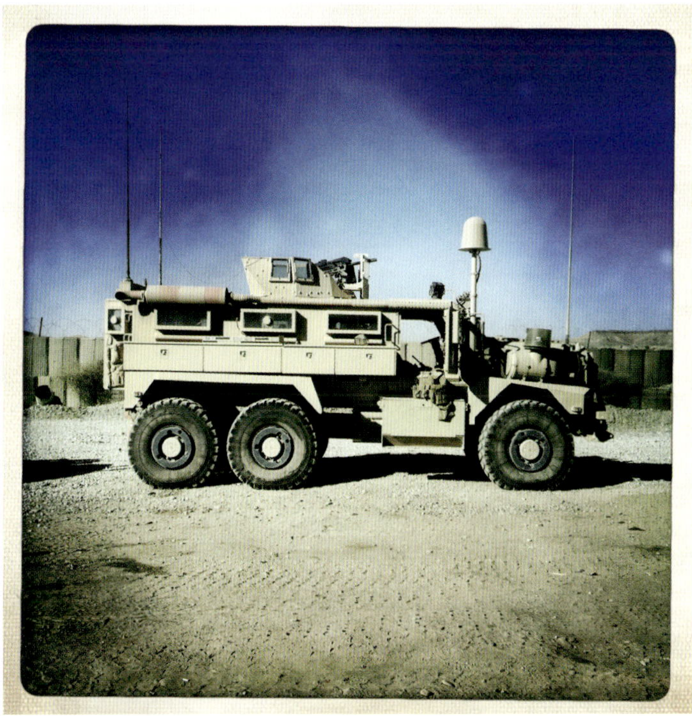

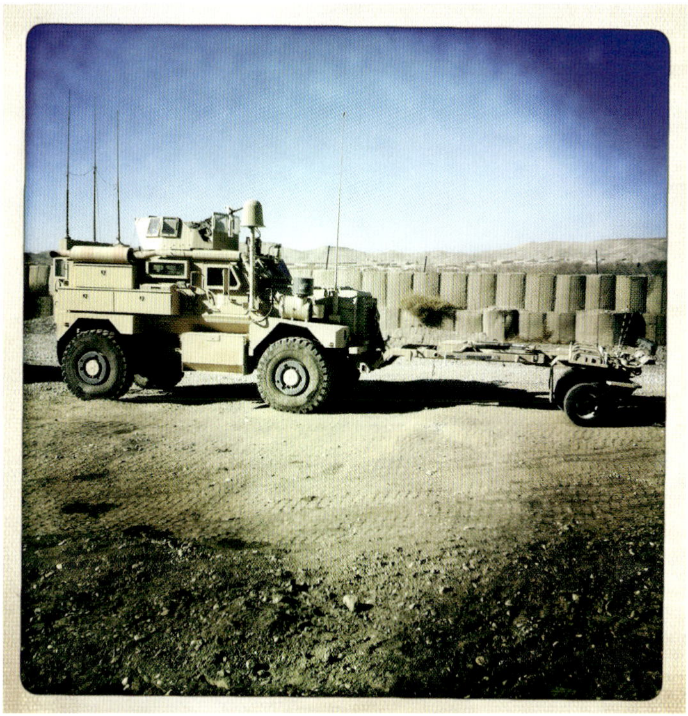

The changing face of warfare has led to the development of smaller, more manoeuverable “survivable vehicles” known as MRAPs (Mine Resistant Ambush Protected). Since it was established in October 2006, the Joint MRAP Vehicle Program has delivered more than 26,000 MRAP vehicles to Iraq and Afghanistan.[76]

Armoured vehicles save lives, as long as the military personnel remain inside. The problem with staying inside the MRAP is that you can’t meet the population and win over their hearts and minds. In recognition of this conundrum, the then ISAF Commander, General David H. Petraeus of the United States Army, directed military personnel on deployment to dismount from their vehicles more often. As cited in the Counterinsurgency Guidelines, August 2010:

“Walk. Stop by, don’t drive by. Patrol on foot whenever possible and engage the population. **Take off your sunglasses.** Situational awareness can only be gained by **interacting face-to-face,** not separated by ballistic glass or Oakleys.

"Secure and serve the population.
**The decisive terrain is the human terrain.
The people are the center of gravity.**
Only by providing them security and earning their trust and confidence can the Afghan government and ISAF prevail."

GENERAL DAVID H. PETRAEUS
COMMANDER, ISAF
UNITED STATES FORCES-AFGHANISTAN
AUGUST 2010
("COMISAF'S COUNTERINSURGENCY [COIN] GUIDANCE") [77]

Not surprisingly, more dismounting means more injuries and more casualties. **As with body armour, you're damned if you do and damned if you don't.**

iProbe 05_**Figure + Ground**

The camera is an extension of the eye; a prosthetic device of the beholder.

"The main obstacle to a clear understanding of the effects of the new media is our deeply embedded habit of regarding all phenomena from a fixed point of view."

(MARSHALL MCLUHAN AND QUENTIN FIORE, *THE MEDIUM IS THE MASSAGE: AN INVENTORY OF EFFECTS*) [78]

A Marine and senior officer, visiting the Musa Qala base for the first time, looked out over the landscape and the busy Friday market beyond the fortified walls of the base, where merchants and traders gathered, having arrived on foot or on donkey carts. "It's amazing to think of how little these people have accomplished in thousands of years compared to what America has accomplished in just a few hundred," he said. I wondered how much or how little he knew about Afghanistan.

I took these photographs through the windows of armoured vehicles.

It was the closest thing to "surveillance" photography I've ever done: the people I was photographing could not see me.

Armoured vehicles prevent you from being killed, but they also prevent you from being seen.

Because I was strapped in by a seat belt with my back to the window, I couldn't turn all the way around, and I held the iPhone over my shoulder, flat up against the window for the picture. Because the iPhone processor took about 20 seconds between shots, the images I got were mostly luck. The only real editing I did was to wait until we passed through a village where there would likely be people before I pressed the shutter-button icon.

The thick, dirty panes of bulletproof glass obscured the photos so that what was beyond the window was murky.

The first image I looked at on my iPhone elicited in me a feeling that, in McLuhan's terms, would be attributed to the resonating intervals of meaning that are the result of recognizing an unfixed perspective of an artefact.

This is the relationship of Figure to Ground, described in the Prologue of this book.

Figure and Ground are in a constant state of **abrasive interplay.**

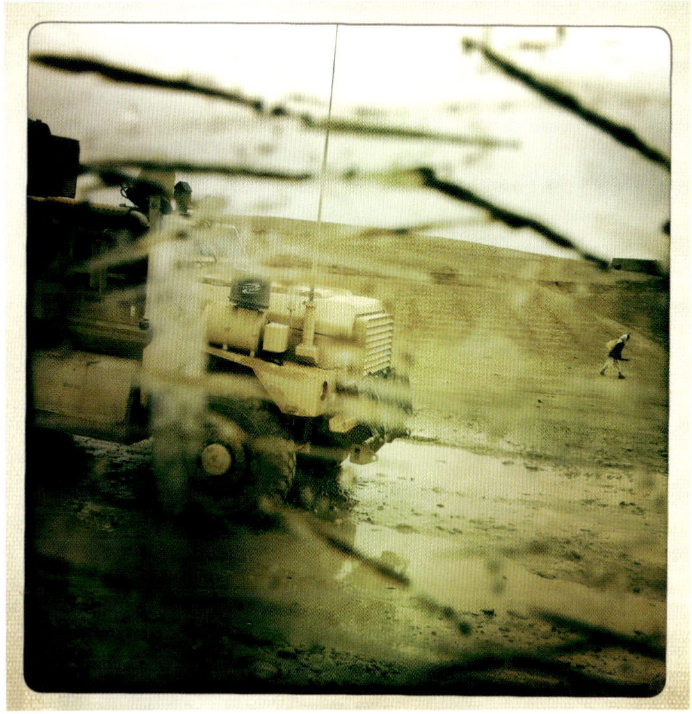

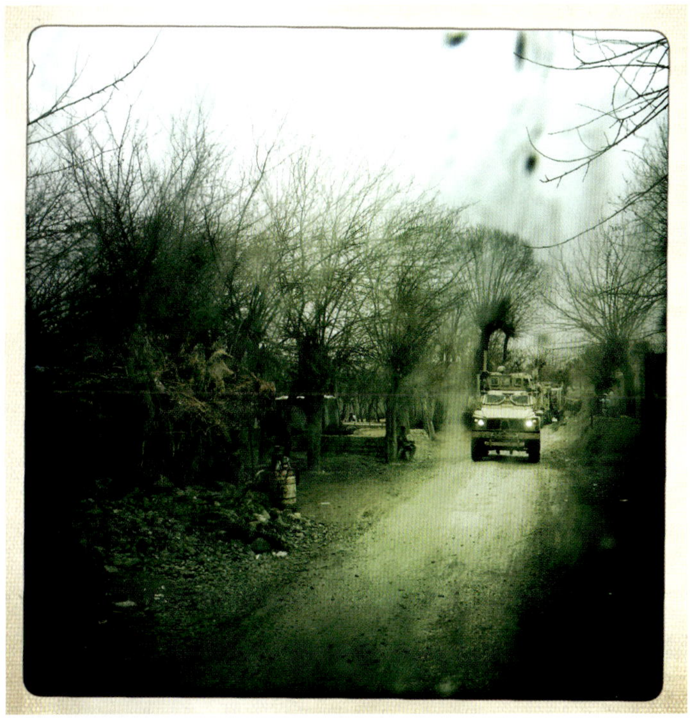

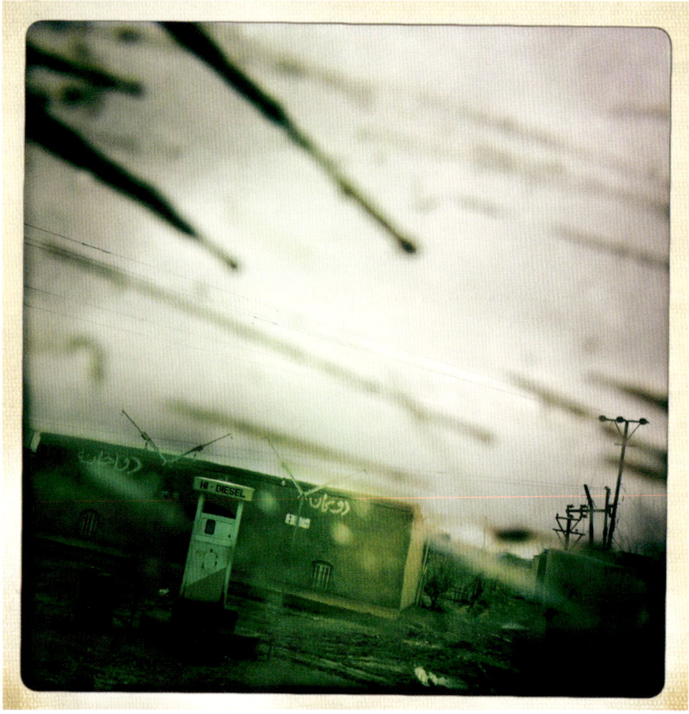
HI - DIESEL

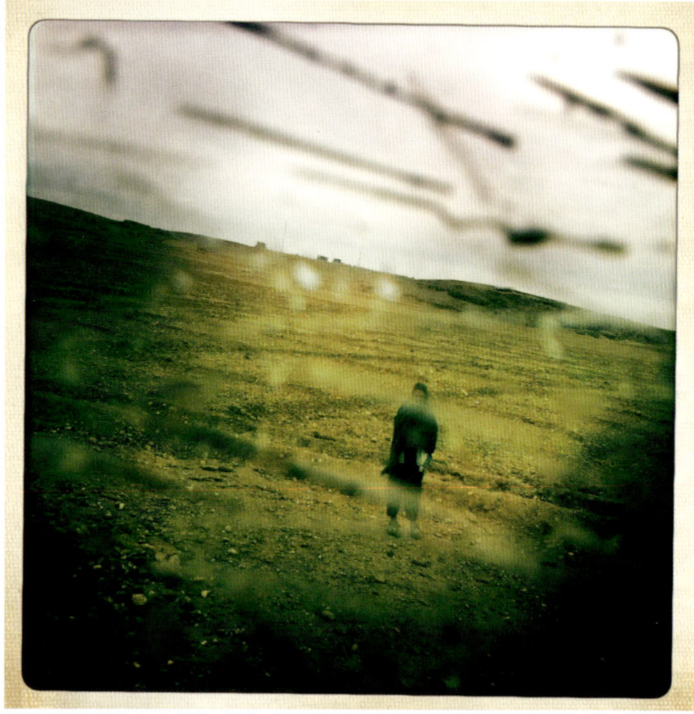

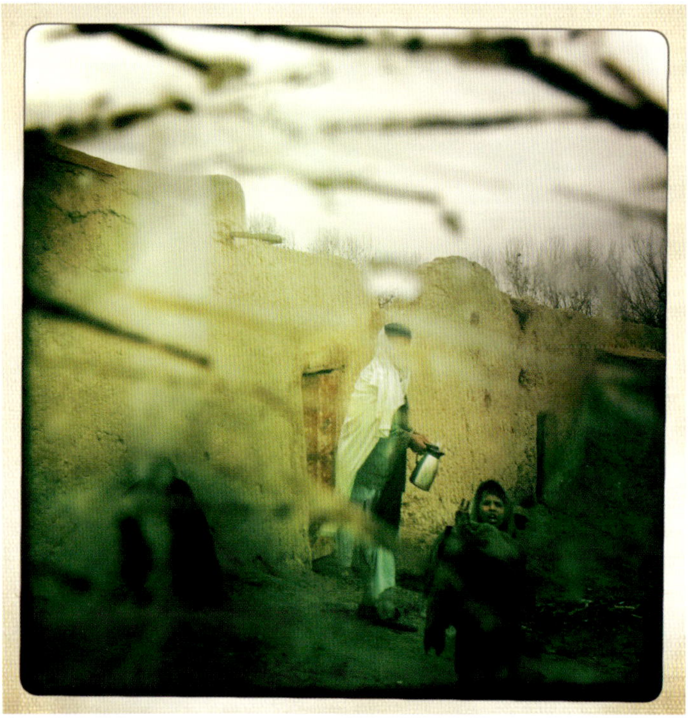

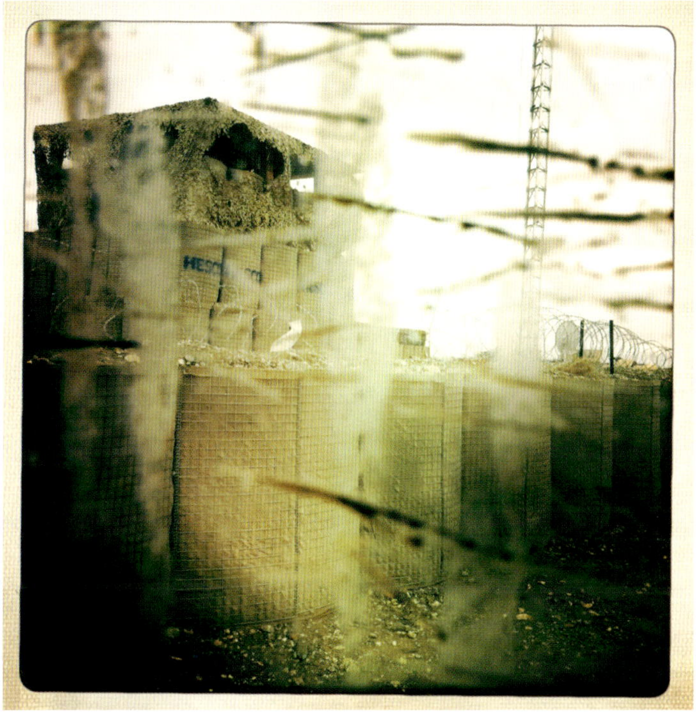
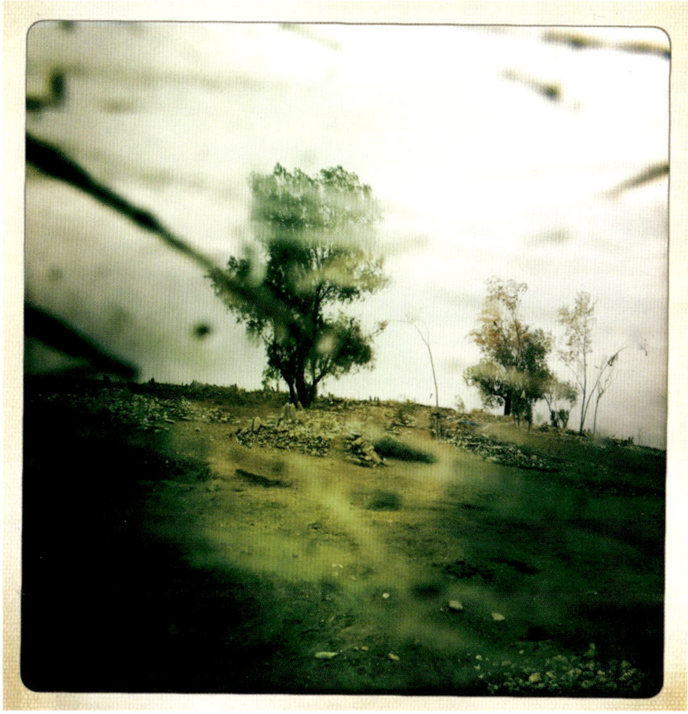

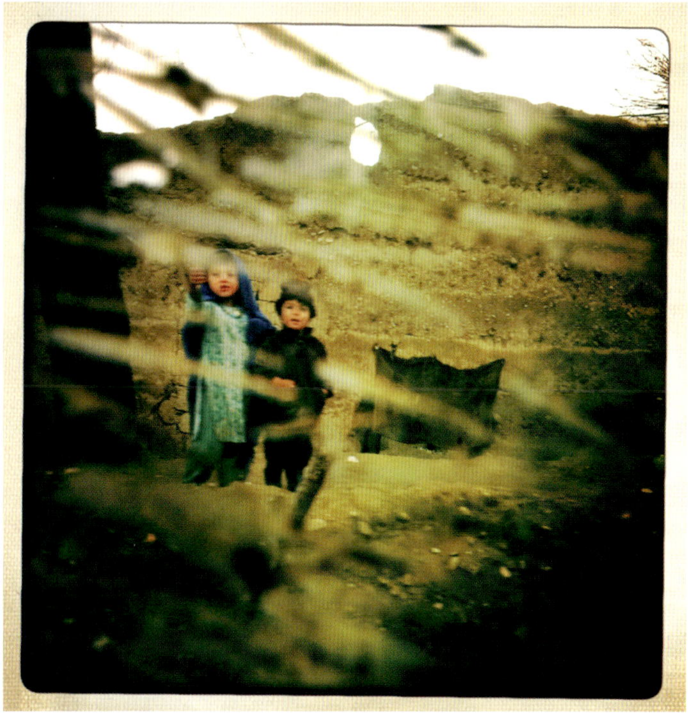

In these strange, painterly iPhone Hipstamatic images, I felt that something had been captured of the complex, inaccessible relationship between the Marines and the Afghans.

All technologies are "self-amputations of our own being."

(MARSHALL MCLUHAN AND QUENTIN FIORE, *WAR AND PEACE IN THE GLOBAL VILLAGE*) [79]

Photographing through the window of an armoured vehicle dismembers the camera (which is already a self-amputation) from the photographer. The subject out the window is not looking back at a photographer (another human being) carrying a machine, but at the machine directly. The gaze is not therefore at us, but at an idea of us as embodied by machinery, in this case an armoured vehicle.

The passers-by couldn't see I was taking their pictures, but because they know the military is there keeping watch on things, they knew they were being watched.

From the point of view of people on the outside, there is no difference between the armoured vehicle and the personnel on the inside of the armoured vehicle.

There is a metaphoric, or poetic, relationship between the outside and the inside. Each is to the other both Figure and Ground, foreground and background, in a resonating relationship:
I am looking at you
looking at me
looking at you.

It is symbolic of how one side never sees the other side except as a kind of stereotype: on the one side you have American military personnel wrapped inside armoured vehicles (or perched atop a military base judging all of history based on a single point of view), and on the other side you have figures of Afghans resolving into view against a desert landscape. No language is exchanged between the two. Even if the Marines dismount, anything they say is filtered through an interpreter, or else there are small gestures, like handing out candies or buying a chicken.

You can tell that both sides want to communicate with each other. But there are too many obstacles between them. **It is just too hard.**

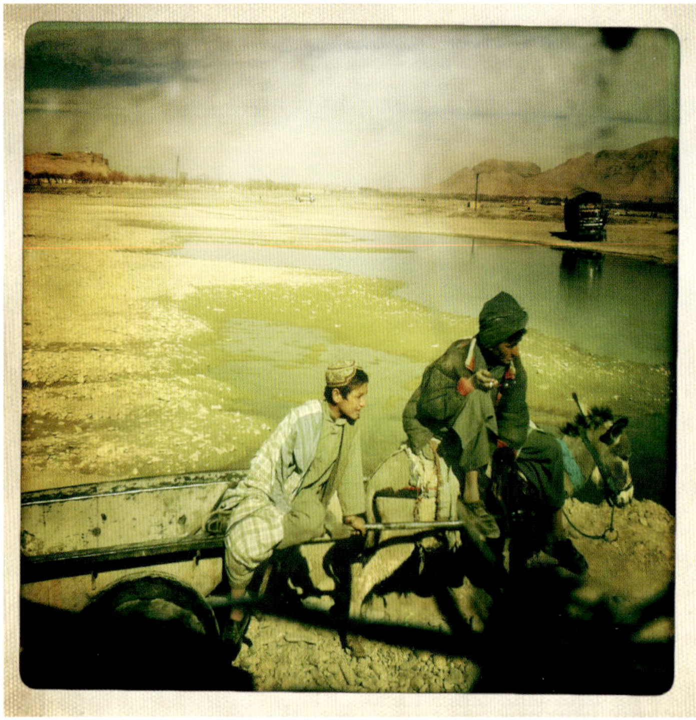

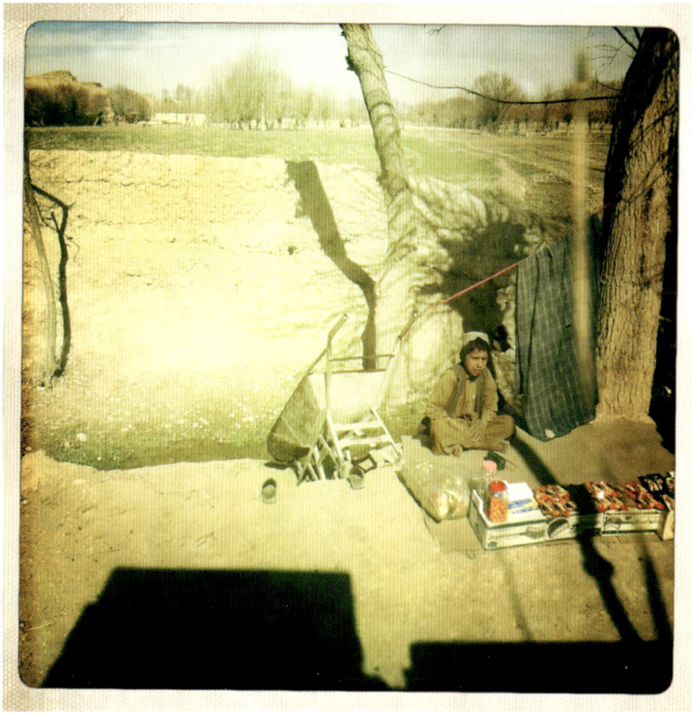

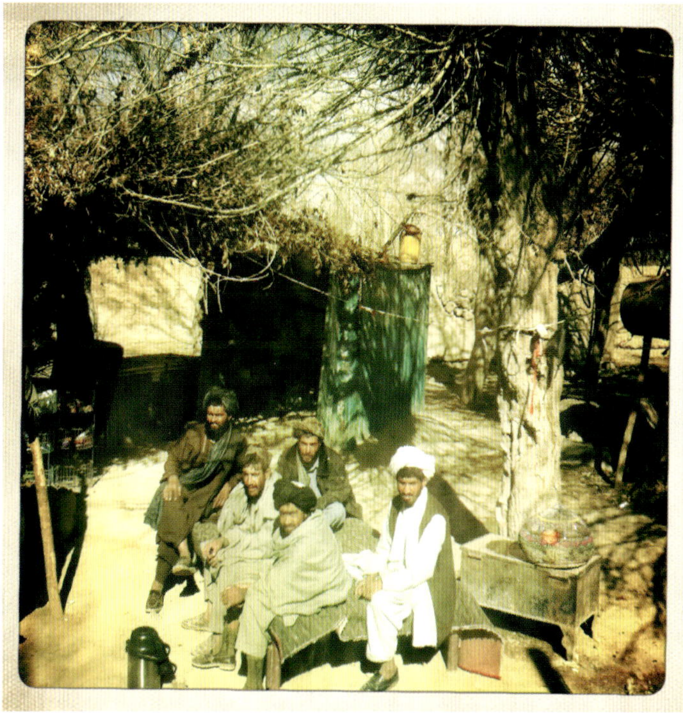

iProbe 06_Improvised Explosive Devices (IEDs) Made of Wood

IEDs are extensions of the finger and of the forest—forests converted to wood converted to energy, detonated with a finger.

The initial technology for improvised explosive devices (IEDs) was given to the mujahideen in Afghanistan by the United States in the 1970s to help the Afghans fight the Russians (during that protracted, proxy war). The mujahideen would later disperse (it's a complicated story)[80] and re-emerge as a kind of second-generation, mostly Pashtun and Pakistani "religious freedom fighters" who call themselves the Taliban ("the Students").[81]

Today, about 1,000 IEDs are planted in Afghanistan every month.[82]

They are the signature weapon of the Taliban and are responsible for the majority of American, International Security Assistance Force (ISAF) and Afghan National Army (ANA) casualties and injuries. They also accounted for nearly 1,000 civilian deaths in 2011.[83] The Marines had a couple of expert contractors on base whose only job was to analyse IEDs.

The typical IED in Afghanistan is a rudimentary home-made device. A few wires, some farm fertilizer, some kind of flat pressure plates and a few household batteries are about all that is needed. I was shown some IEDs (pictured here) that were made mostly of wood.

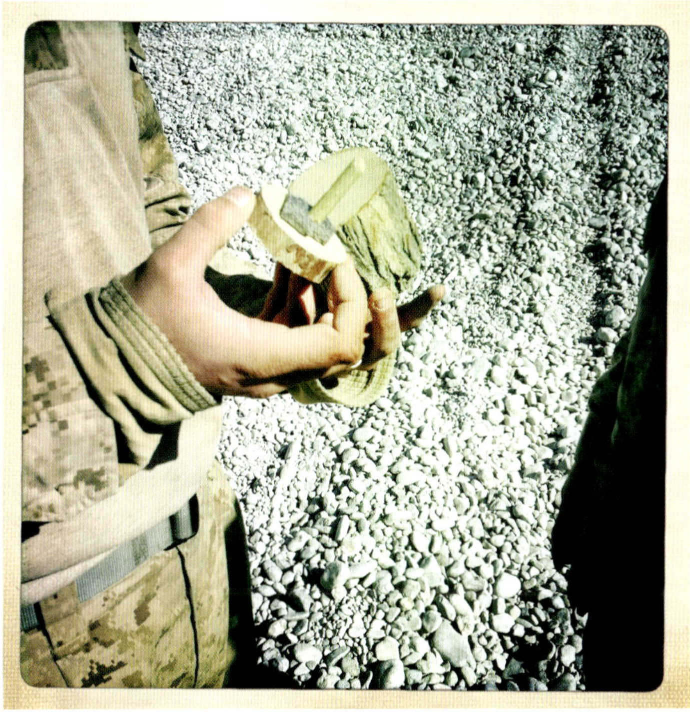

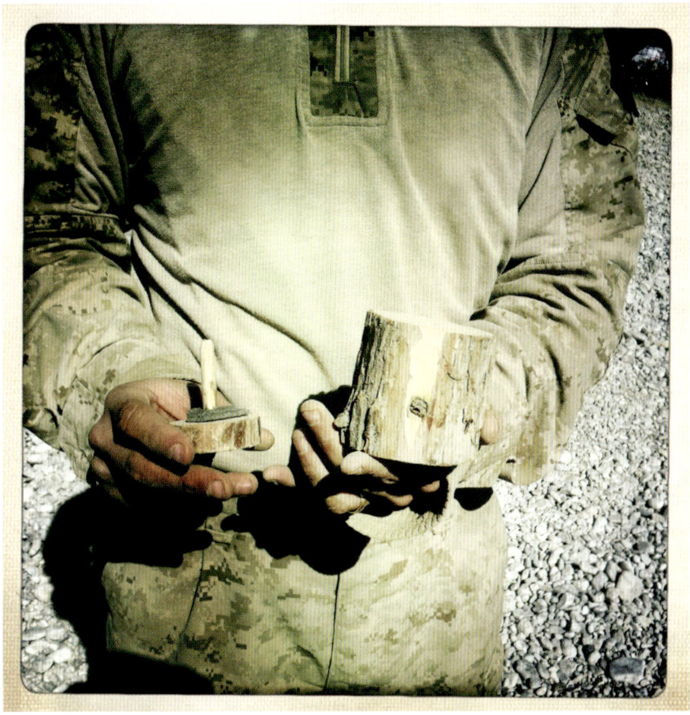

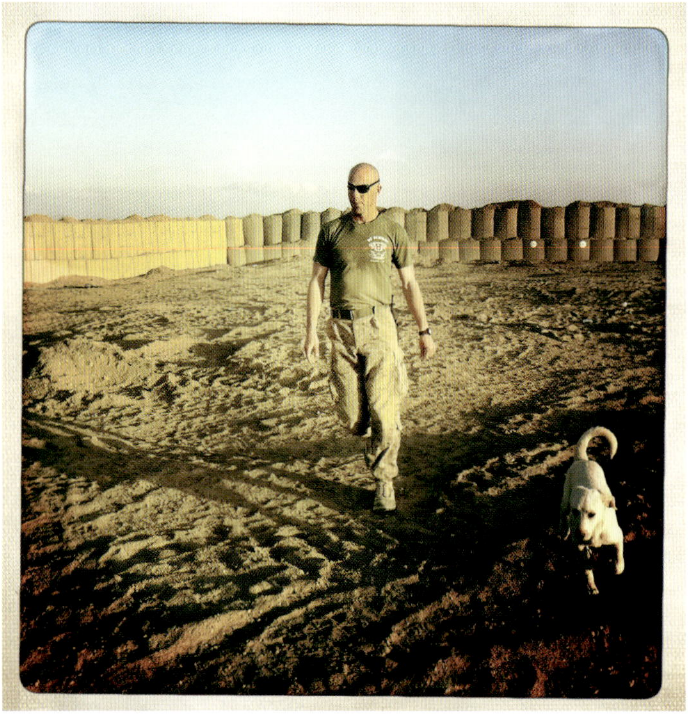

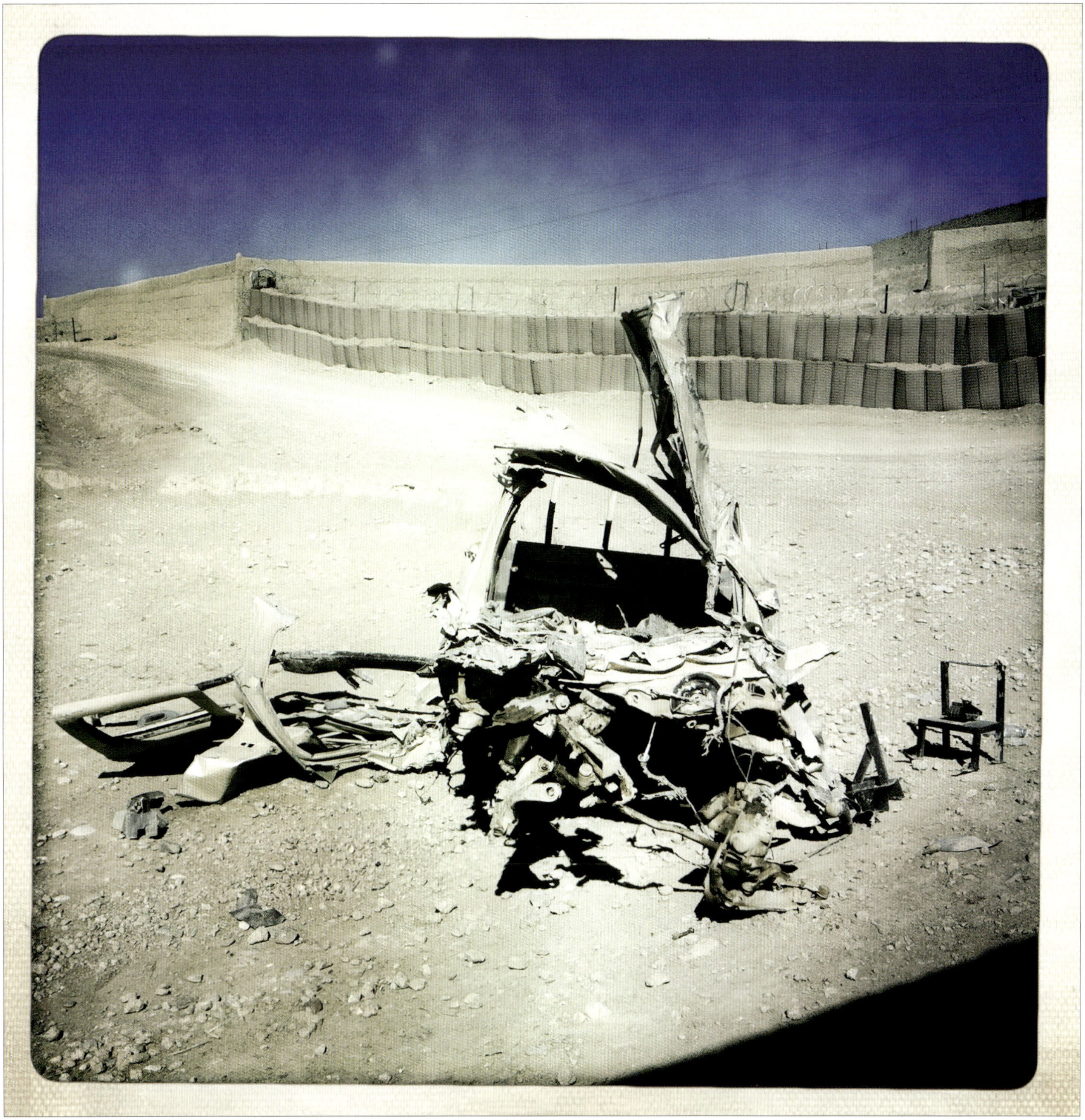

IEDs can be detonated on contact—stepping on or driving over—or by remote signals, including mobile phones.

Radio-wave jammers and sophisticated mine detection devices traditionally used to detect IEDs and land mines have become obsolete against these crude IEDs which contain only scarce amounts of metal or electronic parts.

They are cheap and easy to make. Many are mass manufactured in Pakistan, just across the border to the south.

As it turns out, specially trained sniffer "war dogs" have proven that the best tool for detecting these IEDs is not technological,

but canine.

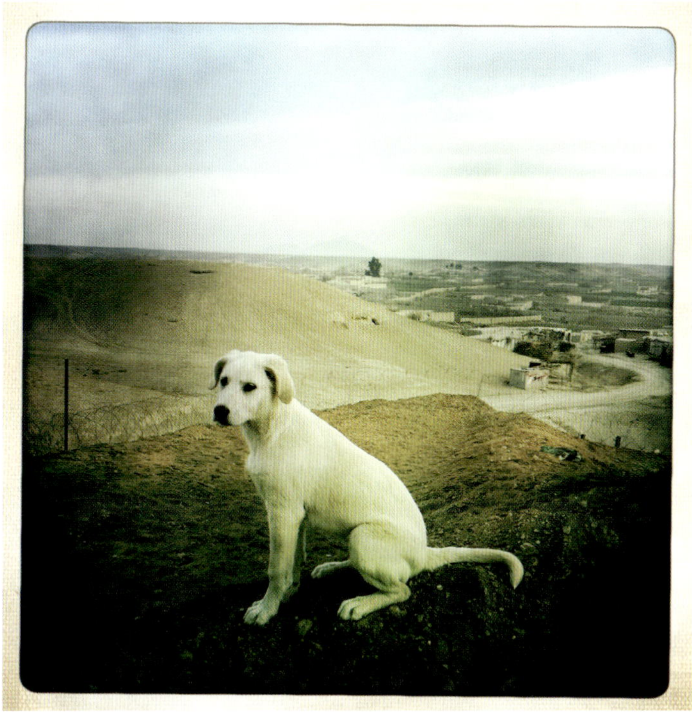

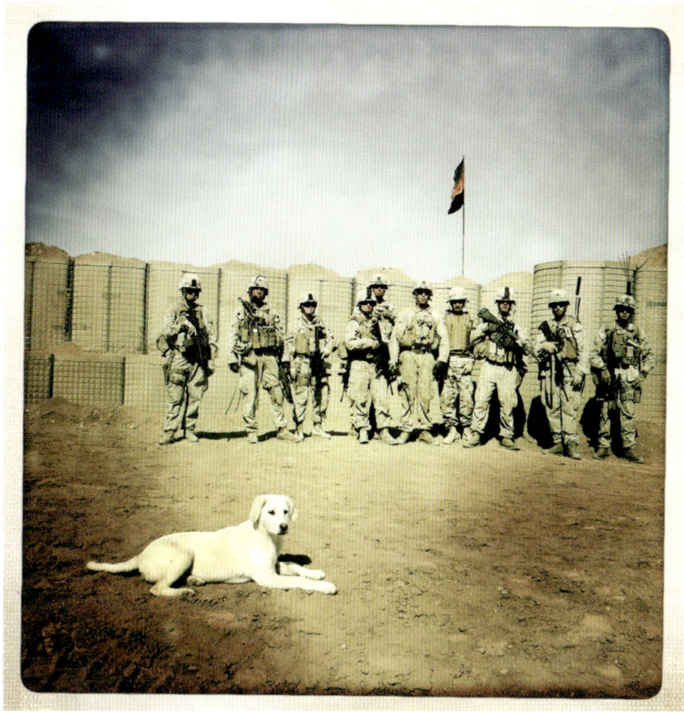

Fuel dispensers are extensions of energy and measurements.

Afghanistan is energy poor.

But there are vast natural gas reserves to the north, in the Caspian Sea, Turkmenistan and Kazakhstan.

Afghan istan = Energy Bridge

84

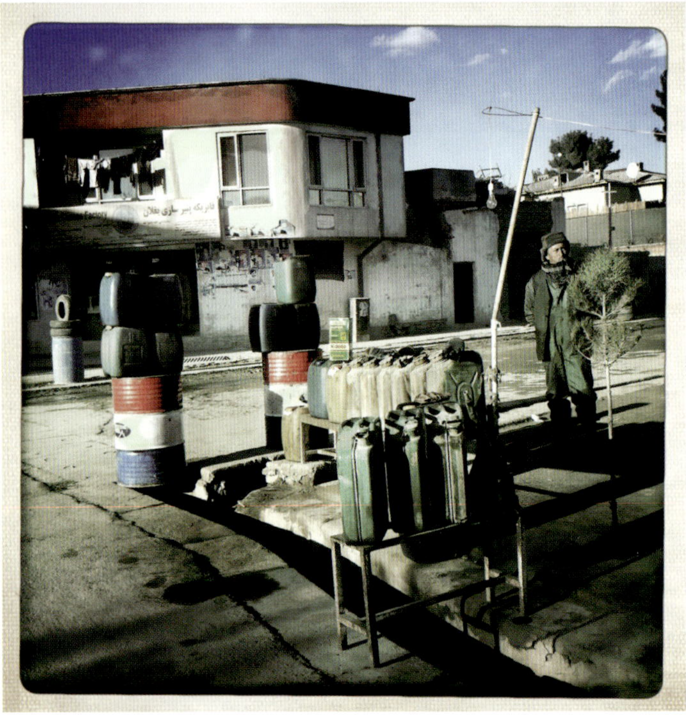

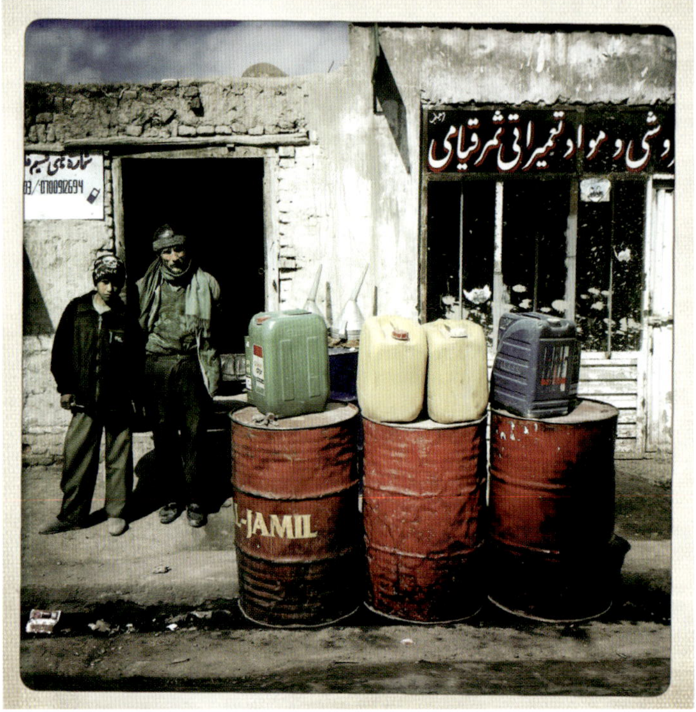
L-JAMIL

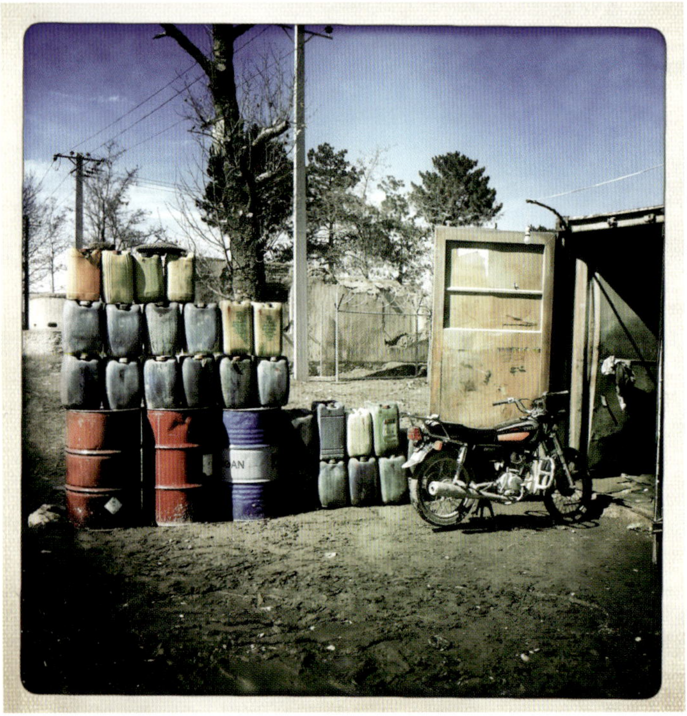

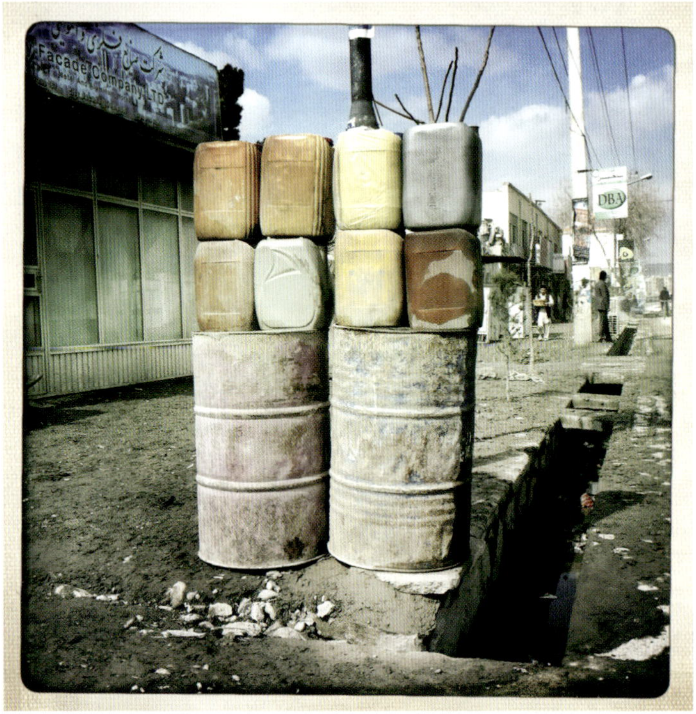
Facade Company LTD
DBA

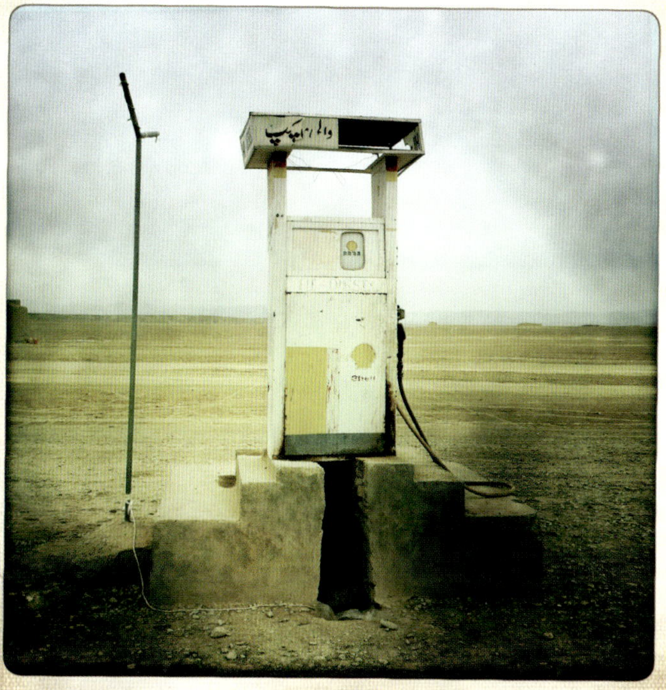
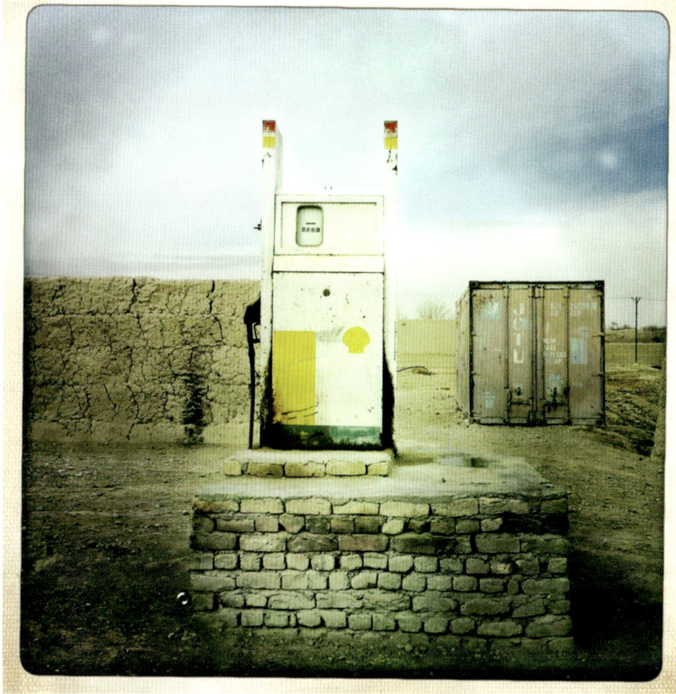
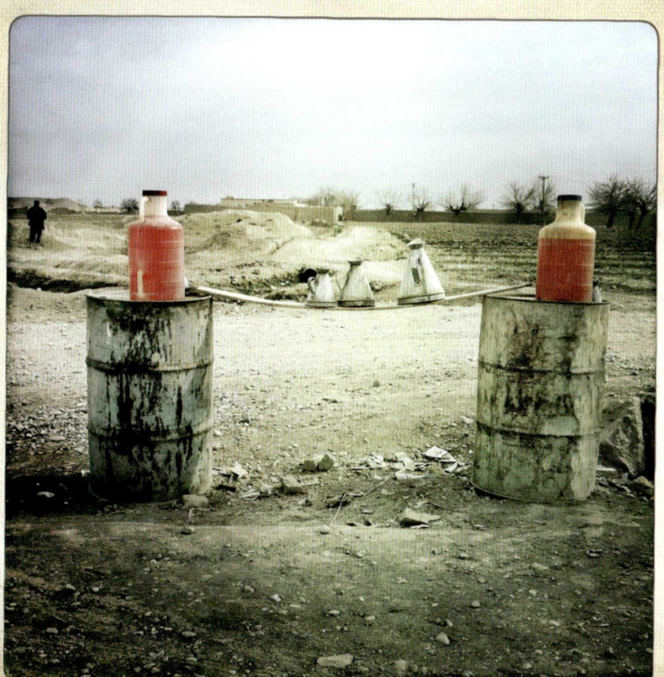
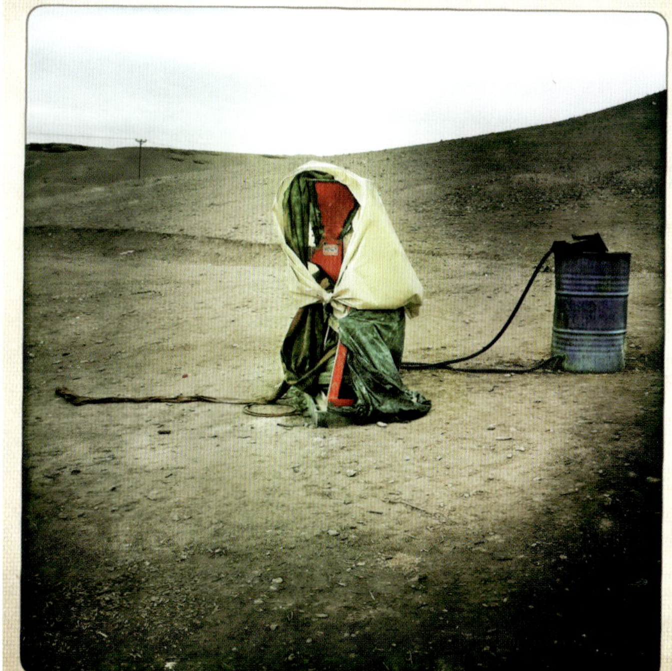

Gas pumps are mechanical-electrical and, nowadays, digital devices used to dispense and measure fuel. The fuel reserve is usually hidden in an underground tank. We expect it to never run dry.

We don't think about where the fuel comes from, or how the fuel is delivered to the fuel dispensers. **It's just dispensed, like out of nowhere.**

Afghanistan is oil and natural gas poor. Fuel is a hot commodity, and in the restive south, if you sell fuel, you probably have to deal with the Taliban. In my section on Musa Qala, I quoted journalist Gretchen Peters saying that Taliban commanders treated the opium storehouses of Musa Qala like ATM machines.[85] It is not a far leap to imagine fuel dispensers being used in a similar way.

You can't fight a war without fuel, and

the job of transporting fuel from south of the border in Karachi, Pakistan, to combat vehicles in remote parts of Afghanistan is expensive.

Sometimes it has to be transported by air because of difficult terrain or because of risk of ambush. Pentagon reports in 2010 put the "fully burdened cost of fuel" for supplying American combat vehicles at $400 per gallon.[86]

I know first-hand the cost of moving fuel in conflict zones.

In Iraq in 2004, travelling with my good friend and colleague Adnan Kahn, I drove into the tail end of an ambushed fuel convoy south of Baghdad (Adnan reported this experience in a feature article for *Maclean's Magazine*). We saw two oil tankers that had been destroyed and the bodies of at least three dead American military personnel strewn on the ground, before we took some photographs, were subsequently captured by insurgents, and eventually escaped with our lives.

The role of oil in the war in Afghanistan is almost never discussed by the U.S. or Canadian governments, but it is written about at length in the Asian press, as well as by Pakistani journalist Ahmed Rashid—who has dubbed the fight for control over fuel in the Caspian region as "The New Great Game"[87]—and by Canadian John Foster, an international energy economist with forty years of experience in energy and international development.

Afghanistan has been at the centre of the geopolitical rallying for control over energy in the Middle East since 1991, when Russia ceased to have total control over these regions. Up until about a month before the attacks of 9/11, the U. S. and the Asian Development Bank (in which Canada is the seventh largest shareholder) were negotiating with the Taliban (from 1997 to 2001) over a pipeline from Turkmenistan to the north, through Afghanistan, and to Pakistan and India to the south. Start dates for the TAPI pipeline (named for the countries it would travel through) are forever being pushed ahead because of the situation in Afghanistan. Meanwhile, Iran has almost completed its pipeline in the region (the Iran–Pakistan–India or IPI pipeline), and China's Turkmenistan–China gas pipeline is well underway—two facts that obviously make the building of an "American friendly" pipeline a pressing geopolitical concern.

(JOHN FOSTER, "A PIPELINE THROUGH A TROUBLED LAND: AFGHANISTAN, CANADA, AND THE NEW GREAT ENERGY GAME," FOR THE CANADIAN CENTRE FOR POLICY ALTERNATIVES) [88]

Turkmenistan to the north, through Afghanistan, and to Pakistan and India to the south.

Route of Planned TAPI Natural Gas Pipeline

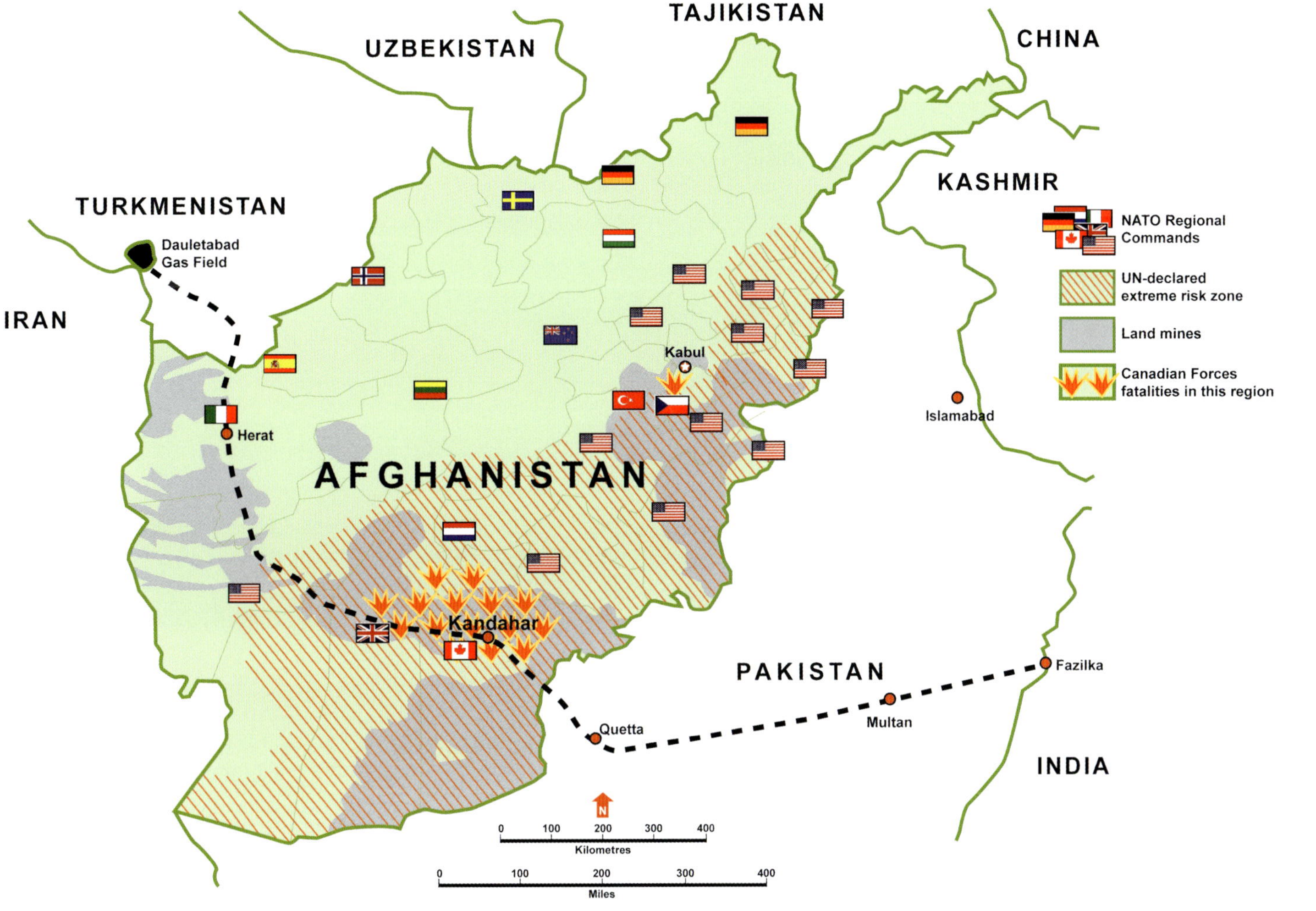

Map courtesy of the Canadian Centre for Policy Alternatives

The First Spike?

The great communications and railway boom in Central Asia in the late 19th century bypassed Afghanistan, which has never had a railway. This has contributed significantly to Afghanistan's isolation in the region, and to the isolation of Afghans from each other.

Proponents of the TAPI pipeline argue that a by-product of the pipeline would be the creation of a transportation infrastructure in Afghanistan, including a railway. But there are many caveats of which to be aware. Critics worry that foreign contractors would get most of the work and that locals would not really get jobs in the end. This is what has happened in Iraq. Moreover, it seems highly unlikely that the security necessary for such an undertaking will be possible any time soon—given that ten years of military intervention already have failed to achieve any security goals. And even if the pipeline were to go ahead, what kind of commitment would the United States and its partners in the Asian Development Bank, including Canada, have to make to protect it? The average lifespan of a pipeline is about fifty years—which is a very long commitment to be sure.

In McLuhan's terms, Afghanistan would become the medium of fuel transportation—an expanded metaphor of the fuel dispensers. What is the effect on a country that is being used as an "energy conduit," as Foster calls it—in other words, as a hub primarily, with any secondary benefits to the country itself simply offshoots of the primary goal of supplying its neighbours?

Is Afghanistan merely a fuel dispenser?

Loudspeakers are an extension of the mouth.

They are artefacts of the persistence of oral culture.

"Fight the information war aggressively. Challenge disinformation. Turn our enemies' extremist ideologies, oppressive practices, and indiscriminate violence against them. **Hang their barbaric actions like millstones around their necks."**

GENERAL DAVID H. PETRAEUS
COMMANDER, ISAF
UNITED STATES FORCES-AFGHANISTAN
AUGUST 2010
("COMISAF'S COUNTERINSURGENCY [COIN] GUIDANCE") [89]

"They make strategies for people who they don't talk to . . . They sit behind the razorwire walls of the Embassy. And the rest make their strategy from behind desks thousands of miles away . . . **They don't seem to realize that the strategy has to be about the people."**

NANCY HATCH DUPREE
FOUNDER, THE LOUIS AND NANCY HATCH DUPREE
FOUNDATION, KABUL, 2009 [90]

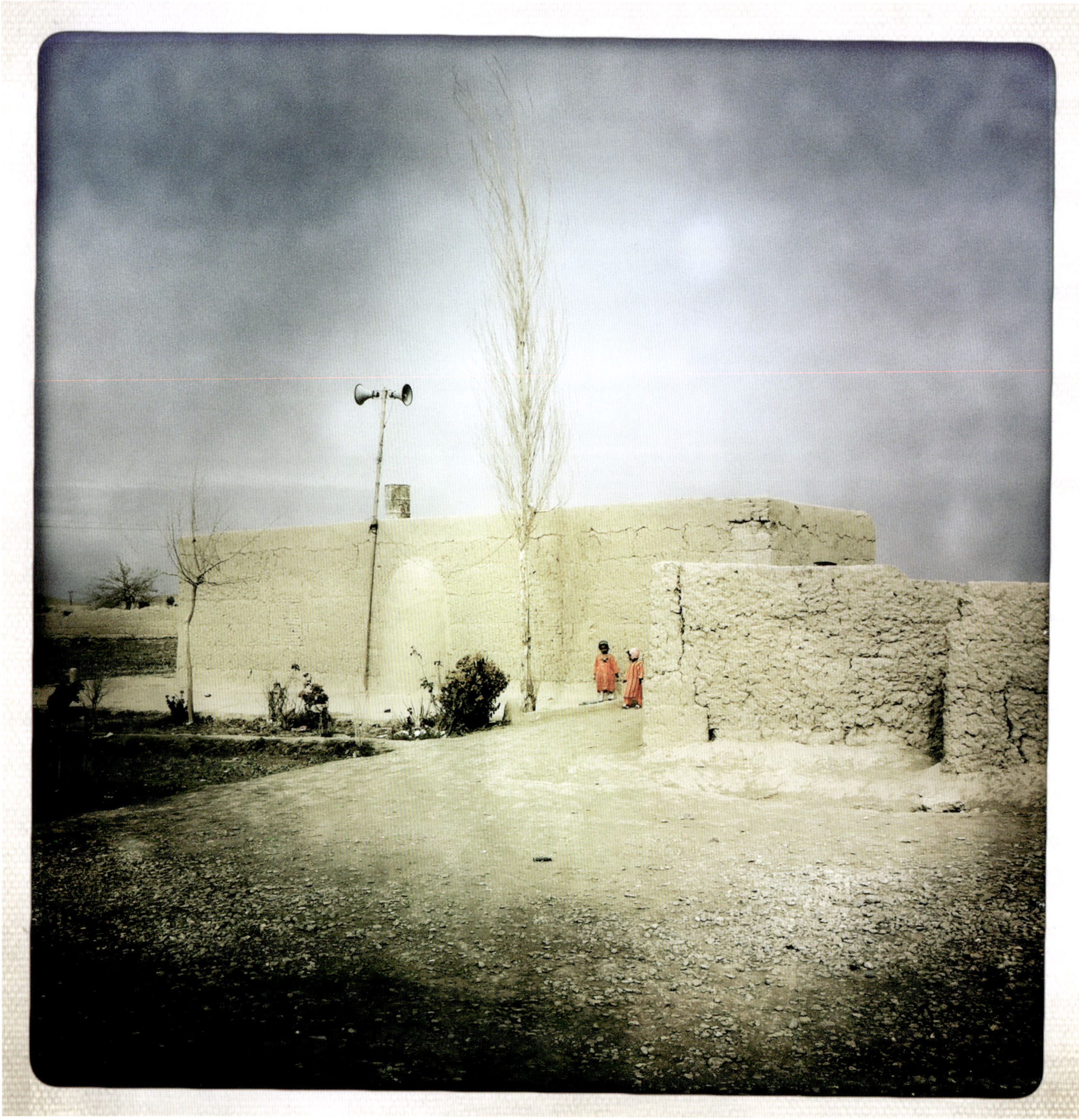

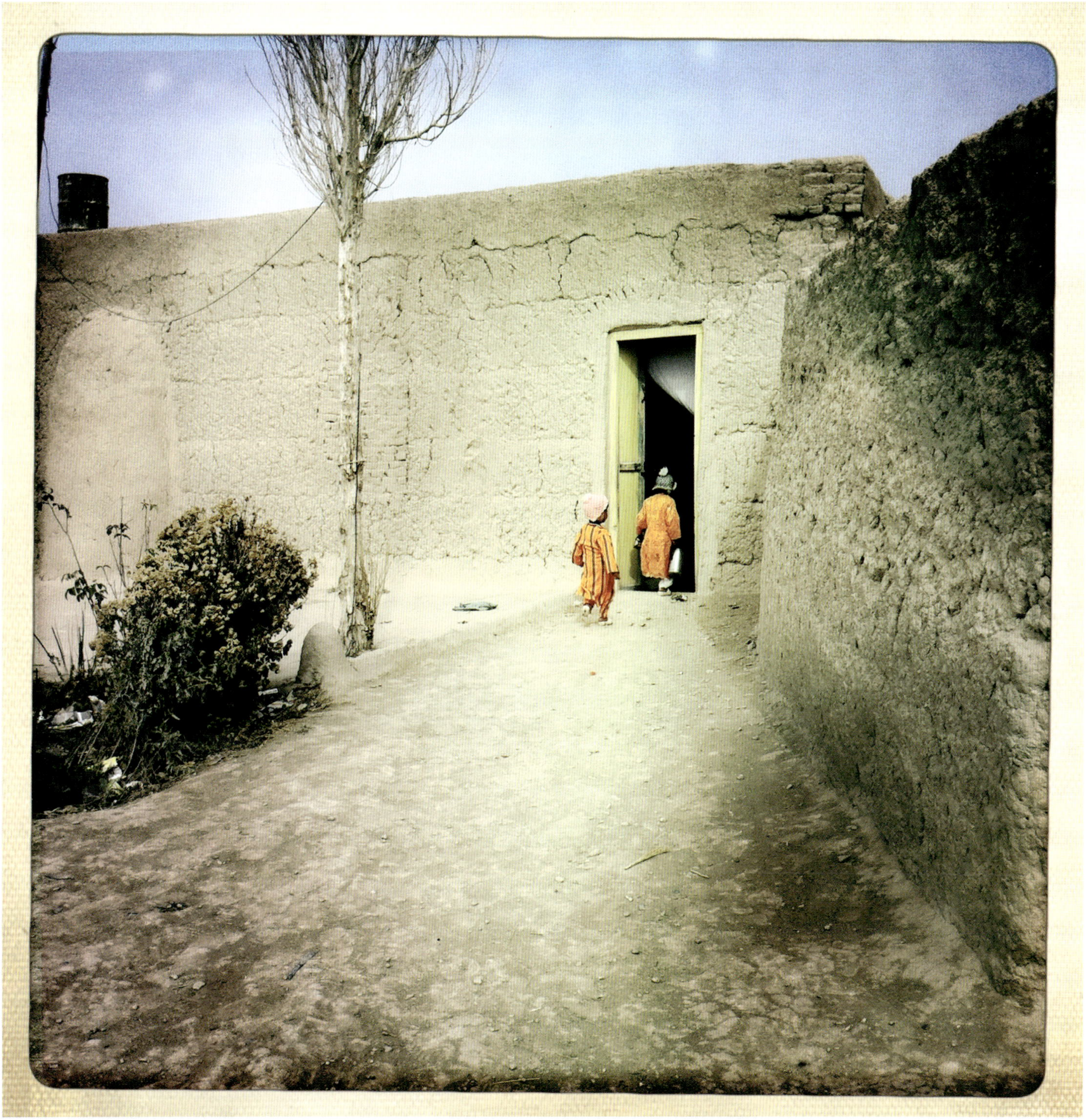

There are some fifty thousand mosques in Afghanistan, including many small, private ones like these in Shir Ghazay. All are equipped with loudspeakers—used to announce the call to prayer as well as to preach religious and political messages. In smaller communities, where many people do not have radios or televisions, and the vast majority are nonliterate, the mosque loudspeaker is where they get most of their news and ideas.

"In no institution does the disparate attitudinal dichotomy of literate vs. non-literate have as much cogency or meaning as it does in religion."

(LOUIS DUPREE [1925–1989], ONE OF THE FOREMOST AUTHORITIES ON AFGHANISTAN, IN HIS SEMINAL HISTORY, *AFGHANISTAN*)[91]

In iProbe 10_The Written Word, I discuss in more detail how the family of Indo-Iranian languages—to which the main two Afghanistan languages Dari and Pashto belong—came to be written in the Arabic script as a direct result of the Arab Conquest of Persia in the 7th and 8th century ce. But while the *Quran* and the Arabic script in which it was written eclipsed the existing writing and religion, the spoken language persevered. Arabic was then, and remains, the language of religion, but the language of the people in many Islamic countries is not Arabic. And so, in the case of a country like Afghanistan, where over 75 percent of the population is nonliterate, not only can they not read or write their own languages, but they must rely on interpretations of the *Quran* read to them by others. Many of the self-appointed imams who can pronounce or mouth the Arabic writing in a *Quran* but not understand it, rely on the oral accounts that have been handed down to them.

Dupree argues that the religion practised in these mostly nonliterate communities has little to do with Islam, and far more to do with local, pre-Islamic tribal traditions and rituals.

An extreme example would be the practice of blood vengeance, which contradicts the *Quran* to the word: "It is not for the believer to kill a believer" (Sura 4:92–4:93). Technically, in Islam, every man can be a religious leader; self-appointed village mullahs are often young, nonliterate men who have never read the *Quran*.[92] This has nothing to do with the oratorical tradition of Quranic study. When we talk of nonliterates who have never read the *Quran*, we are referring to people who have never had it read or recited to them either. The value of oral tradition and recitation is deeply embedded in Islamic culture (*Quran* memorization contests are popular throughout the Islamic world), and "anyone knowing the *Qor'an* by heart (often blind men) is referred to [as a "guardian" or] *Hafiz*."[93]

In his thorough history of language, *Empires of the World: A Language History of the World*, Nicholas Ostler explains how

"language was used in a unique way in the spread of [Islam]. The authentic utterances of the prophet, himself illiterate, were soon, in some undocumented way, reduced to writing. The text so arrived at was immediately holy and absolutely authoritative;

it could not be changed, although it was permissible (as in the Hebrew scriptures) to annotate it with some dots and dashes to mark the vowel sounds, for the benefit of those whose Arabic was not native, and who consequently might need some help in reading the bare consonants. It was known as the *Quran*, 'recitation', based on 'qr', the common Semitic root for reading aloud, and famously begun when the Angel Gabriel commanded Mohammed: 'Recite, in the name of your Lord who created, created man from embryo.'"[94]

In 2010, Afghan journalist Habib Zahori, on assignment with Joshua Paltrow for the *Washington Post*,[95] reported on sermons at several mosques in Kabul. Almost universally, the messages were anti-foreigner, anti-occupation and, not surprisingly, anti-Christian and anti-Jew—although

Jews,
Muslims and Christians
are all

"people of the book,"

or

ahl-i-kitab:

those with divinely inspired written scriptures with the same source.

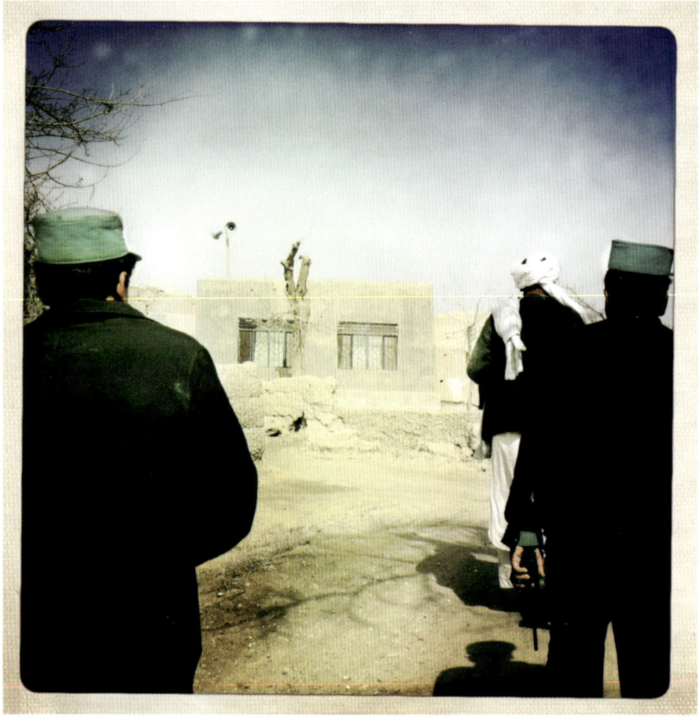

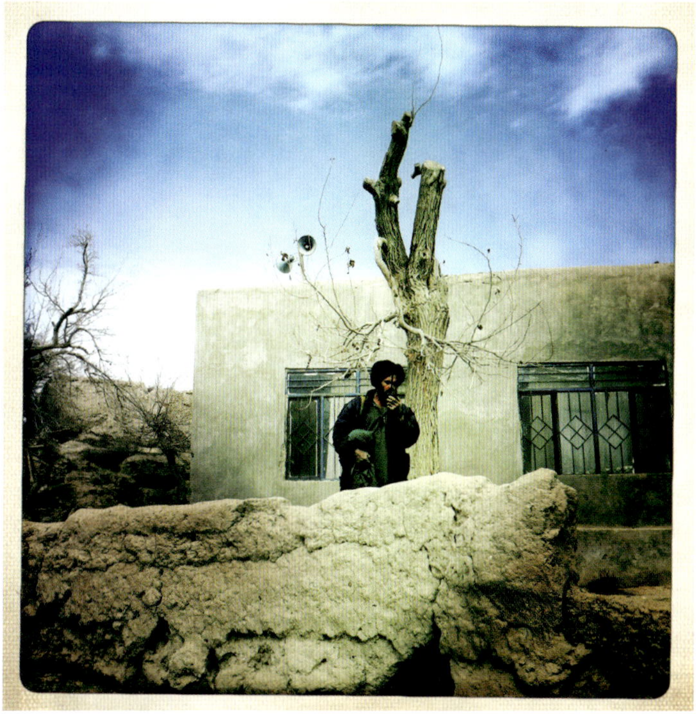

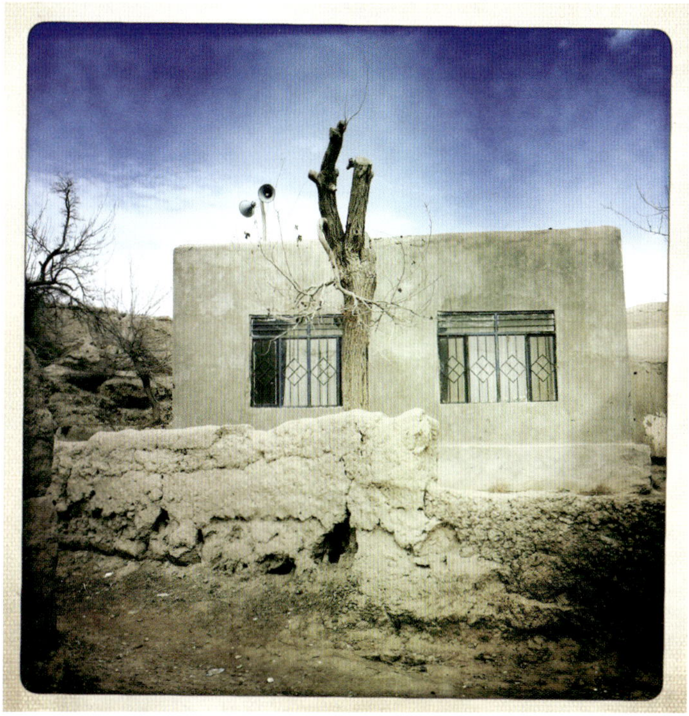

The language / dominant religion correlation

is in evidence throughout the history of the Abrahamic religions (Judaism, Christianity and Islam). From Hebrew to Greek to Roman (Latin) to Arabic to American English (*The Book of Mormon*), language has always been a factor in man's desire for *dominance of* or *autonomy from* the prevailing religion and culture. A recent example is Mormonism, born in the United States circa 1829 and, it follows, transcribed into American English by an American Prophet chosen by God to relay to mankind what He really meant to say. Joseph Smith claimed to have been led by the Angel Moroni to a hillock in western New York State where he found golden tablets on which were engraved God's words, written in the long-dead language of an ancient Egyptian race that had lived in New York before Biblical times (this account is summarized from descriptions in Jon Krakauer's brilliant and fascinating read, *Under the Banner of Heaven*).[96] Smith couldn't read the Egyptian hieroglyphs, so the Angel Moroni provided him with a set of divinely endowed spectacles called "interpreters"[97] that enabled Smith to translate the script into American English. Krakauer also describes how Smith got *The Book of Mormon* published: "Joseph took the manuscript to the publisher of the local newspaper, the Palmyra-based *Wayne Sentinel*, and asked him to print and bind five thousand copies of the book."[98]

The original tablets were lost, making American English the new official language of God.

From the papyrus scrolls of the first Biblical texts, to Gutenberg's historic Bible set in moveable type, to the *Book of Mormon* being published by a newspaper press; to TV and radio evangelists, to imams preaching through the loudspeakers atop mosques … technology has played a role in religion.

It would not be surprising for the next big religion to be revealed on an iPhone app. That is why I still hold on to my Apple stocks.

The persistence of oral culture and the Oz-like power of the imams is a difficult obstacle for western military strategists,

who have become reliant on literacy and the institutions and technologies that have come out of it. Radio is one of these technologies. In keeping with the Commander of the International Security Force (COMISAF)'s order to ramp up the information war against the Taliban propaganda machine, more and more makeshift radio stations helmed by the U.S. Military and ISAF are being established throughout Afghanistan—some right inside the foreign bases. Radio towers are one of the first defining features of any permanent or semi-permanent Patrol Base.

However, with mosque loudspeakers remaining the last impenetrable media outlet, the next best conduit for propaganda and counter-intelligence (COIN) in Afghanistan may not be radio, but mobile phones—a topic I take up in my next iProbe.

iProbe 09_Mobile Telephony: Can You Hear Me Now?

Mobile Telephony is an extension of the ear and of the mouth and of the finger.

I took this first photo of an Afghan National Army soldier making a call on his mobile phone almost as soon as Monica Campbell (my dear friend and colleague) and I arrived at the Shir Ghazay Patrol Base. I could hardly believe the image when I saw it, and even less so now, even though the photo is a kind of evidence. It looks painted, and for an essay about mobile phones and phonecams, it seems staged. I didn't know at the time that it would become an iconic image of my forays into Marshall McLuhan, technology and war.

"The decision to use the hot printed medium in place of the cool, participational, telephone medium is unfortunate in the extreme."

(MARSHALL MCLUHAN, *UNDERSTANDING MEDIA: THE EXTENSIONS OF MAN*) [99]

After narcotics, mobile phone networks are Afghanistan's second largest industry.[100] An Afghan friend who works with mobile phone companies in Kabul asked me a rhetorical question. "Why don't the phone companies set up an office in Kabul with a few hundred employees who just phone people with good advice, like 'Allah would want you to be good to your wives and daughters today'?" I'll tell you; the reason they don't do it is money," he said. "The bottom line is always money."

Mobile person-to-person communication could be helpful in winning the war over hearts and minds. But, as McLuhan said, the idea of using an old-fashioned telephonic person-to-person voice technology is radical and goes against the trend of using the latest technologies in war.[101]

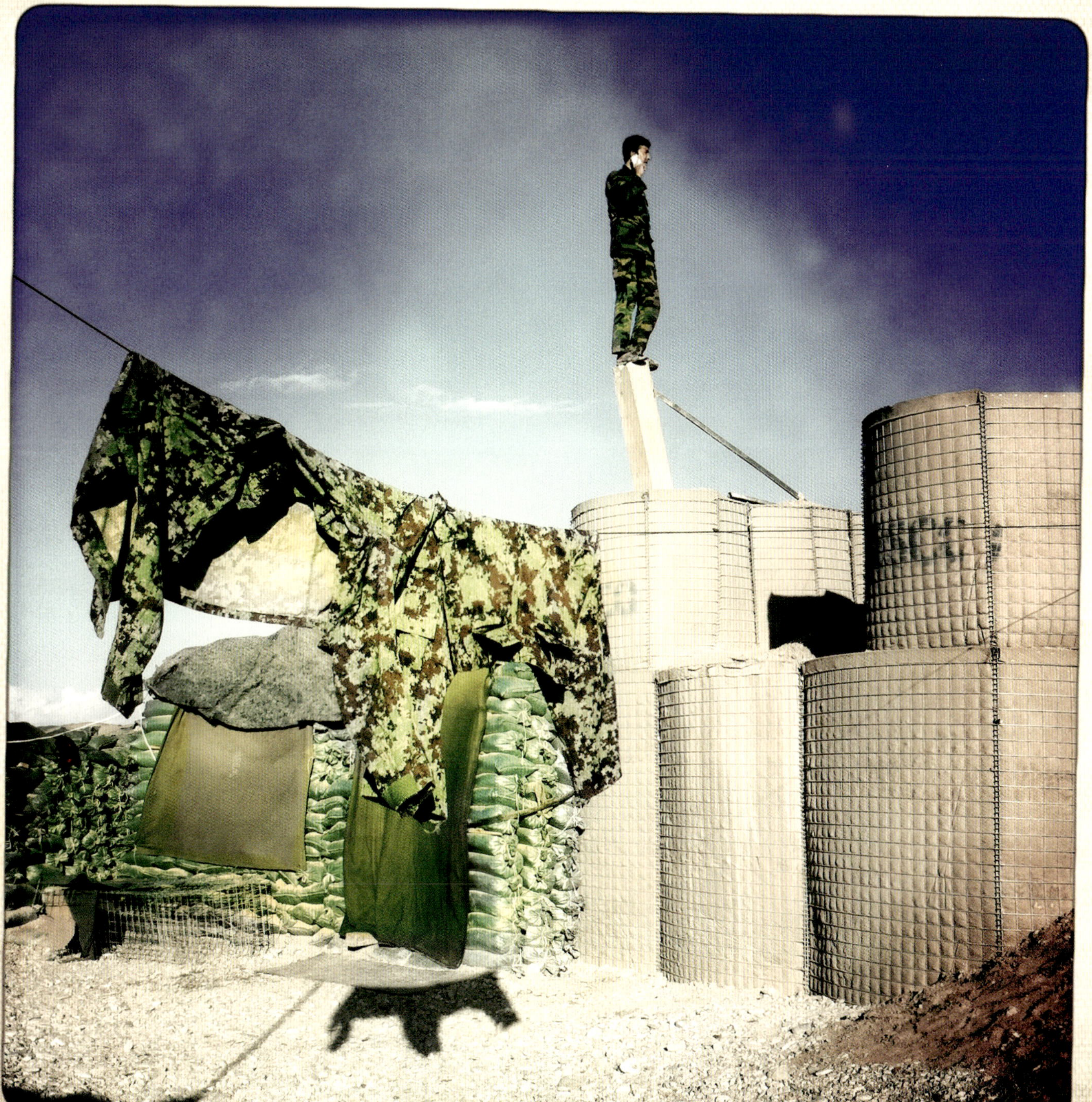

According to interviews conducted by Gretchen Peters in 2008,

"three of the four main Afghan telecom firms . . . pay monthly protection fees in each province, or face having their transmission towers attacked."[102]

I was also told by my friend in the Afghanistan telecom business that the Taliban routinely demand mobile phone companies shut down service at night so that Taliban movements cannot be traced by mobile phone locations. Most companies comply with the threats, but sometimes the Taliban disable the mobile towers themselves. When the towers are down, Afghans in remote communities become even more isolated, underscoring the gap between mobile phone technology and the next available communications technology or service in a household.

An anecdote related in the *Wall Street Journal* in 2010 describes how an elderly man in Kandahar province falls ill, but because the local mobile tower was bombed by the Taliban, his children are unable to phone for help. They carry their father to the hospital in Kandahar city on the back of a donkey[103] For this family, the next best form of communication they had after their mobile phone was a donkey. This is what McLuhan would call an

"overheated medium" flipping back into a previous medium of communication:

Mobile phone creates reliance on support network...

support network fails;

fall back to riding on the back of a donkey.

"Osama bin Laden escaped the Tora Bora siege down a smugglers' trail, 'reportedly on the back of a donkey.'"

(MARY ANN WEAVER, CITED IN GRETCHEN PETERS, *SEEDS OF TERROR: HOW DRUGS, THUGS AND CRIME ARE RESHAPING THE AFGHAN WAR*)[104]

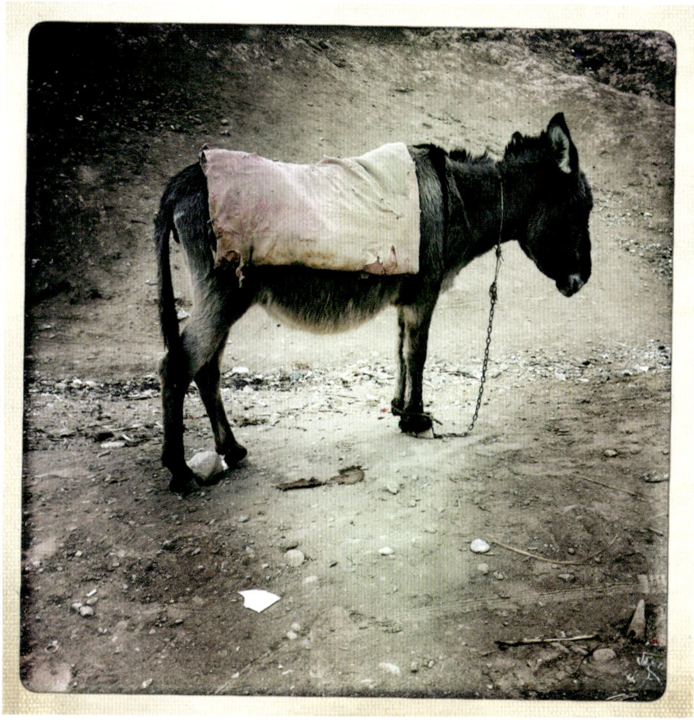

There are other reasons to be wary of (or grateful for) mobile phones.

They are, after all, used as signalling devices:

- "American convoy on its way toward you; get ready to detonate the explosive."
- "Foreigner travelling on road ahead Kidnap first, ask questions later."
- "Taliban threatening attacks. Do not leave the house."
- "Stay away from the mall today."

Many mobile phone users prefer texting to talking—it's faster and cheaper and silent;

and it has created a whole new discipline of phone texting linguistics along with proponents and opponents of The New Art of Texting (see iProbe 02_Phone Texting for more on this). But what about places like Afghanistan, where, outside of major cities (where education levels are vastly higher than the national average), most people cannot read or write text messages?

Mobile phones are voice devices that flipped into writing devices and are flipping back into voice devices with new voice recognition software.

Typically, the most advanced technologies, including voice recognition, are first introduced in rich countries like Canada, and not in Afghanistan, where because of high rates of illiteracy, it might mean the difference between life and death. While 75 percent of Afghans are non-literate (a much higher percentage in rural areas), in 2010 about 50 percent of Afghans (or 13 million subscribers for a total of 29 million citizens) had mobile phones.[105] (There are no statistics to measure what percentage of these phones belong to literate vs. non-literate, or men vs. women). Afghanistan does have an interactive voice recognition and response system called m-paisa available in Dari, Pashto and English that could potentially remove non literacy as a barrier to cellphone use—but for now it is mostly limited to banking.

Amid high-tech surveillance and counter-intelligence devices, the social, political and propaganda potential of simpler, good old-fashioned voice-to-voice communication has yet to be exploited to its full potential.

Writing is an extension of the hand and of the eye; writing is a visual artefact that stands in for man; the written word replaces the ear with the eye.

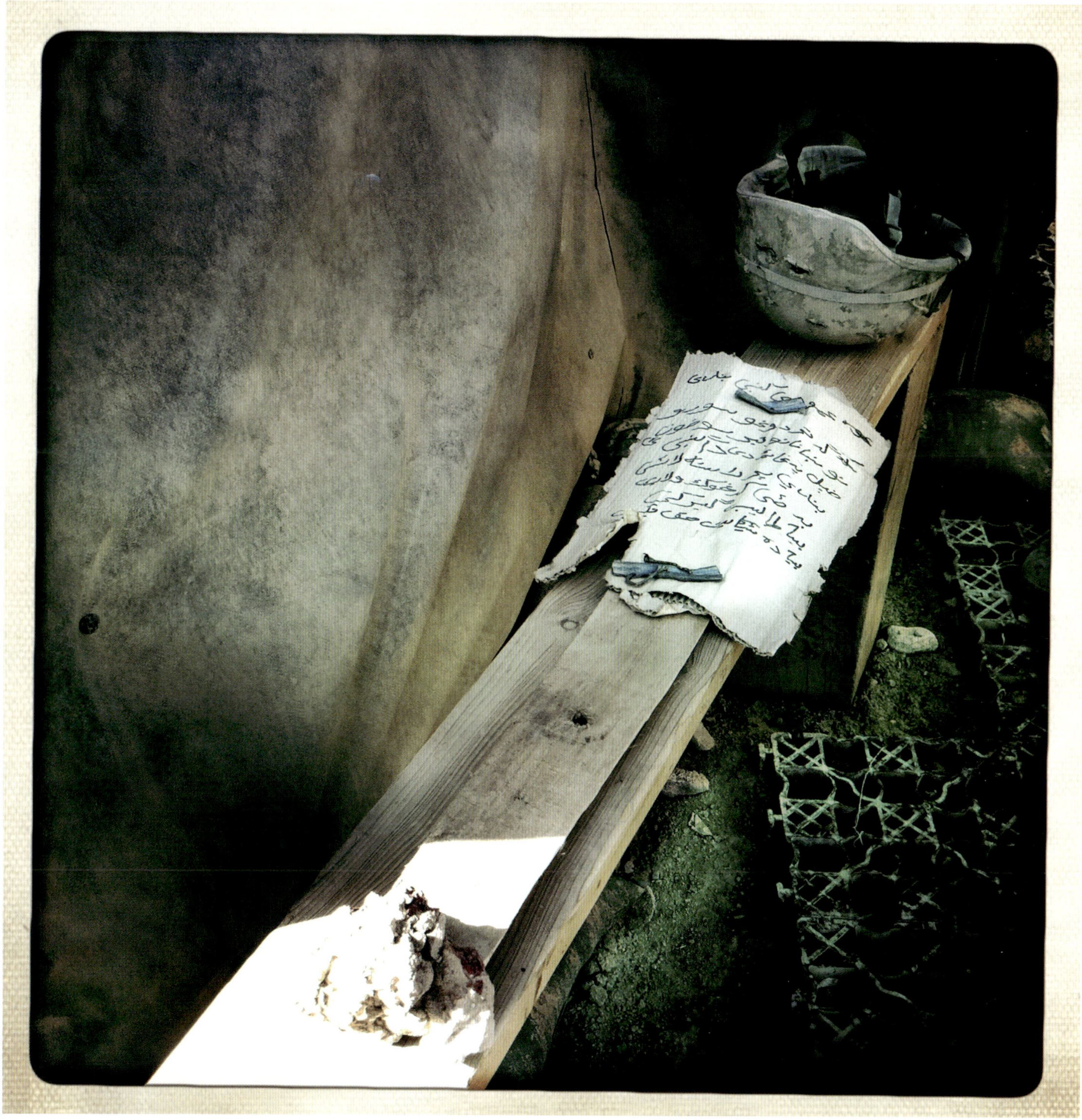

Photographs of signage explicitly show how written language is a visual artifact, a central theme of Marshall McLuhan's *The Gutenberg Galaxy*. Grammar and style are kinds of behaviour that can reveal, through a close reading (exegesis), the sources of the texts.

"Writing was the basic metaphor with which the cycle of civilization began, the step from the dark into the light of the mind."

(MARSHALL MCLUHAN AND QUENTIN FIORE, *THE MEDIUM IS THE MASSAGE: AN INVENTORY OF EFFECTS*) [106]

The written word (like unmanned aerial vehicles) is a way of conveying a message from a (safe) distance.

McLuhan calls writing

"an eye for an ear," [107]

because writing comes from the oral and the acoustic (not the other way around). And while you can have a flourishing oral or "non literate" culture with no written script, you can't have the reverse.

McLuhan believed that in some ways this gives non literate cultures an advantage over literate ones—

their dependence on oral communication forces a closeness in the community, a kind of tribalism and unity, and simultaneously a resistance to written artefacts (language or propaganda) originating from outside the tribe.

During the 2006 Hezbollah–Israel War, unmanned aerial vehicles (AMVs or "drones") dropped reams of leaflets warning the people of Lebanon against supporting Hezbollah leader Hassan Nasrallah. In Afghanistan, where the nonliteracy rate is over 75 percent, and much higher in the remote areas most likely to support the Taliban, disseminating these kinds of flyers would be futile.

The Taliban benefit enormously from non-literacy because it reduces the likelihood of individuals assimilating rogue information and separating from the tribal hive.

One day, some Marines returned to the Shir Ghazay FOB (Forward Operations Base) with a sign they'd found while on patrol. They'd gone out without an interpreter, so they carried it back to base to have it translated. It was handwritten in black marker on corrugated cardboard in a form of Arabic script, presumably Pashto (the dominant language of southern Afghanistan), and was fastened to a two-by-four with some nails and cut pieces of tire rubber.

They said that when they found it, it was surrounded by three rocks that someone had painted red.

Interpreters are prime targets for the Taliban,

who see them as enemy collaborators, and so for their own safety it's not uncommon to go on routine patrols without them. Photojournalists protect the identities of interpreters for the same reason, blacking out their faces if they should appear in any photographs that might be published.

It's hard to find enough Afghans with sufficient language skills willing to take the enormous risks of working for foreign militaries. Although most educated Afghans to some extent speak both official languages (Dari and Pashto), the vast majority of interpreters are from the north and Dari (also known as Afghan Persian) is their mother tongue. Dari and Pashto are both of Indo-European origin and both use a modified Arabic script for their writing, but the two languages are not mutually intelligible. The anthropologist Louis Dupree explains that "the difference between Dari and Pashto is analogous to the range of differences between English and German, or French and Spanish." [108]

One of the two interpreters on base struggled with the sign.

"It's very badly written," he said.

"I can't fully make it out. But it is a warning of some kind from the Taliban." The Marines mistook this to mean that the interpreter couldn't read his own language, and they told him so. Another interpreter gave it a try and determined the sign had something to do with blocking the way—the three red painted rocks seemed to confirm that interpretation.

Even had the Marines wanted to return the sign so that others might heed its warning, it would have been too dangerous to go back.

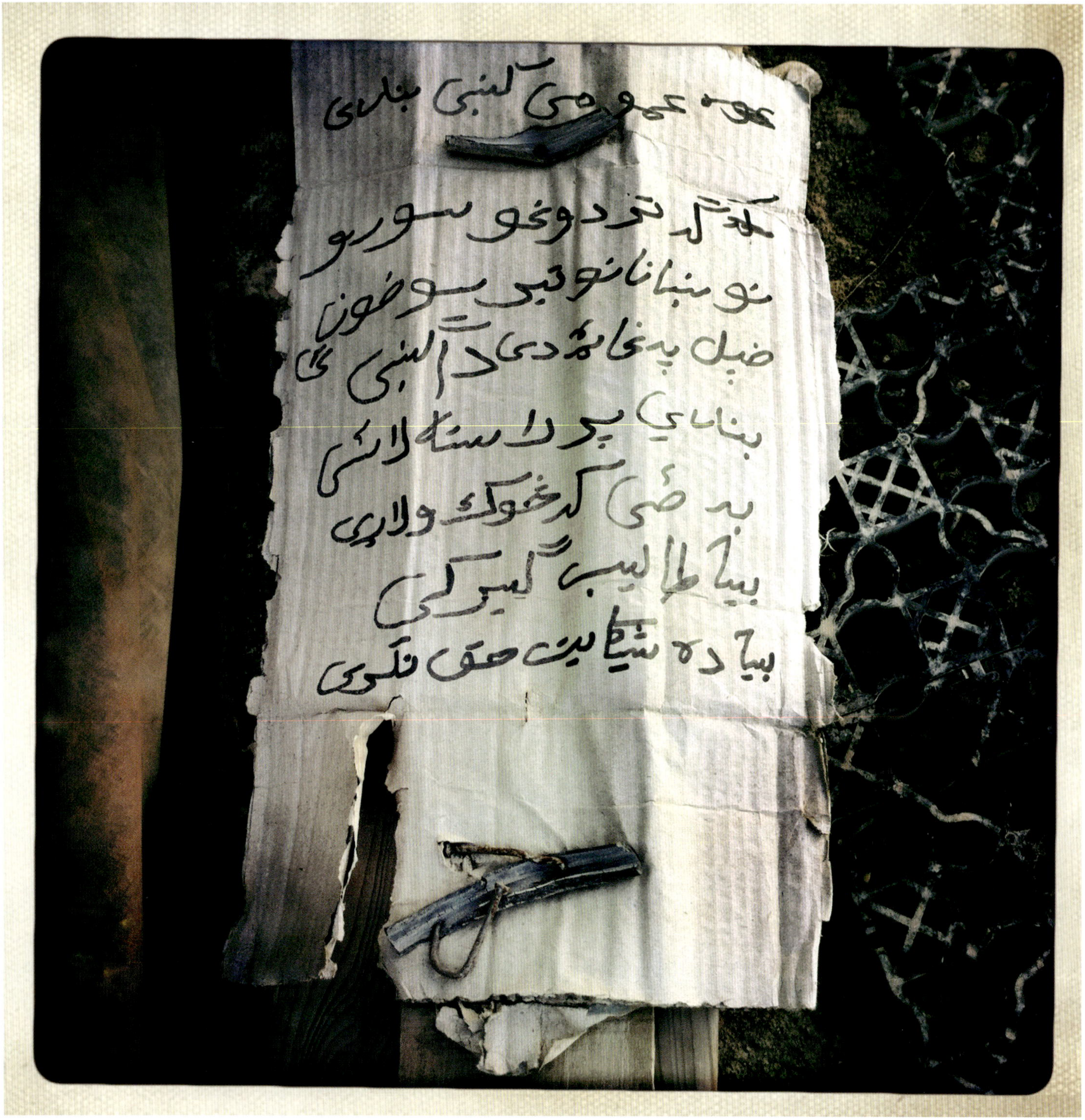

GO BEYOND
THIS POINT
AT YOUR OWN RISK

IF YOU ARE
CAPTURED
BY THE TALIBAN

YOUR BLOOD
IS ON
YOUR OWN HANDS

I told this story to my friend François Lachance in Toronto, who wrote part of his PhD dissertation on McLuhan. The first thing he asked was:

"Why didn't the Marines just take a photograph of the sign?"

It was as if they'd forgotten that writing is a visual artefact, and a camera is a photocopier.

Later, I showed my photograph of the sign to an Afghan scholar in Toronto—who is fluent in Pashto, Dari and Urdu (a language of northern Pakistan where many Taliban come from)—to see what she could make of it. I had already been told a few different things about the language of the sign, including that part of it was written in what looked like Urdu. As it turns out, the sign is written in a kind of corrupted rural Pashto dialect by someone who had learned reading and writing outside the formal education system, probably at a madrasa (the village, or non-official, schools run by the mullahs, the religious preachers).

Nor is the actual script an official Pashto, Dari or Urdu alphabet, but some kind of variant created at the madrasas.

(The translator, who was contacted through a third party, asked to remain anonymous. Even though she lives in Toronto, she is still afraid to be identified and have her name associated with this project. Instead of credit for her translation work, she asked only to express her wishes for peace in Afghanistan, and that she hoped her work would in some way contribute to that purpose.)

> "Each language draws a magic circle round the people to which it belongs."
>
> (MARSHALL MCLUHAN AND ERIC MCLUHAN, *LAWS OF MEDIA: THE NEW SCIENCE*) [109]

The local nature of the writing on the sign meant that it would be nearly impossible for a native Dari speaker to accurately navigate.

It would be something like a native English speaker with some formal education in French trying to decipher a French-based pidgin or Creole like Haitian, or the language of the Labrador Inuit.

Yet the experience of phonetic literacy (as with the Arabic, Cyrillic, Devanagari, Greek and Roman alphabets) is a fundamental characteristic of those who possess it—which is one of McLuhan's fundamental tenets.

So,

however different we may be from whoever wrote that sign, the fact we share phonetic literacy is a more important commonality than that for which we might give credit.

Here is a literal translation of the text:

Prohibited (prevent) for all,

If move from these holes (cavities or red points), her, him blood is at own hand (own neck).

This prevention (blockade) point is going to the right side – then – if someone wanted to go, if arrested (captured) by Taliban, DO not have the rights to complain.

We will never know if there were any consequences to removing the sign.

I am not the first person to point out that Coalition Forces overseas could use more preparatory training in local languages and customs.

It was not so far-fetched that some of the U.S. Marines thought the Afghans spoke Arabic—many had served in Iraq, and recognized the alphabetic signs of Arabic writing they had seen there.

The similarity of a few common greetings, from the *Quran*, reinforced the misconception. They didn't know that

Dari and Pashto are actually closer relatives to their fellow Indo-European languages, including English, as well as to the languages of northern India, than they are to Arabic.

"The Persian [and Dari] word for *is* is still *ast*, like Latin *est*, German *ist*, Russian *yest* and Sanskrit *asti*."

(NICHOLAS OSTLER, *EMPIRES OF THE WORLD: A LANGUAGE HISTORY OF THE WORLD*) [110]

As language historian Nicholas Ostler points out,

"the present-day globalized world is full of Arabic . . . and its ironic similarity to Hebrew,

newly revived in the land of Canaan, is a standing reminder of how the bitterest conflicts set long-lost cousins at each other's throats; *salam* contends against *shalom*, but the common meaning, 'peace', continues to elude them." [111]

(See charts in iProbe 02_Phone Texting pp. 116-119.) [112]

Persian (or Farsi) only began using the Arabic script after the Arab Conquest of Persia (now the Islamic Republic of Iran) in the 8th century ce[113] (which also saw the dominant religion of the region for nearly 2,000 years, Zoroastrianism, succumb to Islam). A comparable mistake to the Americans mistaking Dari for Arabic, might be for a Dari or Arabic speaker who could recognize but not read the Roman alphabet used in English (and not speak or have an ear for English) to land in Malta and think the language there was also English, even though Maltese is completely unintelligible to an English speaker. However, an Arab speaker can easily understand spoken Maltese! Maltese could roughly be described as Arabic written in the Roman alphabet—indeed it is the only Semitic language written in Latin script. Maltese is descended from a dialect spoken in Sicily after the Tunis raided the mostly Greek Orthodox island in the 7th and 8th centuries. Even after the Norman Conquest in 1061–90, the people of Malta continued to speak Arabic, but they adopted the Latin alphabet. While modern Maltese contains words recognizable from Italian and English, the language in its spoken form is largely understandable to Arabic speakers.

The history of world languages is full of examples of languages that have adopted foreign phonetic alphabets.

One of the greatest powers of phonetic alphabets is that they can be fitted to other tongues. Vietnamese has been written in a variant of the Roman alphabet ever since it was introduced to them by the Portuguese in the 16th century. Even Chinese, which is the most successful language in the world in terms of numbers of people who speak it as a first language, increasingly uses Pinyin, a phonetic transliteration system based on the finite Roman alphabet, which is much easier to learn than the thousands of picto-phonetic symbols of Chinese.

The Marines were not trained in language,

let alone its correlative arts, translation and exegesis; and in Afghanistan they were severely disadvantaged by not having enough translators.

As a simple explication of the text and writing of the sign shows,

there is more to learn from a few handwritten words than meets the eye.

The myth of Cadmus and the dragon's teeth

In my iProbe on Phone Texting I looked at the power of the alphabet, about which McLuhan said,

"The alphabet is an aggessive and militant absorber and transformer of cultures."[114]

Cadmus, a Phoenician prince, was credited in Greek Myth with bringing the phonetic alphabet to Greece. The story goes that

en route to Thebes, Cadmus slays a dragon, and in so doing angers the Greek Goddess Athena. Athena (tricking him) orders Cadmus to sow the dragon's teeth in the fields of Thebes. From the dragon's teeth spring up armed men, carrying with them both the might of the sword and the influence of language.

(SUMMARIZED FROM MARSHALL MCLUHAN, *UNDERSTANDING MEDIA: THE EXTENSIONS OF MAN*) [115]

"The alphabet meant power and authority and control of military structures at a distance. When combined with papyrus [the portable transmitter of language: the smart phones of antiquity] the alphabet spelled the end of the stationary temple bureaucracies and the priestly monopolies of knowledge and power."

(MARSHALL MCLUHAN, *UNDERSTANDING MEDIA: THE EXTENSIONS OF MAN*) [116]

The letters of the alphabet are extensions of the teeth (symbolized by the dragon's teeth).

"That the power of letters as agents of aggressive order and precision should be expressed as extensions of the dragon's teeth is natural and fitting. Teeth are emphatically visual in their linear order. Letters are not only like teeth visually, but their power to put teeth into the business of empire-building is manifest in our Western history."

(MARSHALL MCLUHAN, *UNDERSTANDING MEDIA: THE EXTENSIONS OF MAN*) [117]

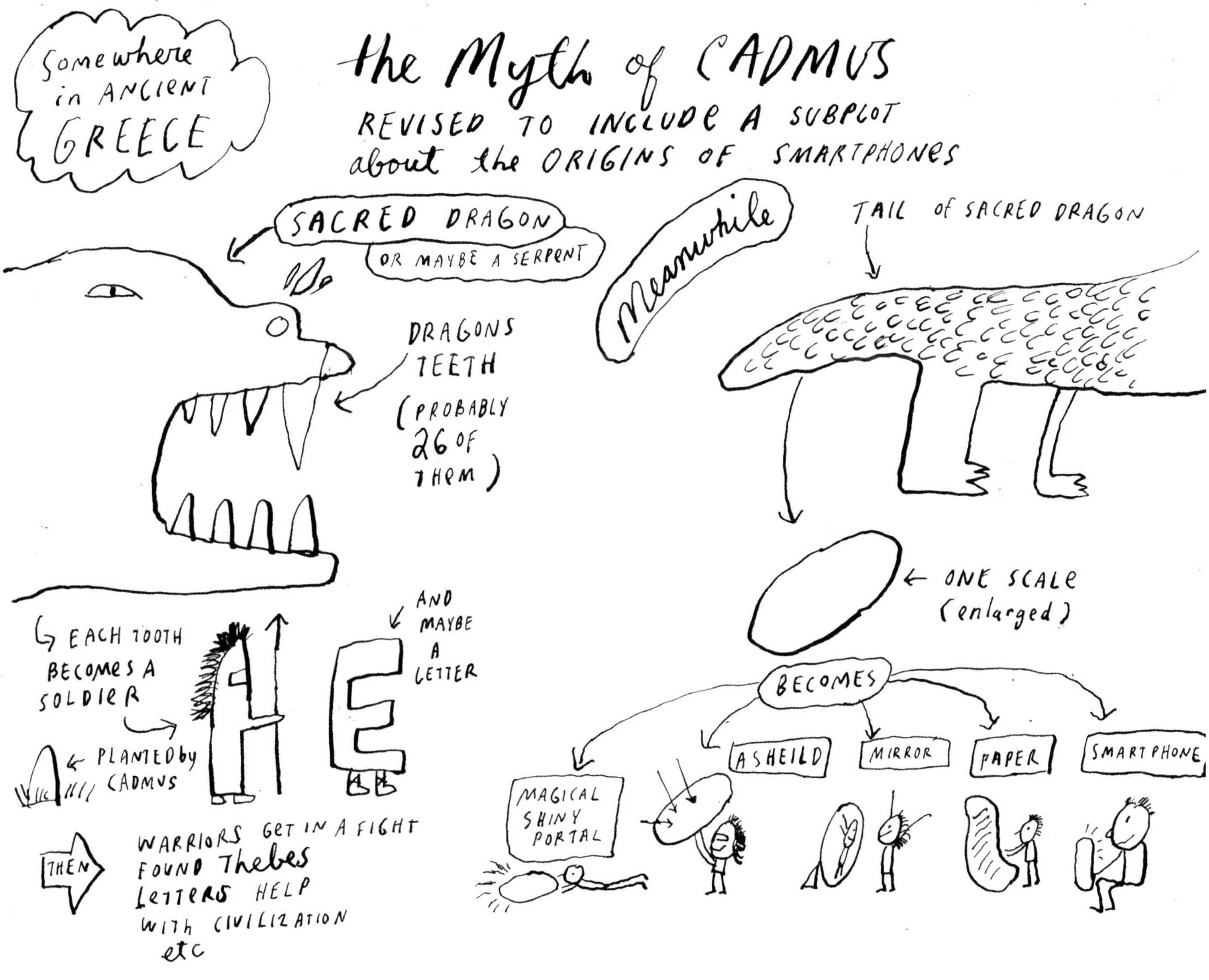
Somewhere in ANCIENT GREECE
the Myth of CADMUS
REVISED TO INCLUDE A SUBPLOT about the ORIGINS OF SMARTPHONES
SACRED DRAGON
OR MAYBE A SERPENT
DRAGONS TEETH
(PROBABLY 26 OF THEM)
Meanwhile
TAIL OF SACRED DRAGON
ONE SCALE (enlarged)
BECOMES
MAGICAL SHINY PORTAL
A SHEILD
MIRROR
PAPER
SMARTPHONE
EACH TOOTH BECOMES A SOLDIER
AND MAYBE A LETTER
PLANTED by CADMUS
THEN
WARRIORS GET IN A FIGHT
FOUND Thebes
LETTERS HELP WITH CIVILIZATION
etc

We now know without a doubt that the military classes were among those who spread the first alphabet around 1850 bce because of

military rock writing and graffiti

discovered by Yale archaeologists John and Deborah Darnell (in 1993) at the Wadi el-Hôl[118] along an ancient caravan route from Abidos (in upper Egypt) to Thebes[119] —

a recent archaeological fact McLuhan would not have had the benefit of knowing, but which would not have surprised him a bit.

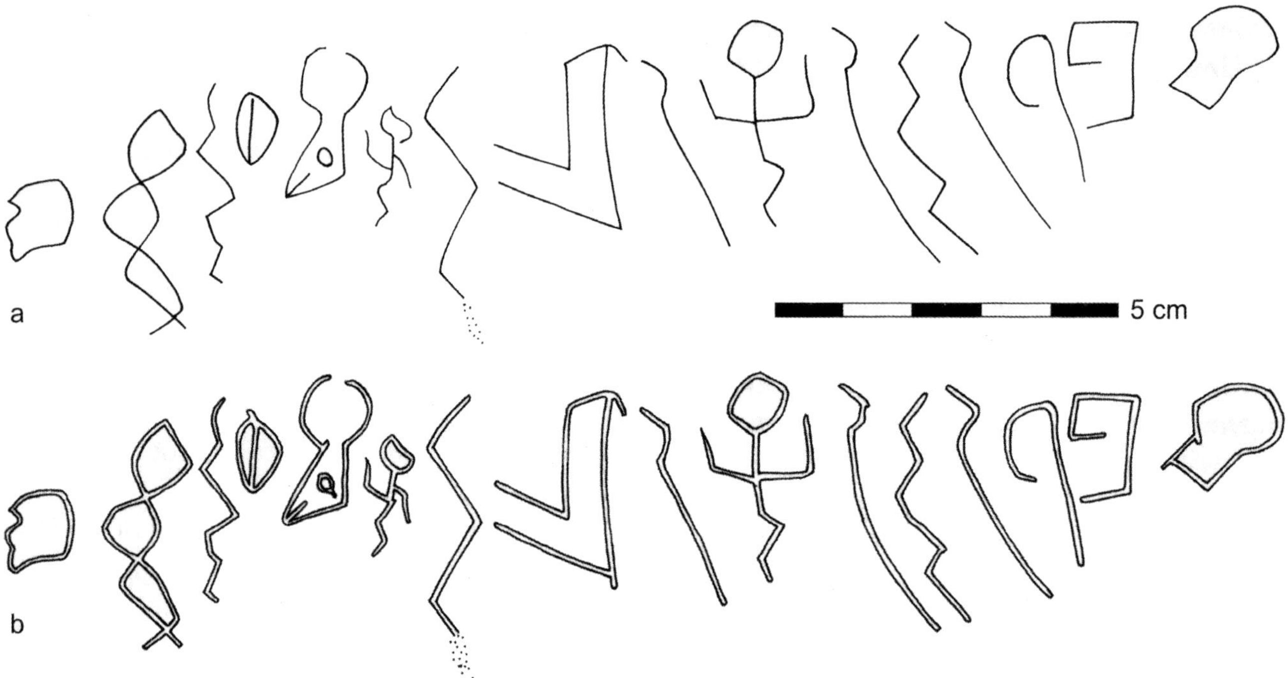

Wadi el-Hôl Alphabetic Inscription 1:
the Horizontal Inscription.
a) facsimile of the base of the inclined lines;
b) facsimile of the outer edges of the incised lines.

Wadi el-Hôl Alphabetic Inscription 2:
the Vertical Inscription.
a) facsimile of the base of the incised lines;
b) facsimile of the outer edges of the incised lines.

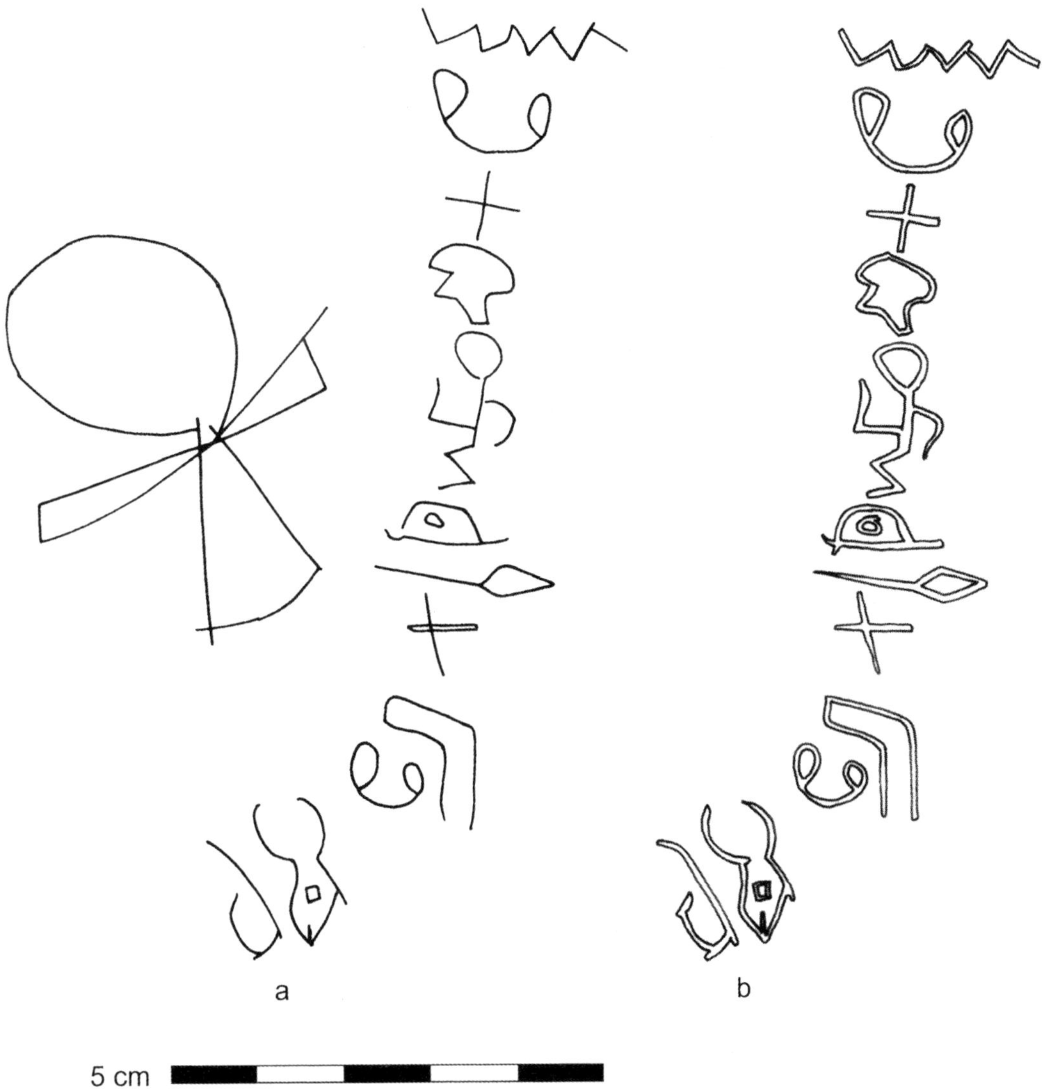

FROM JOHN COLEMAN DARNELL, F. W. DOBBS-ALLSOPP, MARILYN J. LUNDBERG, P. KYLE MCCARTER AND BRUCE ZUCKERMAN WITH THE ASSISTANCE OF COLLEEN MANASSA. "TWO EARLY ALPHABETIC INSCRIPTIONS FROM THE WADI EL-HÔL: NEW EVIDENCE FOR THE ORIGIN OF THE ALPHABET FROM THE WESTERN DESERT OF EGYPT," IN *THE ANNUAL OF THE AMERICAN SCHOOLS OF ORIENTAL RESEARCH*, VOLUME 59. BOSTON: AMERICAN SCHOOLS OF ORIENTAL RESEARCH, 2005.[120]

Unmanned Aerial Vehicles are an extension of the eye, of the finger, of the body.

“You do definitely get the sense that you are sort of a guardian angel. You’re like an eye-in-the-sky.”

(U.S. AIR FORCE CAPTAIN CATHERINE PLATT, PREDATOR DRONE SENSOR OPERATOR
CREECH AIR FORCE BASE, NEVADA, USA)[121]

Unmanned Aerial Vehicles—popularly called “drones” because the buzzing noise of their propellers can be heard from the ground—were first developed by Israel for surveillance purposes. Today they are the most talked-about weapon in use by the U.S. military. Pilots, operating on what look like video game monitors at ground control stations in the Mojave Desert, fly the drones by remote to and from take-off and landing sites thousands of miles away.

They fly too high to be seen with the naked eye, but close enough to the ground that sometimes you can hear them buzzing overhead

24–7.

“The drones were terrifying.

"From the ground, it is impossible to determine who or what they are tracking as they circle overhead. The buzz of a distant propeller is a constant reminder of imminent death."

(*NEW YORK TIMES* JOURNALIST AND TALIBAN KIDNAP VICTIM DAVID RHODE DESCRIBING "THE FEAR THE DRONES INSPIRED AMONG HIS CAPTORS, AS WELL AS AMONG ORDINARY CIVILIANS," AS QUOTED BY TAYLOR OWEN IN "DRONE'S DON'T JUST KILL.")[122]

In the last few years, stories of drone error have become a staple in the news and it's becoming increasingly clear that while drones very often do get their intended targets, they also kill a lot of innocents.

"We've killed 4,700 . . .

Sometimes you hit innocent people,

and I hate that, but we're at war, and we've taken out some very senior members of Al-Qaeda."

(Republican Senator Lindsey Graham, to a crowd at the Easley Rotary Club in South Carolina, February 19th, 2013) [123]

So-called principles of

proportionality

that weigh the negative effects of collateral damage against military advantage have long been part of the narratives of war strategy.

In McLuhan's terms of Figure and Ground or Foreground and Background,

military advantage is Figure,

and

collateral damage is Ground.

Humans, by nature, tend to focus on the figure, and the military is no exception to this: like the Republican Senator from South Carolina, they overweigh the figure, and underplay the effects taking place (literally and figuratively) on the ground.

In other words,

they don't see the forest for the trees (or don't want to).

There is no way of measuring how much damage these unintended kills cause to public relations, or how many new Taliban recruits they create. In fact the whole current war in Afghanistan can be attributed to lack of foresight (or willful blindness) during the Cold War era U.S–Soviet Union proxy war in Afghanistan in the 1980s. The Americans exploited the fighting fervor among Fundamentalist Islamist Groups, many from neighbouring Pakistan.

An excellent source on this subject is long-time Pakistan and Afghanistan correspondent Kathy Gannon's *I is for Infidel . . . J is for Jihad, K is for Kalashnikov*. As Gannon puts it:

"An alliance was born [between the U.S. and the their new allies]. Afghanistan's anti-Soviet fighters were called mujahedeen—holy warriors—and their war was a jihad or holy war." [124]

The Americans armed the mujahideen to the hilt and piled hundreds of millions of dollars into their pockets in exchange for ousting the Russians.

These are some of the groups that eventually became allied with Bin Laden. Moreover, the ongoing fighting created thousands of refugees on the Pakistan border—mostly poor, rural Pashtuns, some of whom would later become Taliban recruits.[125]

For a comparable example of Figure and Ground gone horribly awry, consider the Henry Kissinger-sanctioned American secret bombings of Cambodia (1969–70), which killed some 40,000 rural Cambodians living near the Vietnamese border, and rendered hundreds of thousands more homeless and disenfranchised. It was all part of fighting the Communists in Vietnam and Cambodia, but even at the time it was apparent that the massive B-52 attacks took their greatest toll on the civilian population.

Someone had decided that the civilian casualties

were *proportionally* worth it.

The American bombings created the fertile ground for recruitment into the then-rogue extremist Maoist group the Khmer Rouge. Had the Americans not bombed Cambodia as part of their proxy war against the Russians in Vietnam, the Khmer Rouge would not have been able to garner enough support to implement their insane, nightmarish agenda, responsible for the deaths of an estimated 1.5 million Cambodians between April 1975 and January 1979. Most Cambodians I talked to when I lived there in the late 1990s believed that the Nobel Peace Prize-winning Kissinger was a war criminal.

Taylor Owen, the research director of the Tow Center for Digital Journalism at Columbia University and a senior editor of OpenCanada.org, describes what I'll call the "Cambodia effect" taking place in Afghanistan as a direct result of drone activity:

"The broader impacts of drone use are revealing. They expose the false dichotomy between civilians and militants that underlies both the tactical decision-making process and much of the public debate about that process. Drones do not only affect their intended "kills"—they affect the civilians literally caught in their kill zones, and those living under them in fear day and night."

(TAYLOR OWEN, "DRONE'S DON'T JUST KILL,")[126]

Taylor writes perceptively and passionately about how the current debate on drones often misses the main point, which is that

"ubiquitous drone use blurs the line between citizen and militant."[127]

Owen also points out some of the unintended effects of the drone operations that would have McLuhan pricking up his ears:

"[Because of drone-induced anxieties], most kids in Waziristan no longer attend school."[128]

If we can still say that part of the plan in Afghanistan (and northern Pakistan) is to win hearts and minds, build schools and support education, then this is a clear example where the effect of the action is opposite to the intent of the action.

Some of the Marines I met liked to tell the story of how Afghan farmers thought the ultra-automated, unmanned drones were flown by specially trained mice.

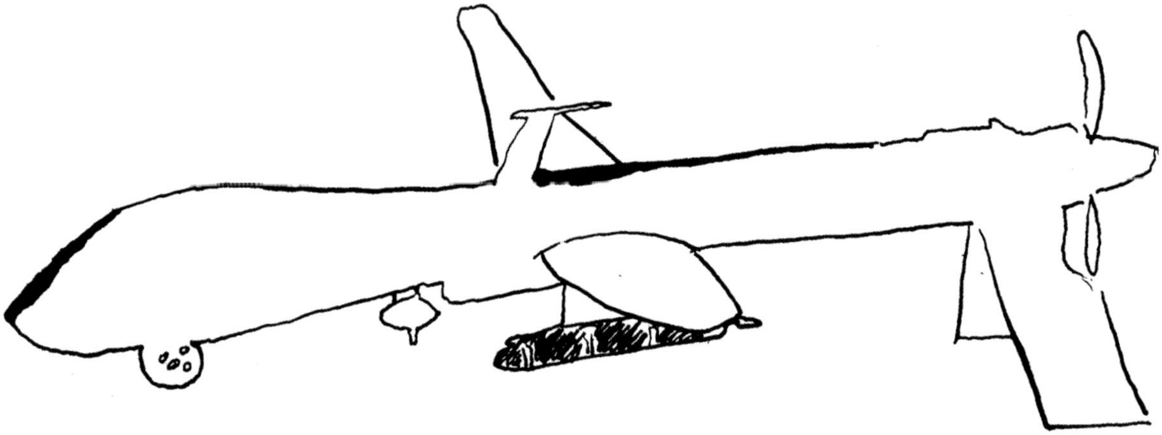

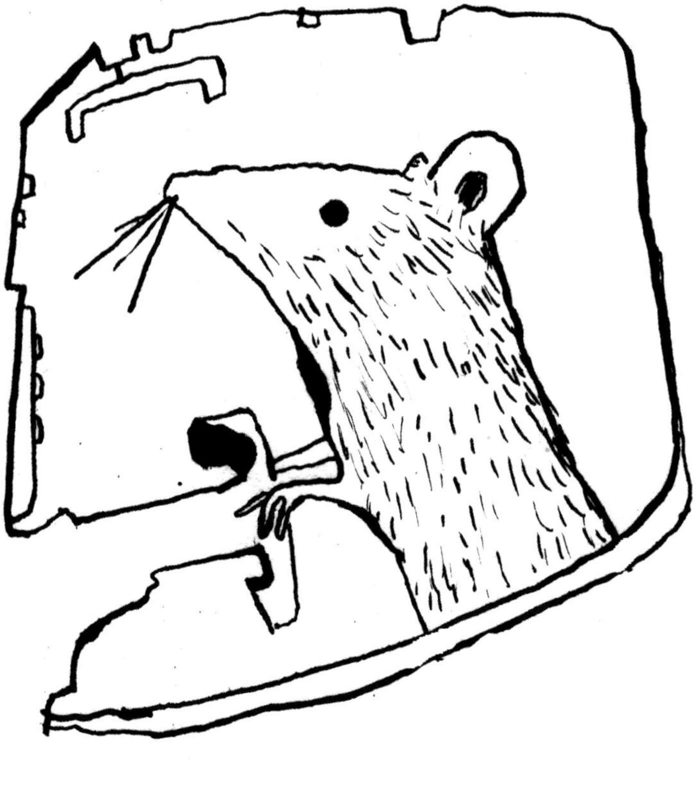

Drones are heard but not seen from the ground (so I couldn't photograph one). I asked my friend, the Canadian artist Jason Logan, to draw me one, based on the Marines' story.

I imagine it had become a sort of urban myth, told and retold, its original, apocryphal source irrelevant.

The story fed their psyches by perpetuating the idea that the technological gap between their enemies and them was unbridgeable

to the point of absurdity. But the correlative to their misplaced faith in super-technologies is an opposite and equally significant loss of understanding of, and appreciation for, the more "primitive," primary technologies and tools of communication, like simple handwritten signs, loudspeakers atop mosques or improvised explosive devices (IEDs) made of wood (see iProbe 06_Improvised Explosive Devices [IEDs] Made of Wood and iProbe 10_The Written Word).

It was important for the Marines to believe they would win at war because of their superior technologies, and drones, with their remote-controlled, super-accurate targeting and high-resolution cameras, are a perfect symbol of everything that can make humans capable of fighting a war without actually putting their physical selves at risk.

"The biggest noticeable difference is your lack of sensory output."

(U.S. AIR FORCE MAJOR JAMES ACKERMAN, PREDATOR PILOT—ON PILOTING DRONES VS. OTHER AIRCRAFT.)[129]

"Firearms and bombs, which permit deadly action at great distances, seem to relieve the user of responsibility."

(MARSHALL MCLUHAN AND ERIC MCLUHAN, *LAWS OF MEDIA: THE NEW SCIENCE*)[130]

What happens when soldiers are totally detached from the bodily, sensory, physical actualities of war?

Some enemies consider the use of unmanned weaponry as cowardice—if you're not willing to die for the cause, how important is it to you? Moreover, little is yet known about how post-traumatic stress and other disorders will affect people who kill at such great distances. The received belief is that it's easier to kill someone you can't see. In *Laws of Media*, McLuhan noted this with regard to World War II fighter pilots, citing psychiatrist Anthony Storr in his study, *Human Aggression*:

"The distance between [a bomber pilot a few hundred feet above a village] and the people he is bombing makes them into an impersonal target, no longer human beings like himself with whom he can identify."[131]

But the reverse is also true, and the pilots seem inhuman to the people being bombed on the ground. In the case of drones, the attacker really is not human. In his comprehensive book on robotics and warfare, *Wired for War*, P. W. Singer interviews John Pike of GlobalSecurity.org about the roboticization of war. Pike compares it to the *Terminator* movies:

"This [robotics revolution] opens up great vistas, some quite pleasant, others quite nightmarish. On the one hand, this could make our flesh-and-blood soldiers so hard to get that traditional war—a match of relatively evenly matched peers—could become a thing of the past. But this might also rob us of our humanity. We could be the ones that wind up looking like Terminators in the world's eyes." [132]

Moreover, if we follow McLuhan's logic that our technologies alter our identities, that every new technology brings with it an identity crisis and provokes a psychic change, then the effect of remote control weapons on the user should be significant. McLuhan wrote that

"radical changes of identity, happening suddenly and in very brief intervals of time, have proved more deadly and destructive to human values than wars fought with hardware weapons."

(MARSHALL MCLUHAN AND ERIC MCLUHAN, *LAWS OF MEDIA: THE NEW SCIENCE*) [133]

And if, as McLuhan would insist, the drones are extensions of the pilots, prosthetics of a sort, then

would not the act of killing, even from thousands of miles away, effect in them phantom traces of what their hands had done?

Removed from action in the field, drone operators are also denied the camaraderie of combat, where the brotherhood of soldiers builds allegiances and support of mythic proportions. War is hideous.

The only thing worse than war is facing war alone, without your brothers in arms.

UAVs obsolesce camaraderie and brothers in arms.

A 2012–13 study by the Armed Forces Health Surveillance Center (AFHSC), written about in the *New York Times*, found that killing at a distance takes its toll too, and "drone pilots are experiencing mental health problems like depression, anxiety and post-traumatic stress at the same rate as pilots of manned aircraft who are deployed to Iraq or Afghanistan."[134] In an interview with James Doa of the *Times*, Jean Lin Otto, who was a co-author of the AFHSC study, explained that "remotely piloted aircraft pilots may stare at the same piece of ground for days . . . They witness the carnage. Manned aircraft pilots don't do that. They get out of there as soon as possible."[135]

It used to be that being a fighter pilot was one of the most dangerous jobs you could have during a war. Asymmetrical warfare has already reduced the dangers of piloting bombers, but drones take physical safety to a new level. By 2015, the U.S. Air Force expects to have more drone pilots than bomber pilots.[136] The flip side of this, which is what McLuhan is always interested in, is that while there will be fewer deaths, there will be vastly more cases of severe psychological trauma—and that carries with it a much higher financial burden on the state (see iProbe 03_Body Armour).

Another result of having fewer military personnel on the ground is that military intelligence becomes increasingly dependent on unknown elements.

With fewer military personnel on the ground to intercede and interpret word-of-mouth information, informants become less reliable.

Local disputes and rivalries can easily lead to misinformation motivated by revenge (something I witnessed in Iraq when I spent three months embedded with the 3/7 Cavalry, 3rd Infantry Division in 2003).

So while the drones seem to offer superpower eyes, the information coming to the ears is diminished in power. As McLuhan would say, they are giving

an eye for an ear.

iProbe 12_Sandbags and HESCO Concertina Barriers

Harnessing the power of earth and sand;

Walls are extensions of the people on the other side.

You can't go to Iraq or Afghanistan without seeing HESCO bastion barriers and sandbags everywhere. The Marines use them to create temporary walls and fortifications against blasts or small arms.

Originally designed as flood barriers, HESCOs are named after the British company that developed them in the 1980s. They are made of collapsible wire-mesh encasings and heavy-duty fabric liners. Like sandbags,

they are a kind of impermanent brick,

filled with local sand, dirt or gravel, so they can be used anywhere on earth where there is earth and sand.

Like the ancient adobe villages in Afghanistan, sandbags and HESCO bastion barriers are extensions of the earth and sand.

Some of the oldest man-made structures in Afghanistan are built of adobe, or sun-dried brick, one of the oldest and most common building materials. It is older than the alphabet.

The word *adobe* can be traced to the Egyptian Middle Kingdom period (c.2000 bce):

djbt meaning "mud or sun-dried brick" becomes *al* "the" *dtub*, "brick," in Arabic, which the Spaniards absorb and by merging the indefinite article al ("the" in Arabic) with the noun *dtub* ("brick") created the word *adobe*—the word that eventually entered the English lexicon sometime in the 18th century.

Adobe is made of sand, water and some kind of bonding material like straw or manure. The mud mixture is dried in brick-shaped molds.

Compared to the historic and enduring traditional Afghan adobe villages, the Marine's temporary bases—built of the very same earthen materials but without binding compounds—seemed like peculiar impermanent versions of civilization.

Yet because they are made of the same material as the ground on which they were built, they strangely both fit into the landscape and did not fit in at the same time. They were situated inside the communities, but separated from the communities. Instead of doors, they had armoured tanks at the front entrances.

Like Nomadic Tribes, the Marines with their HESCO Villages have no intention of staying—leaving the Afghans to fend off the Taliban by themselves.

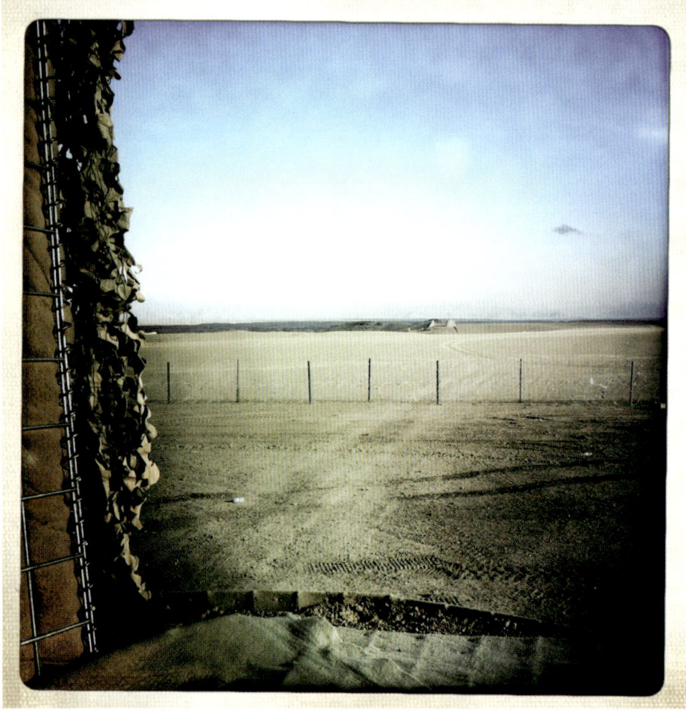

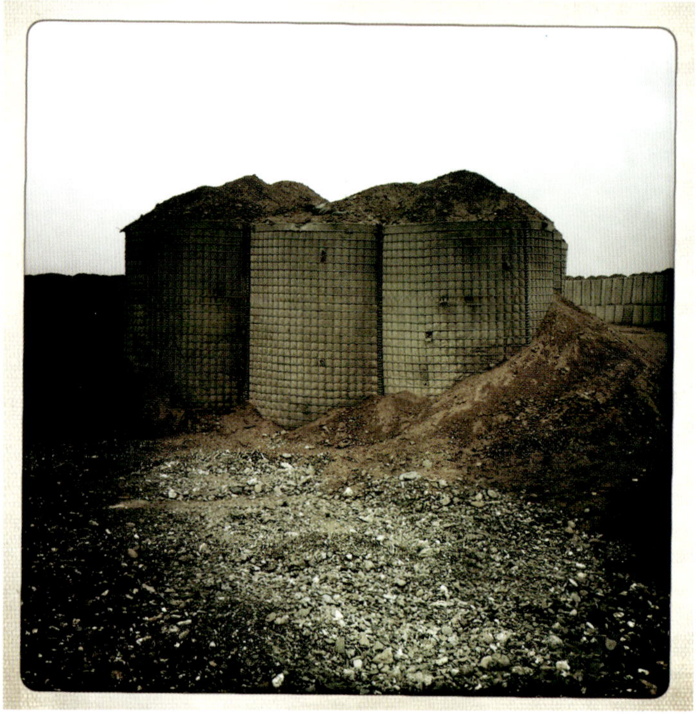

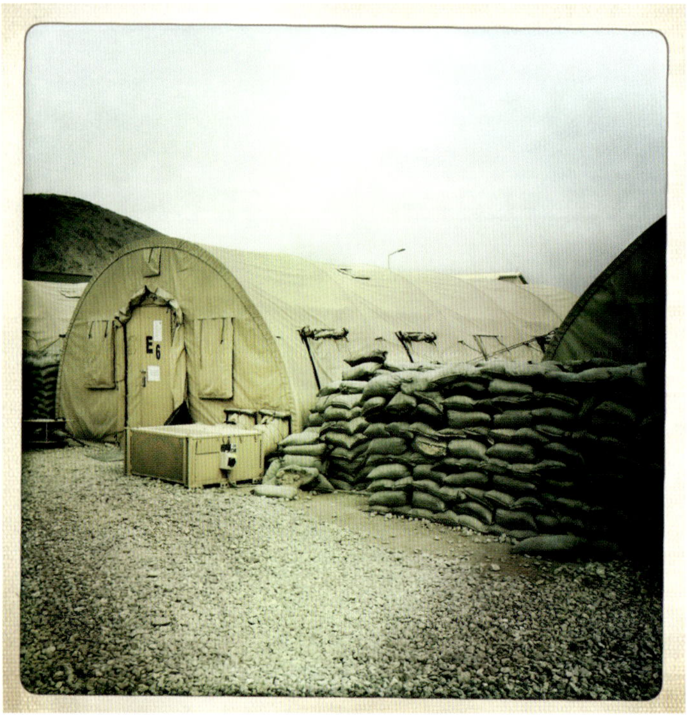
E6

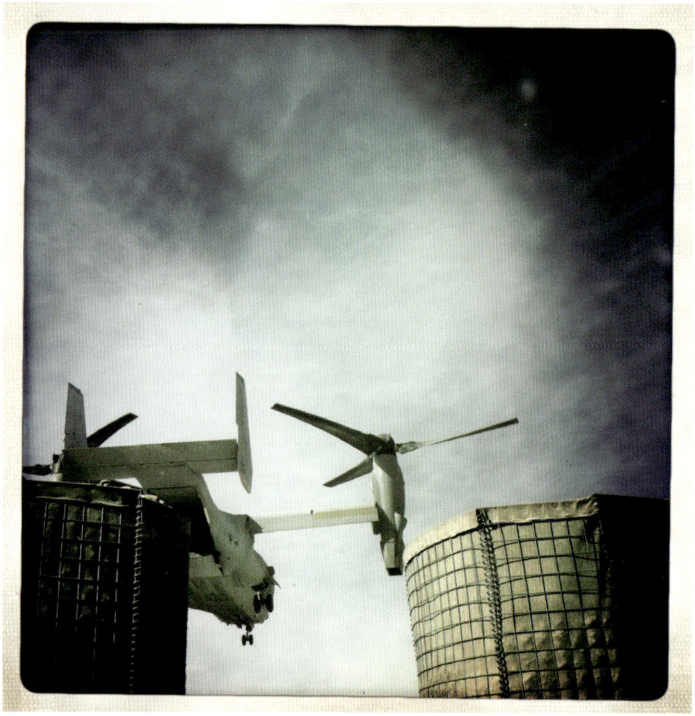

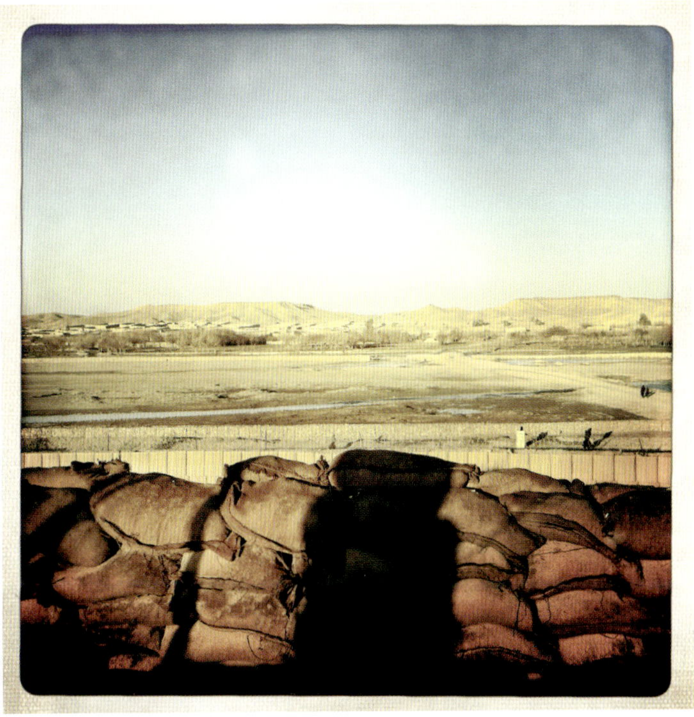
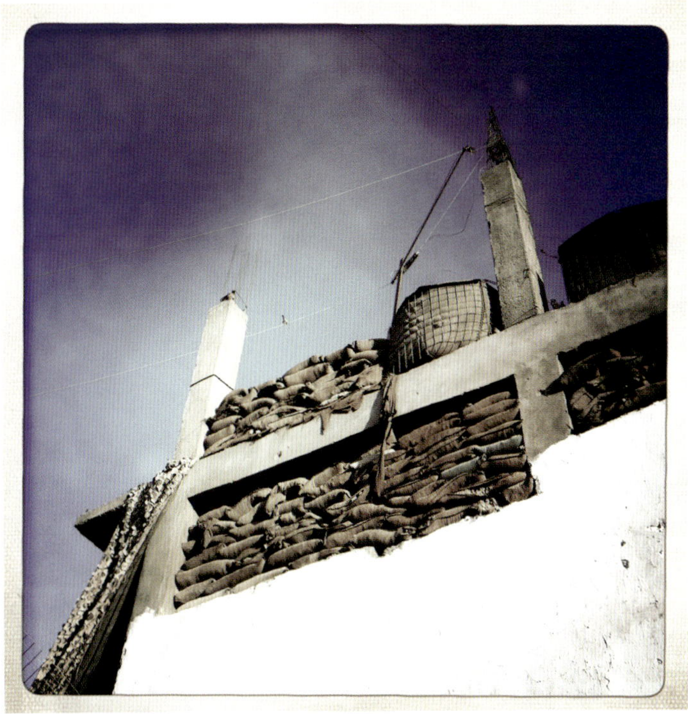
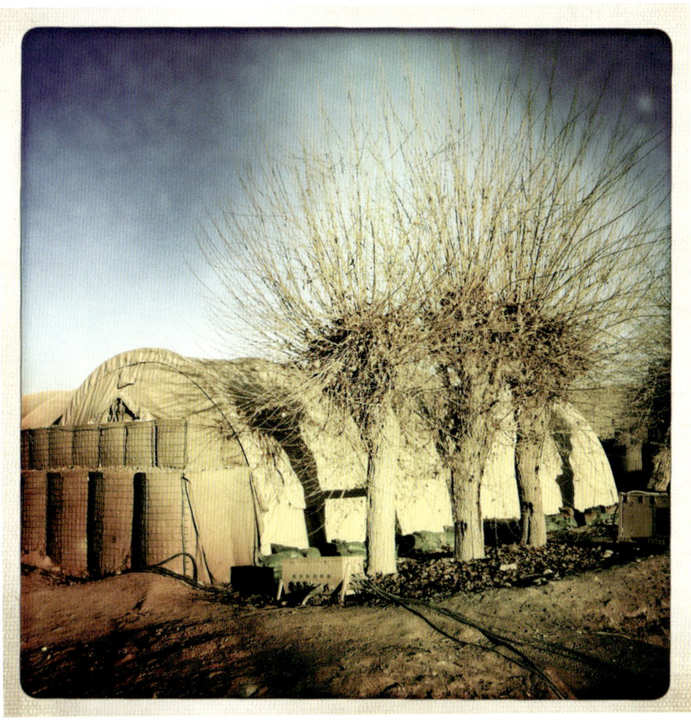
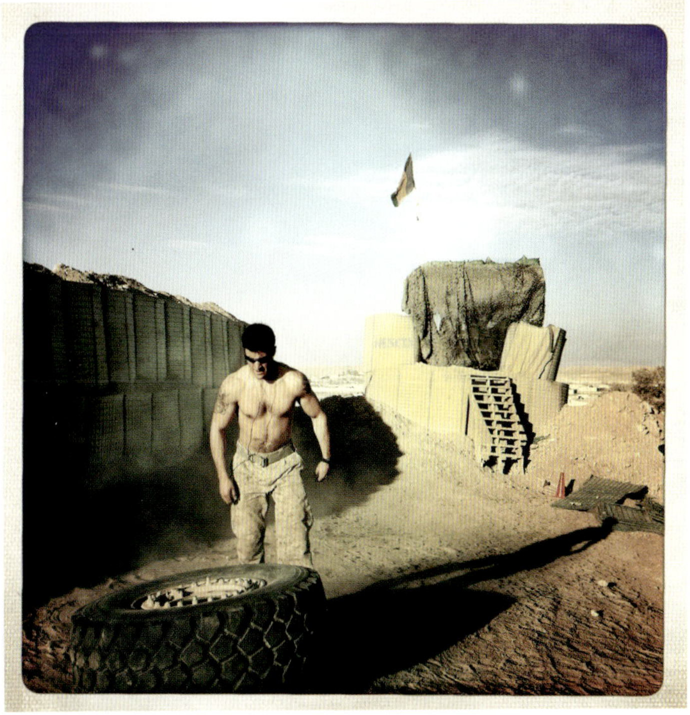

Genesis 11:00–11:10—
The Tower of Babel

Now the whole earth had one language and the same words.

And as they migrated from the east, they came upon a plain in the land of Shinar and settled there. And they said to one another, "Come, let us make bricks, and burn them thoroughly."

And they had brick for stone, and bitumen for mortar.

Then they said, "Come let us build ourselves a city, and a tower with its top in the heavens, and let us make a name for ourselves; otherwise we shall be scattered abroad upon the face of the whole earth." The LORD came down to see the city and the tower, which mortals had built.

And the LORD said, "Look, they are one people, and they have all one language; and this is only the beginning of what they will do; nothing that they propose to do will now be impossible for them. Come, let us go down, and confuse their language there, so that they will not understand one another's speech."

So the LORD scattered them abroad from there over the face of all the earth, and they left off building the city.

Therefore it was called Babel, because there the LORD confused the language of all the earth; and from there the LORD scattered them abroad over the face of all the earth."

(NEW REVISED STANDARD VERSION)

Tetrads: The Laws of Media

“The laws of media in tetrad form

belong properly to rhetoric and grammar, not philosophy. Our concern is etymology and exegesis. This is to place the modern study of artefacts on a humanistic and linguistic basis for the first time.”

(MARSHALL MCLUHAN AND ERIC MCLUHAN, *LAWS OF MEDIA: THE NEW SCIENCE*)[137]

Suggested as a new, scientific way of viewing artefacts,

tetrads are the diagrammatic application of Marshall McLuhan’s theories and laws of media.

The quintessential text on tetrads is Marshall and Eric McLuhan’s *Laws of Media: The New Science*. The following summaries are drawn principally from the last chapter of that book, “Tetrads.”

The simultaneous four-part visual structure of the tetrad removes the sequential, linear limitations of narrative text from the process of grasping the metaphoric outcroppings of artefacts.

A tetrad is also the etymology of an artefact: it concerns its past, present and future effects.

The four parts of the tetrad are

simultaneous, expansive, resonant, appositional, metaphoric . . .

The beauty of the tetrad, like many of McLuhan’s best ideas, is its deceivingly obvious simplicity. As this series of iProbes has shown, we very often neglect to anticipate the unexpected effects of The Things We Make (our technologies and artefacts). The following pages attempt to visualize the iProbes in tetrad form.

Whereas the graphic presentation of the tetrads in *Laws of Media: The New Science* is a fairly straightforward text table, I’ve worked with Jenny Armour to create and customize a new tetrad graphic for *Looking for Marshall McLuhan in Afghanistan*. The goal was to honour Marshall and Eric McLuhan’s concept while emphasizing the visual play of the tetrad.

The four parts of the tetrad—enhances, obsolesces, retrieves, reverses (into)—

are framed as questions.

Figure Ground
Foreground Background
are in a constant state of interplay.

I like to think of McLuhan's tetrads as a game show about technology where contestants win prizes for deducing the subliminal or unintended effects of all things man-made **(artefacts).**

It's The Marshall McLuhan Show!

These are the four questions of the McLuhan Tetrad, which are asked in no particular order:

Enhances

Every technology extends or amplifies some human faculty or organ.

What does the artefact enhance, extend or intensify?

Obsolesces

When one area of experience is heightened or intensified, another is diminished or pushed aside.

What does the artefact render obsolete, or displace?

Retrieves

The content of any medium is another medium.

What does the artefact retrieve that was previously obsolesced?

Reverses (into)

Every form, pushed to the limit of its potential, reverses its characteristics.

What does the artefact produce or become when pressed to an extreme?

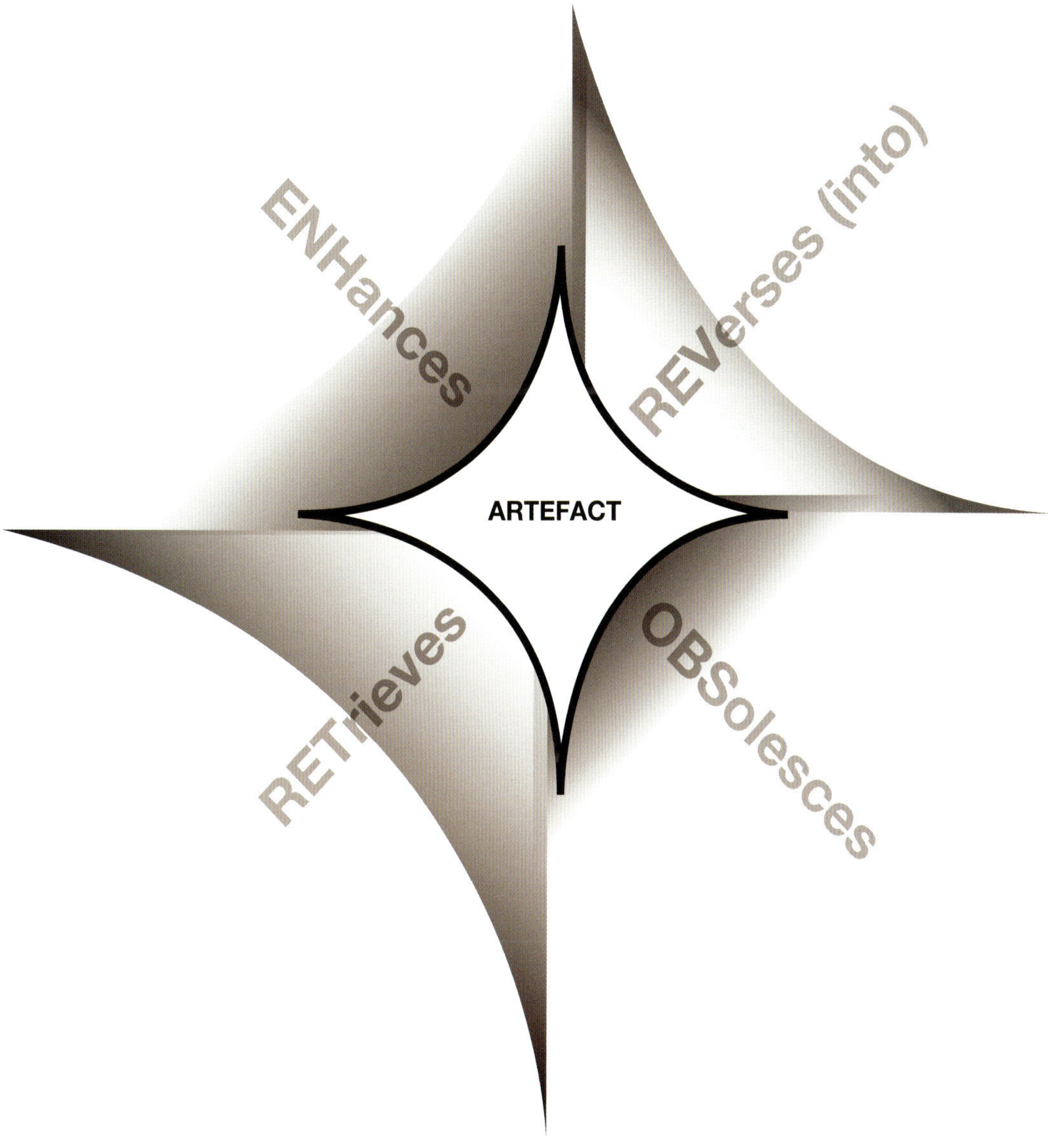
ENHances
REVerses (into)
ARTEFACT
RETrieves
OBSolesces

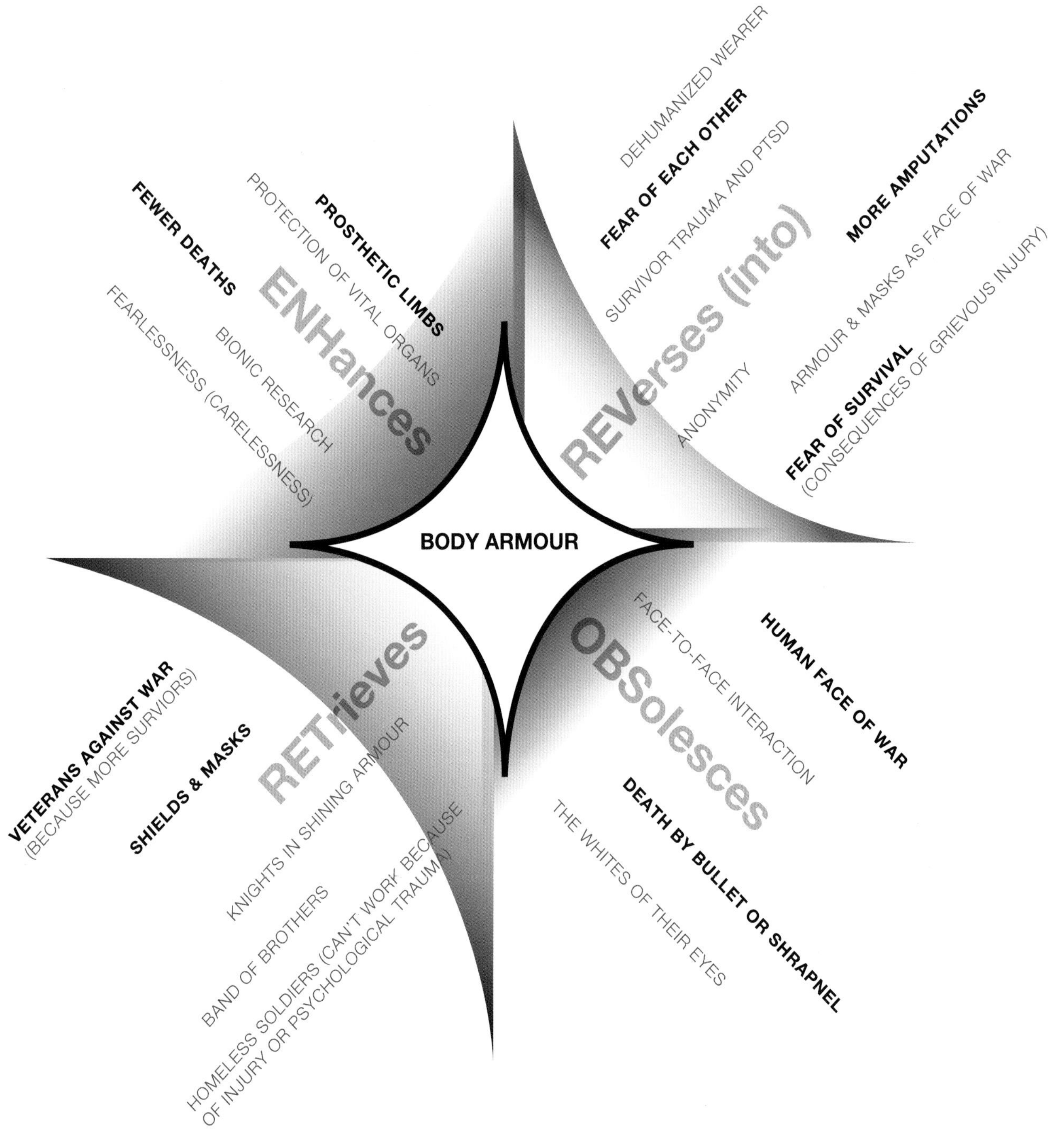
BODY ARMOUR
ENHances
FEWER DEATHS
PROSTHETIC LIMBS
PROTECTION OF VITAL ORGANS
BIONIC RESEARCH
FEARLESSNESS (CARELESSNESS)
REVerses (into)
DEHUMANIZED WEARER
FEAR OF EACH OTHER
SURVIVOR TRAUMA AND PTSD
ANONYMITY
MORE AMPUTATIONS
ARMOUR & MASKS AS FACE OF WAR
FEAR OF SURVIVAL
(CONSEQUENCES OF GRIEVOUS INJURY)
RETrieves
VETERANS AGAINST WAR
(BECAUSE MORE SURVIORS)
SHIELDS & MASKS
KNIGHTS IN SHINING ARMOUR
BAND OF BROTHERS
HOMELESS SOLDIERS (CAN'T WORK BECAUSE
OF INJURY OR PSYCHOLOGICAL TRAUMA)
OBSolesces
FACE-TO-FACE INTERACTION
HUMAN FACE OF WAR
DEATH BY BULLET OR SHRAPNEL
THE WHITES OF THEIR EYES

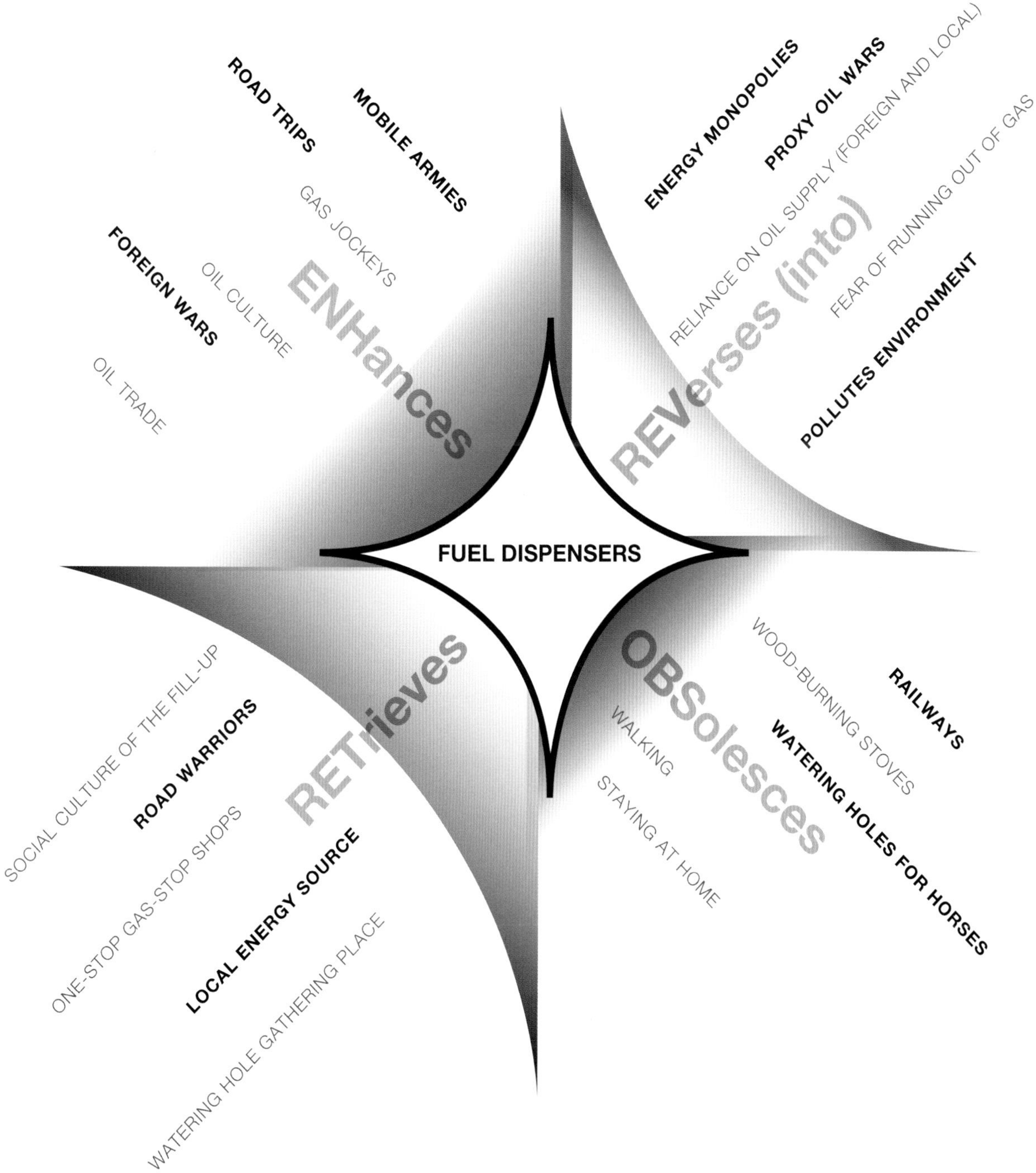
FUEL DISPENSERS
ENHances
ROAD TRIPS
MOBILE ARMIES
GAS JOCKEYS
FOREIGN WARS
OIL CULTURE
OIL TRADE
REVerses (into)
ENERGY MONOPOLIES
PROXY OIL WARS
RELIANCE ON OIL SUPPLY (FOREIGN AND LOCAL)
FEAR OF RUNNING OUT OF GAS
POLLUTES ENVIRONMENT
RETrieves
SOCIAL CULTURE OF THE FILL-UP
ROAD WARRIORS
ONE-STOP GAS-STOP SHOPS
LOCAL ENERGY SOURCE
WATERING HOLE GATHERING PLACE
OBSolesces
WOOD-BURNING STOVES
RAILWAYS
WALKING
WATERING HOLES FOR HORSES
STAYING AT HOME

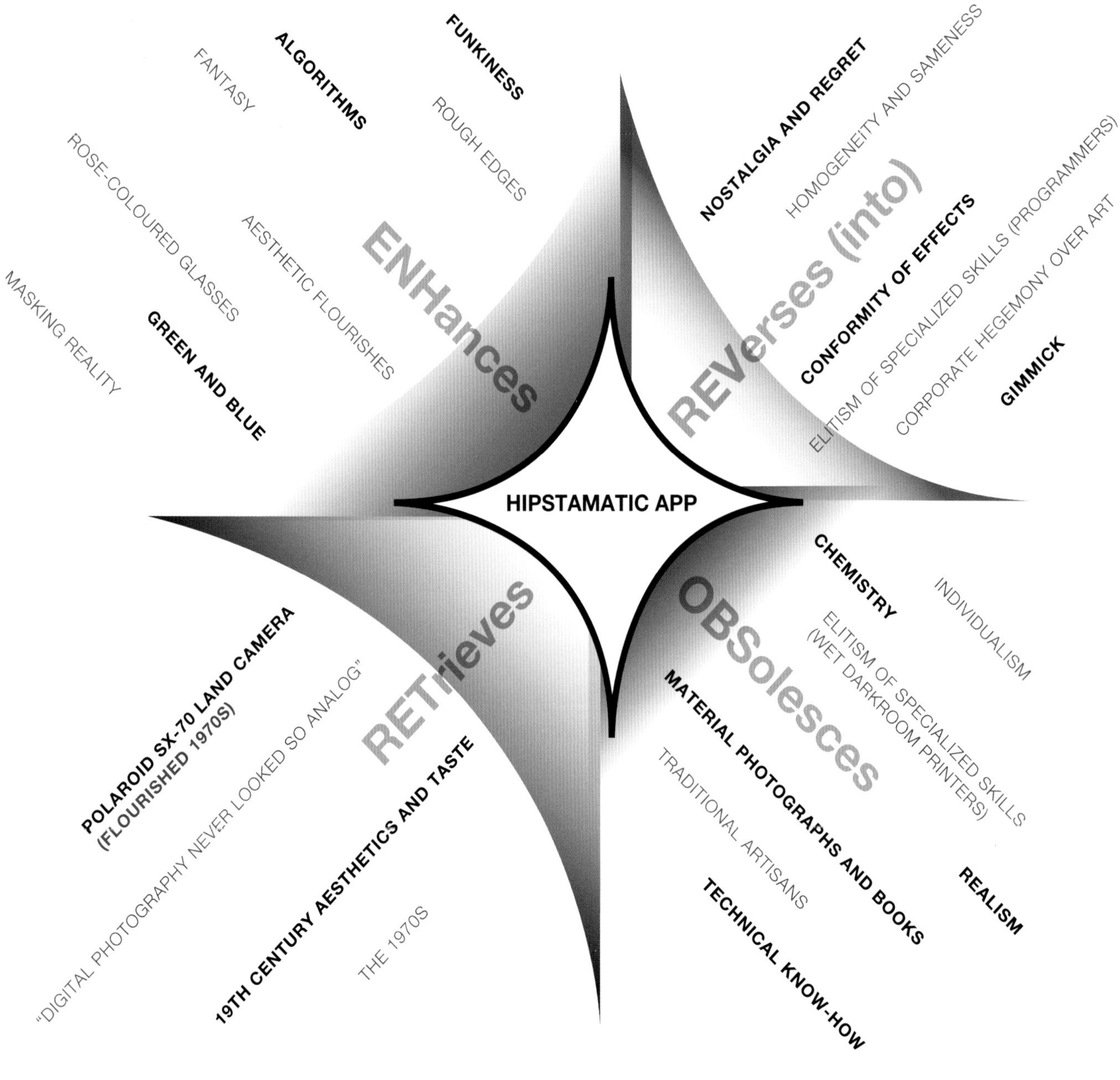

HIPSTAMATIC APP
ENHances
FANTASY
ALGORITHMS
FUNKINESS
ROUGH EDGES
ROSE-COLOURED GLASSES
AESTHETIC FLOURISHES
MASKING REALITY
GREEN AND BLUE
REVerses (into)
NOSTALGIA AND REGRET
HOMOGENEITY AND SAMENESS
CONFORMITY OF EFFECTS
ELITISM OF SPECIALIZED SKILLS (PROGRAMMERS)
CORPORATE HEGEMONY OVER ART
GIMMICK
RETrieves
POLAROID SX-70 LAND CAMERA (FLOURISHED 1970S)
"DIGITAL PHOTOGRAPHY NEVER LOOKED SO ANALOG"
19TH CENTURY AESTHETICS AND TASTE
THE 1970S
OBSolesces
CHEMISTRY
INDIVIDUALISM
ELITISM OF SPECIALIZED SKILLS (WET DARKROOM PRINTERS)
MATERIAL PHOTOGRAPHS AND BOOKS
TRADITIONAL ARTISANS
REALISM
TECHNICAL KNOW-HOW

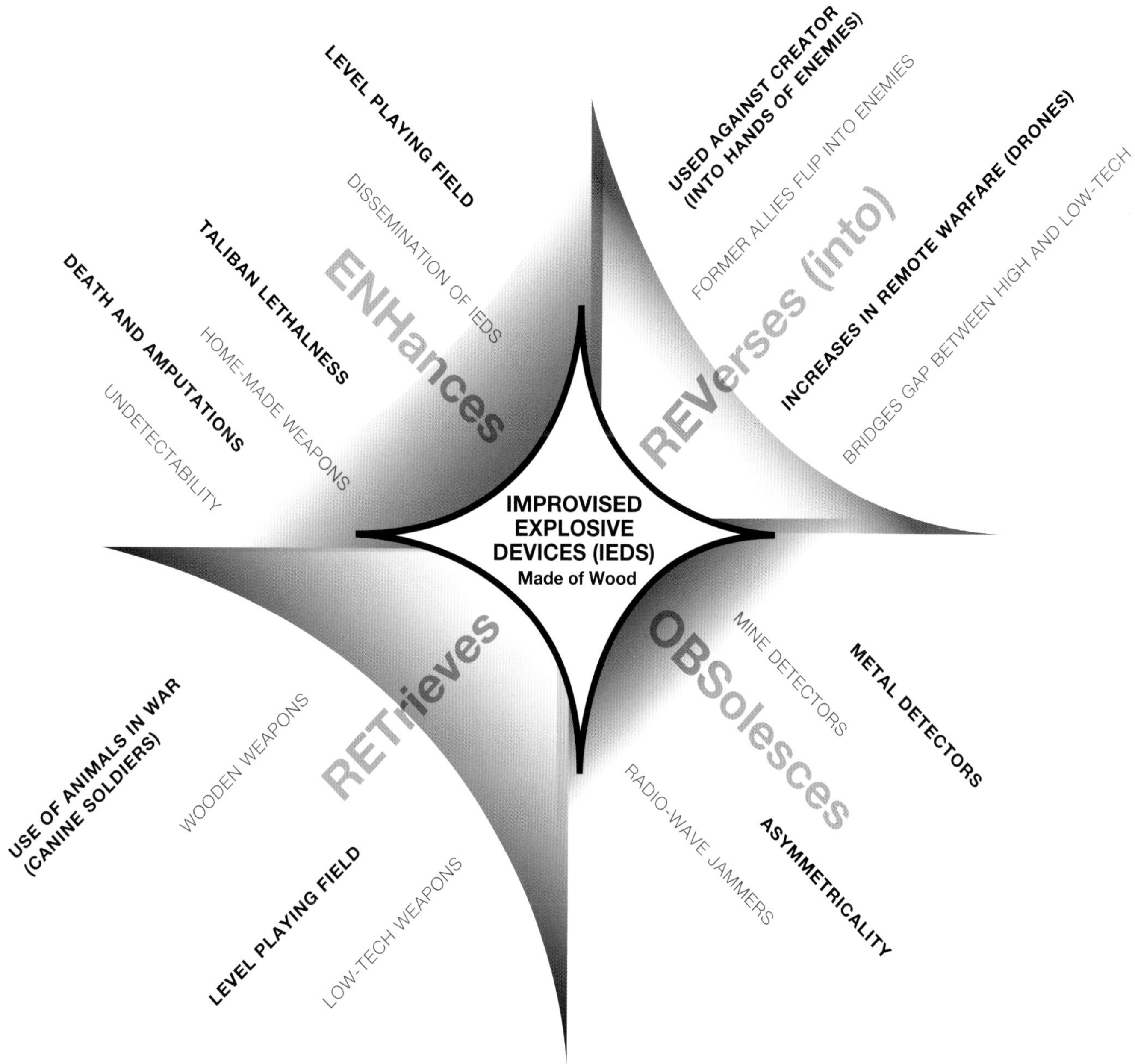
IMPROVISED EXPLOSIVE DEVICES (IEDS)
Made of Wood
ENHances
LEVEL PLAYING FIELD
DISSEMINATION OF IEDS
TALIBAN LETHALNESS
HOME-MADE WEAPONS
DEATH AND AMPUTATIONS
UNDETECTABILITY
REVerses (into)
USED AGAINST CREATOR (INTO HANDS OF ENEMIES)
FORMER ALLIES FLIP INTO ENEMIES
INCREASES IN REMOTE WARFARE (DRONES)
BRIDGES GAP BETWEEN HIGH AND LOW-TECH
RETrieves
USE OF ANIMALS IN WAR (CANINE SOLDIERS)
WOODEN WEAPONS
LEVEL PLAYING FIELD
LOW-TECH WEAPONS
OBSolesces
MINE DETECTORS
METAL DETECTORS
RADIO-WAVE JAMMERS
ASYMMETRICALITY

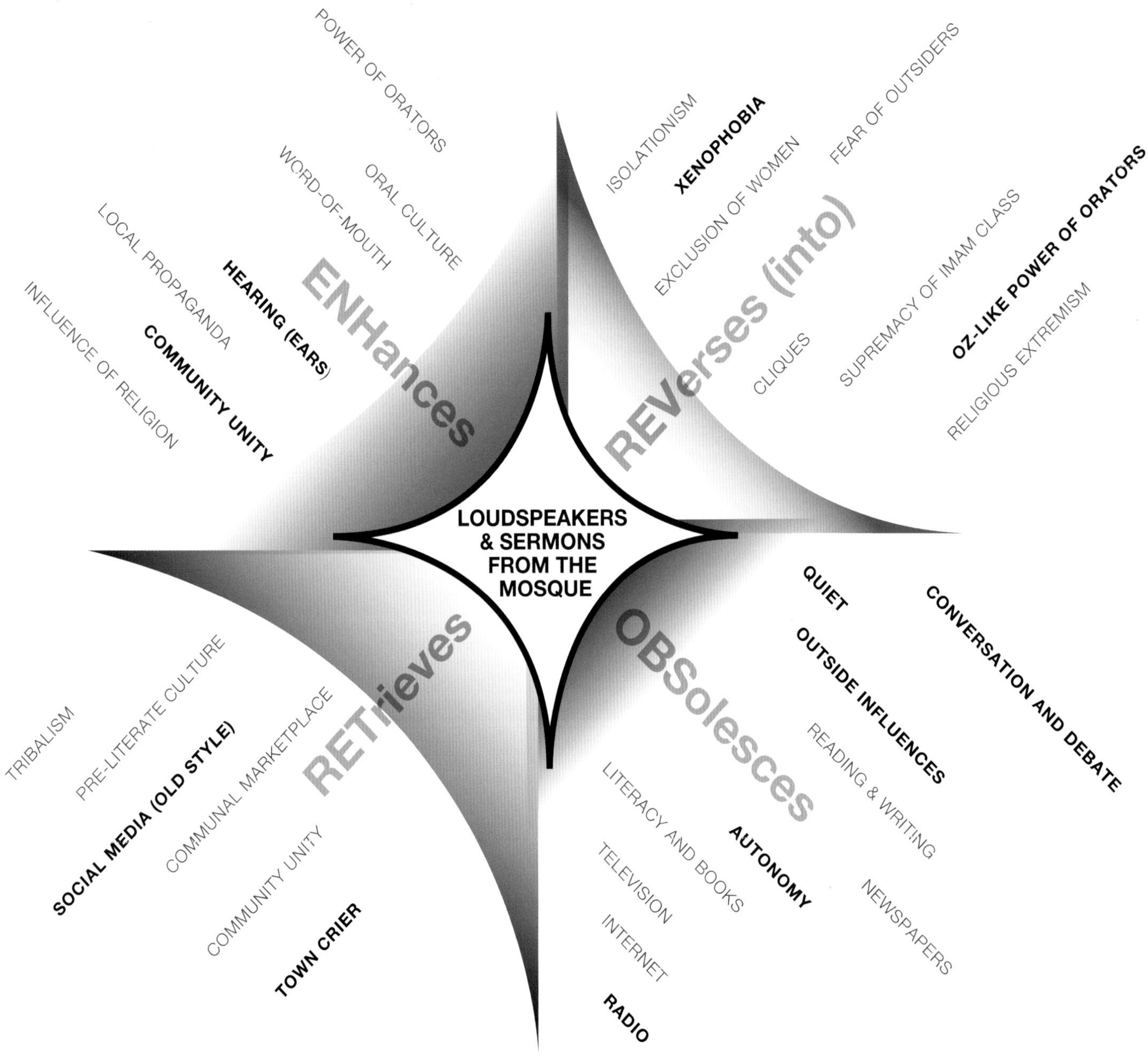
LOUDSPEAKERS & SERMONS FROM THE MOSQUE
ENHances
POWER OF ORATORS
ORAL CULTURE
WORD-OF-MOUTH
HEARING (EARS)
LOCAL PROPAGANDA
COMMUNITY UNITY
INFLUENCE OF RELIGION
REVerses (into)
ISOLATIONISM
XENOPHOBIA
EXCLUSION OF WOMEN
FEAR OF OUTSIDERS
CLIQUES
SUPREMACY OF IMAM CLASS
OZ-LIKE POWER OF ORATORS
RELIGIOUS EXTREMISM
RETrieves
TRIBALISM
PRE-LITERATE CULTURE
SOCIAL MEDIA (OLD STYLE)
COMMUNAL MARKETPLACE
COMMUNITY UNITY
TOWN CRIER
OBSolesces
QUIET
CONVERSATION AND DEBATE
OUTSIDE INFLUENCES
READING & WRITING
LITERACY AND BOOKS
AUTONOMY
TELEVISION
NEWSPAPERS
INTERNET
RADIO

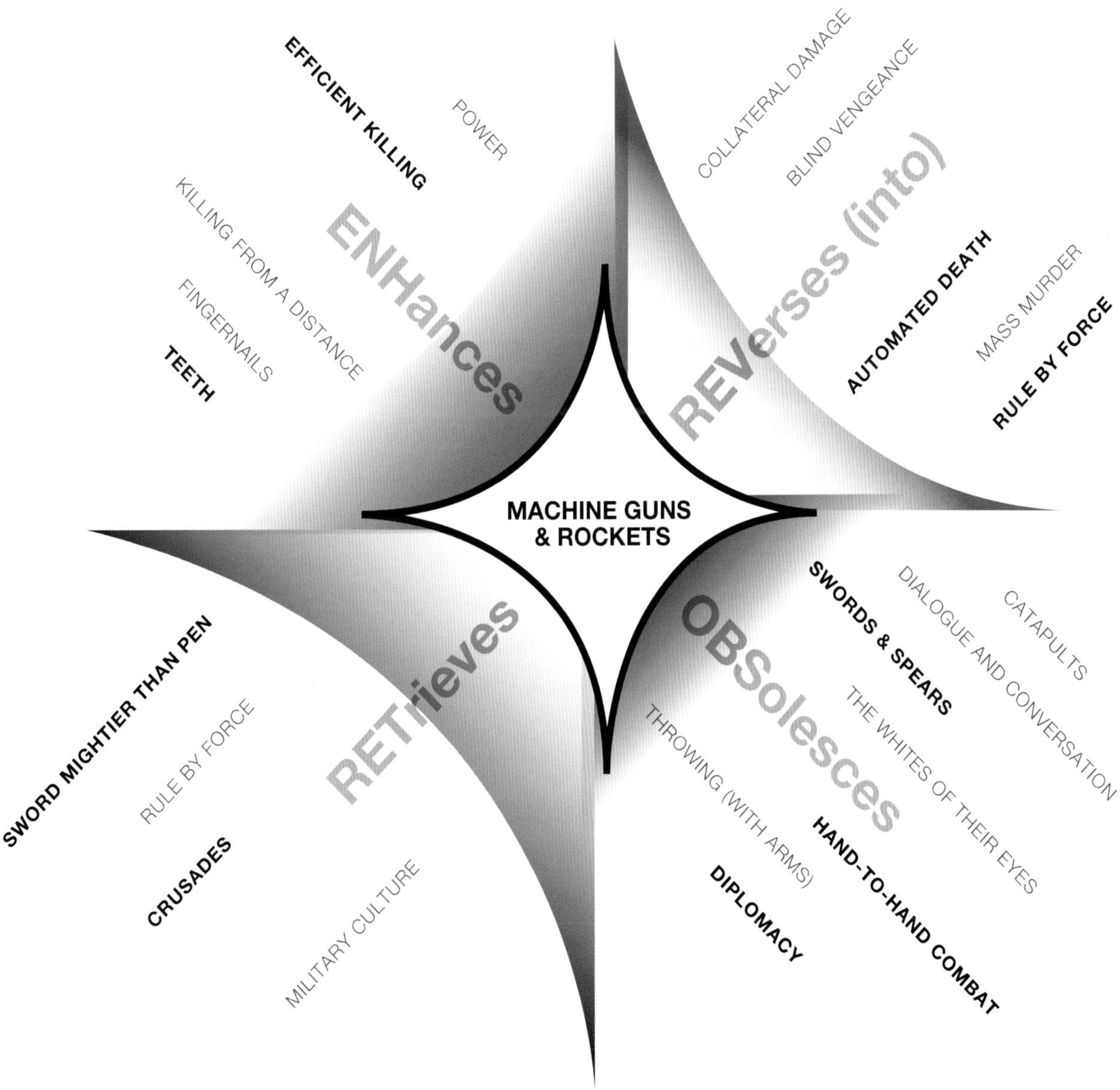
MACHINE GUNS & ROCKETS
ENHances
EFFICIENT KILLING
POWER
KILLING FROM A DISTANCE
FINGERNAILS
TEETH
REVerses (into)
COLLATERAL DAMAGE
BLIND VENGEANCE
AUTOMATED DEATH
MASS MURDER
RULE BY FORCE
RETrieves
SWORD MIGHTIER THAN PEN
RULE BY FORCE
CRUSADES
MILITARY CULTURE
OBSolesces
SWORDS & SPEARS
DIALOGUE AND CONVERSATION
CATAPULTS
THE WHITES OF THEIR EYES
THROWING (WITH ARMS)
HAND-TO-HAND COMBAT
DIPLOMACY

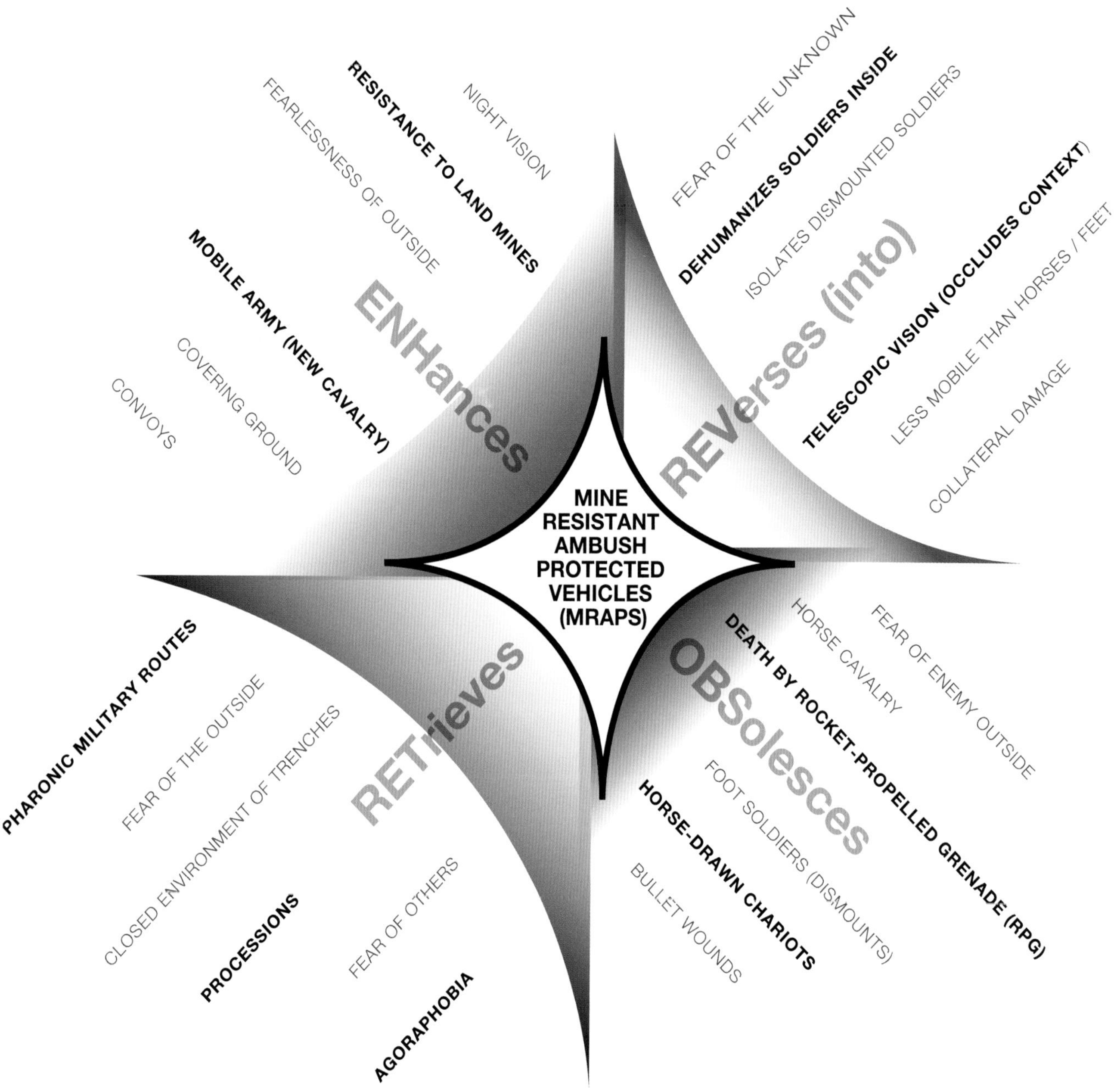
MINE RESISTANT AMBUSH PROTECTED VEHICLES (MRAPS)
ENHances
REVerses (into)
RETrieves
OBSolesces
NIGHT VISION
RESISTANCE TO LAND MINES
FEARLESSNESS OF OUTSIDE
MOBILE ARMY (NEW CAVALRY)
COVERING GROUND
CONVOYS
FEAR OF THE UNKNOWN
DEHUMANIZES SOLDIERS INSIDE
ISOLATES DISMOUNTED SOLDIERS
TELESCOPIC VISION (OCCLUDES CONTEXT)
LESS MOBILE THAN HORSES / FEET
COLLATERAL DAMAGE
PHARONIC MILITARY ROUTES
FEAR OF THE OUTSIDE
CLOSED ENVIRONMENT OF TRENCHES
PROCESSIONS
FEAR OF OTHERS
AGORAPHOBIA
HORSE CAVALRY
FEAR OF ENEMY OUTSIDE
DEATH BY ROCKET-PROPELLED GRENADE (RPG)
FOOT SOLDIERS (DISMOUNTS)
HORSE-DRAWN CHARIOTS
BULLET WOUNDS

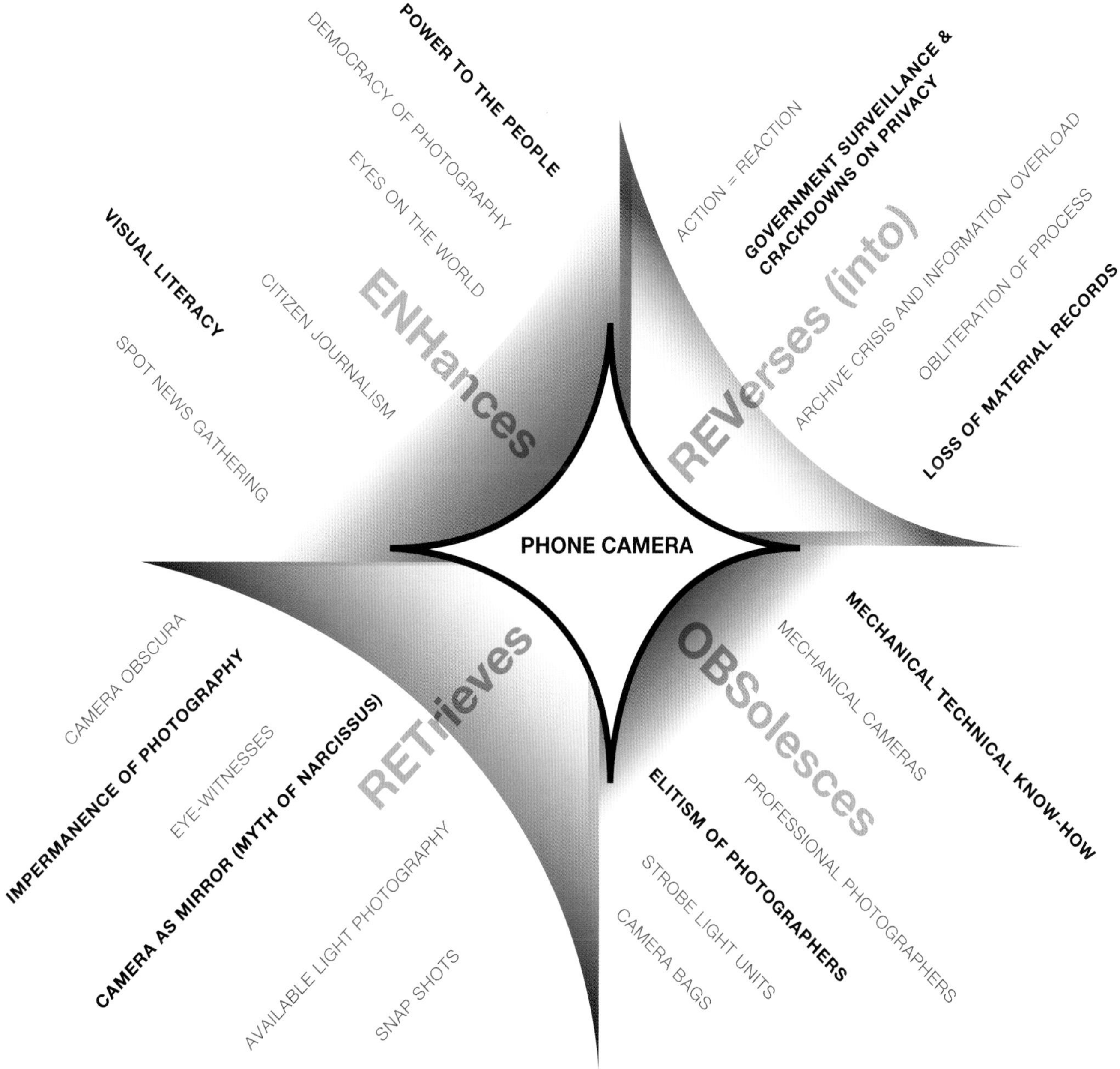

PHONE CAMERA
ENHances
POWER TO THE PEOPLE
DEMOCRACY OF PHOTOGRAPHY
EYES ON THE WORLD
VISUAL LITERACY
CITIZEN JOURNALISM
SPOT NEWS GATHERING
REVerses (into)
ACTION = REACTION
GOVERNMENT SURVEILLANCE & CRACKDOWNS ON PRIVACY
ARCHIVE CRISIS AND INFORMATION OVERLOAD
OBLITERATION OF PROCESS
LOSS OF MATERIAL RECORDS
RETrieves
CAMERA OBSCURA
IMPERMANENCE OF PHOTOGRAPHY
EYE-WITNESSES
CAMERA AS MIRROR (MYTH OF NARCISSUS)
AVAILABLE LIGHT PHOTOGRAPHY
SNAP SHOTS
OBSolesces
MECHANICAL CAMERAS
MECHANICAL TECHNICAL KNOW-HOW
ELITISM OF PHOTOGRAPHERS
PROFESSIONAL PHOTOGRAPHERS
STROBE LIGHT UNITS
CAMERA BAGS

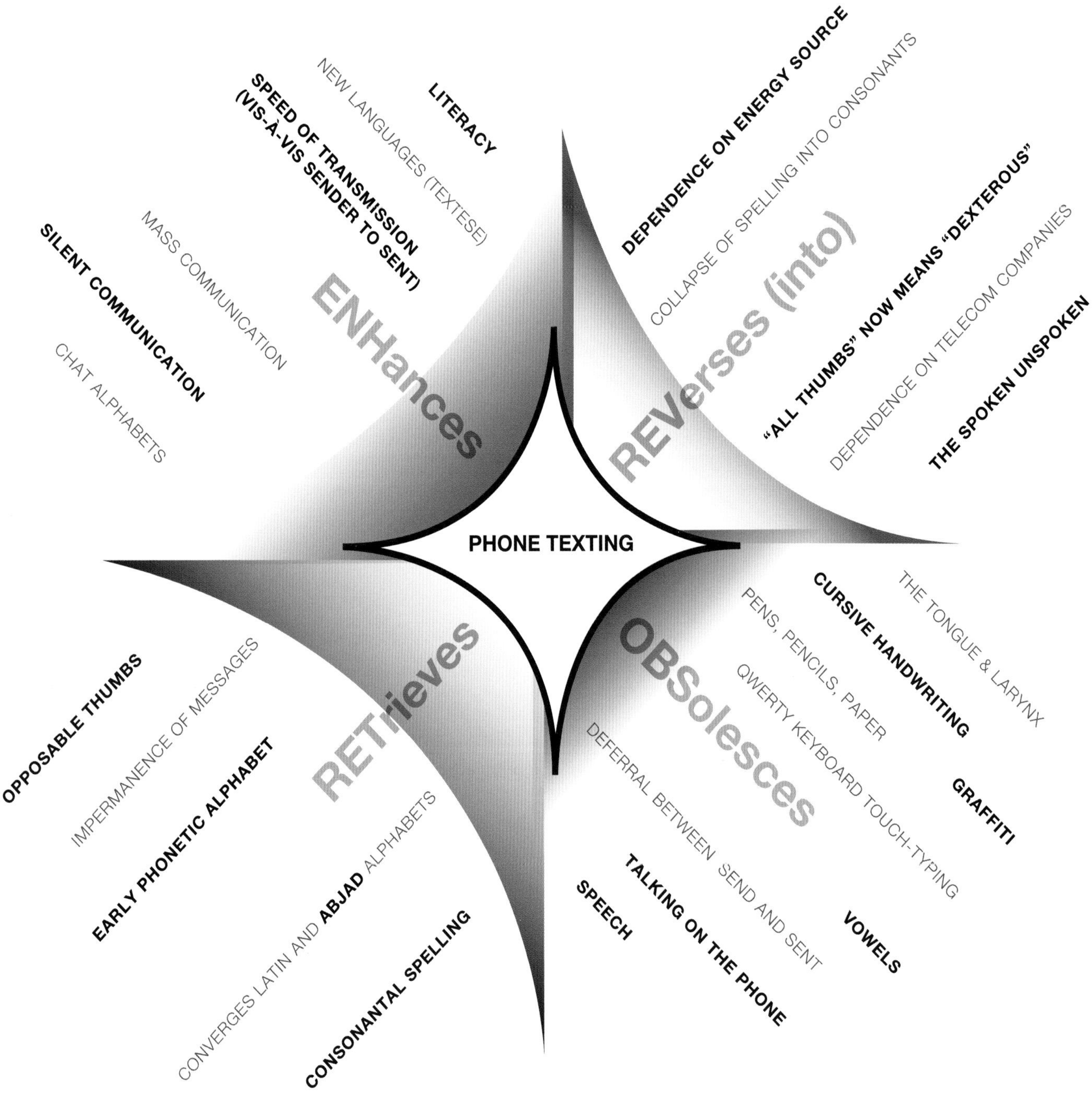
PHONE TEXTING
ENHances
LITERACY
NEW LANGUAGES (TEXTESE)
SPEED OF TRANSMISSION (VIS-À-VIS SENDER TO SENT)
MASS COMMUNICATION
SILENT COMMUNICATION
CHAT ALPHABETS
REVerses (into)
DEPENDENCE ON ENERGY SOURCE
COLLAPSE OF SPELLING INTO CONSONANTS
"ALL THUMBS" NOW MEANS "DEXTEROUS"
DEPENDENCE ON TELECOM COMPANIES
THE SPOKEN UNSPOKEN
RETrieves
OPPOSABLE THUMBS
IMPERMANENCE OF MESSAGES
EARLY PHONETIC ALPHABET
CONVERGES LATIN AND ABJAD ALPHABETS
CONSONANTAL SPELLING
OBSolesces
THE TONGUE & LARYNX
CURSIVE HANDWRITING
PENS, PENCILS, PAPER
QWERTY KEYBOARD TOUCH-TYPING
GRAFFITI
DEFERRAL BETWEEN SEND AND SENT
VOWELS
TALKING ON THE PHONE
SPEECH

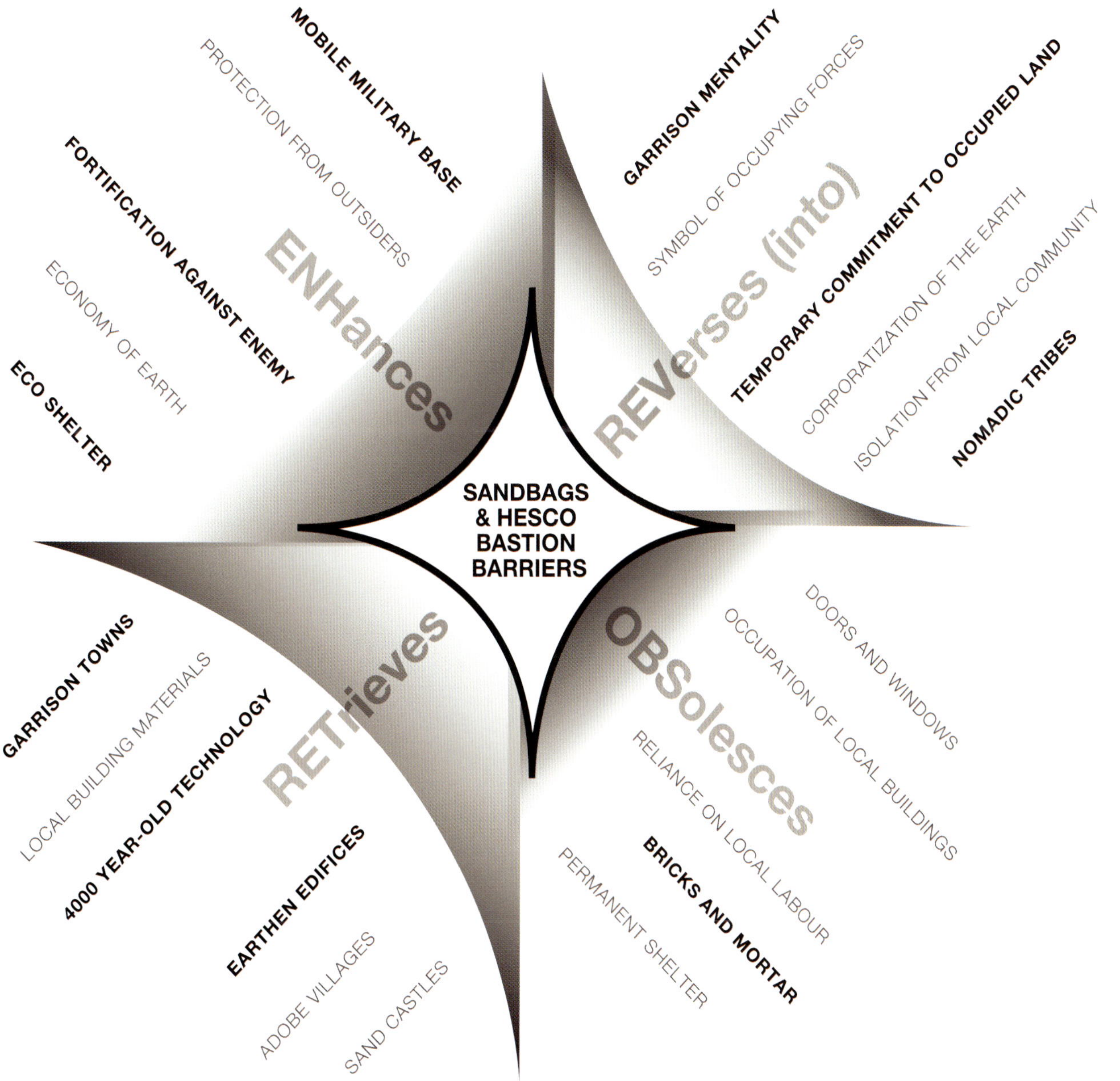
SANDBAGS & HESCO BASTION BARRIERS
ENHances
MOBILE MILITARY BASE
PROTECTION FROM OUTSIDERS
FORTIFICATION AGAINST ENEMY
ECONOMY OF EARTH
ECO SHELTER
REVerses (into)
GARRISON MENTALITY
SYMBOL OF OCCUPYING FORCES
TEMPORARY COMMITMENT TO OCCUPIED LAND
CORPORATIZATION OF THE EARTH
ISOLATION FROM LOCAL COMMUNITY
NOMADIC TRIBES
RETrieves
GARRISON TOWNS
LOCAL BUILDING MATERIALS
4000 YEAR-OLD TECHNOLOGY
EARTHEN EDIFICES
ADOBE VILLAGES
SAND CASTLES
OBSolesces
DOORS AND WINDOWS
OCCUPATION OF LOCAL BUILDINGS
RELIANCE ON LOCAL LABOUR
BRICKS AND MORTAR
PERMANENT SHELTER

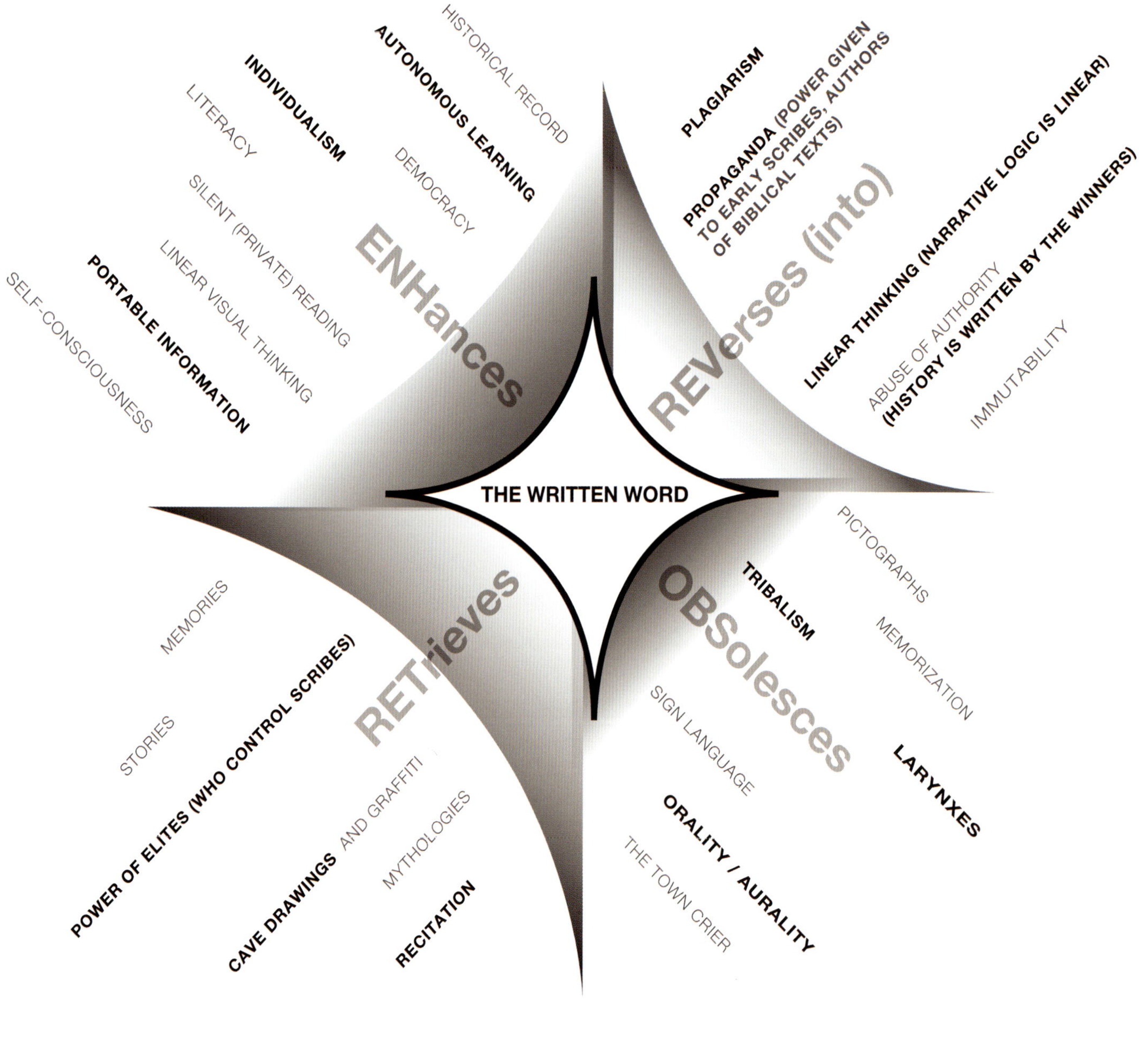
THE WRITTEN WORD
ENHances
HISTORICAL RECORD
AUTONOMOUS LEARNING
INDIVIDUALISM
LITERACY
DEMOCRACY
SILENT (PRIVATE) READING
LINEAR VISUAL THINKING
PORTABLE INFORMATION
SELF-CONSCIOUSNESS
REVerses (into)
PLAGIARISM
PROPAGANDA (POWER GIVEN TO EARLY SCRIBES, AUTHORS OF BIBLICAL TEXTS)
LINEAR THINKING (NARRATIVE LOGIC IS LINEAR)
ABUSE OF AUTHORITY (HISTORY IS WRITTEN BY THE WINNERS)
IMMUTABILITY
RETrieves
MEMORIES
STORIES
POWER OF ELITES (WHO CONTROL SCRIBES)
CAVE DRAWINGS AND GRAFFITI
MYTHOLOGIES
RECITATION
OBSolesces
PICTOGRAPHS
TRIBALISM
MEMORIZATION
SIGN LANGUAGE
LARYNXES
ORALITY / AURALITY
THE TOWN CRIER

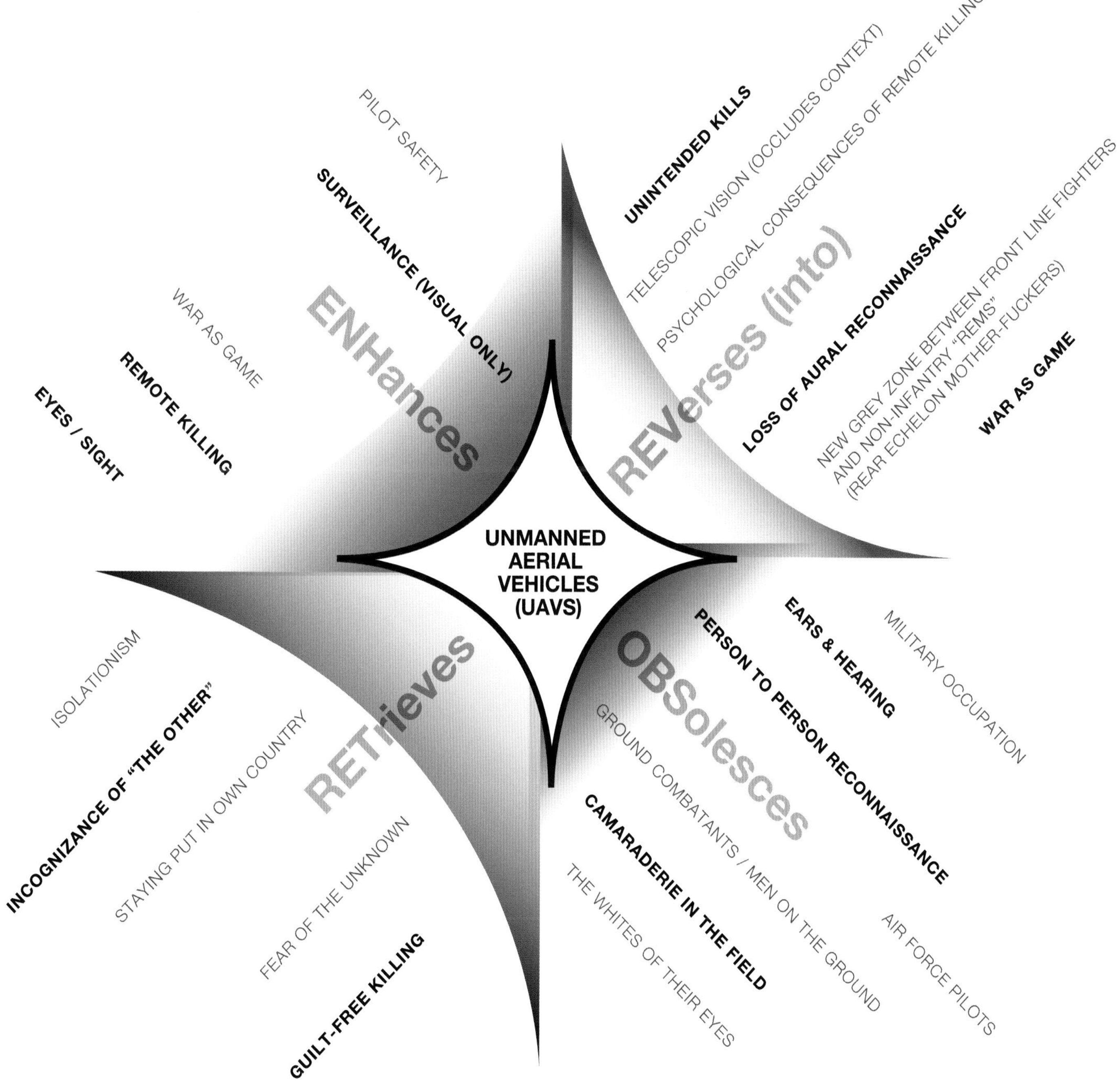
UNMANNED AERIAL VEHICLES (UAVS)
ENHances
PILOT SAFETY
SURVEILLANCE (VISUAL ONLY)
WAR AS GAME
REMOTE KILLING
EYES / SIGHT
REVerses (into)
UNINTENDED KILLS
TELESCOPIC VISION (OCCLUDES CONTEXT)
PSYCHOLOGICAL CONSEQUENCES OF REMOTE KILLING
LOSS OF AURAL RECONNAISSANCE
NEW GREY ZONE BETWEEN FRONT LINE FIGHTERS AND NON-INFANTRY "REMS" (REAR ECHELON MOTHER-FUCKERS)
WAR AS GAME
RETrieves
ISOLATIONISM
INCOGNIZANCE OF "THE OTHER"
STAYING PUT IN OWN COUNTRY
FEAR OF THE UNKNOWN
GUILT-FREE KILLING
OBSolesces
EARS & HEARING
MILITARY OCCUPATION
PERSON TO PERSON RECONNAISSANCE
GROUND COMBATANTS / MEN ON THE GROUND
CAMARADERIE IN THE FIELD
THE WHITES OF THEIR EYES
AIR FORCE PILOTS

Notes

1. Marshall McLuhan and Quentin Fiore, *War and Peace in the Global Village*, 16.
2. Canadian Lieutenant General (Retired) Andrew Leslie, former ISAF Deputy Commander in Afghanistan, at a public lecture held by *The Literary Review of Canada*, December 3rd 2012 in Toronto. A video of the talk can be found at TVO Big Ideas: bigideas.tvo.org.
3. Kathy Gannon, *I is for Infidel . . . J is for Jihad, K is for Kalashnikov*, 118.
4. Marshall McLuhan, *Understanding Media: The Extensions of Man*, 199.
5. Marshall McLuhan and Quentin Fiore, *War and Peace in the Global Village*, 98.
6. Umberto Eco, "Towards a Semiological Guerrilla Warfare," in *Travels in Hyperreality*.
7. Basetrack was a 2010 Knight News Challenge winner, spearheaded by project director Teru Kuwayama. The Basetrack embed team was Teru Kuwayama, Balazs Gardi, Tivadar Domaniscky, Monica Campbell and Rita Leistner (Campbell and Leistner were principally brought in to cover the Female Engagement Teams in the last weeks of the embed). The other Basetrack team members were Matt Farwell, David Gurman, Sadika Hameed, Joshua Levy, Sundev Lohr, Laszlo Malahovsky, Omar Mullick, Amy Pereira and Habib Zahori. For more information, see basetrack.org and Facebook.com/basetrack, and http://www.knightfoundation.org/blogs/knightblog/2011/8/4/war-afghanistan-home-iphone/ and issu.com/basetrack/docs/basetrack.
8. Marshall McLuhan and Eric McLuhan, *Laws of Media: The New Science*, 226.
9. Ibid., 3.
10. Quoted in W. Terrence Gordon, *Marshall McLuhan: Escape Into Understanding*, page 183.
11. Marshall McLuhan and Eric McLuhan, *Laws of Media: The New Science*, 9.
12. Ibid., 25.
13. Marshall McLuhan, *The Gutenberg Galaxy: The Making of Typographic Man*, 102.
14. Ibid., 104.
15. Ibid., 201.
16. Ibid., 216.
17. Gretchen Peters, *Seeds of Terror: How Drugs, Thugs, and Crime are Reshaping the Afghan War*, 126-127.
18. Ibid., 128.
19. Ibid., 131.
20. The Basetrack embed team was Teru Kuwayama, Balazs Gardi, Tivadar Domaniscky, Monica Campbell and Rita Leistner (Campbell and Leistner were principally brought in to cover the Female Engagement Teams in the last weeks of the embed).

21. See www.basetrack.org and www.facebook.com/basetrack

22. Marshall McLuhan, *Understanding Media: The Extensions of Man*, 247.

23. Ibid., 83.

24. Ibid., 339.

25. Marshall McLuhan and Quentin Fiore, *War and Peace in the Global Village*, 12.

26. Marshall McLuhan and Eric McLuhan, *Laws of Media: The New Science*, 98.

27. Marshall McLuhan and Quentin Fiore, *The Medium is the Massage: An Inventory of Effects*, 26.

28. Marshall McLuhan and Eric McLuhan, *Laws of Media: The New Science*, 128.

29. Marshall McLuhan, *Understanding Media: The Extensions of Man*, 35.

30. Ibid., 4.

31. Ralph Waldo Emerson, "Works and Days," in *Society and Solitude*. New York: Houghton Mifflin and Company, 1888. Quoted in Marshall McLuhan and Eric McLuhan, *Laws of Media: The New Science*, 94.

32. Edward T. Hall, *The Silent Language*, Garden City, N.Y.: Anchor Press/Doubleday, 1973 (1959). Quoted in Marshall McLuhan, *Understanding Media: The Extensions of Man*, 94.

33. Marshall McLuhan, *Understanding Media: The Extensions of Man*, 191.

34. Erik Barnouw, *Mass Communication*, New York: Rinehart and Company, 1958. Quoted in Marshall McLuhan, *The Gutenberg Galaxy: The Making of Typographic Man*, 128.

35. Marshall McLuhan, *Understanding Media: The Extensions of Man*, 9.

36. Ibid., 259.

37. Ibid., 262.

38. Ibid., 266.

39. Ibid., 265.

40. Ibid., 267.

41. Ibid., 268.

42. Ibid., 268.

43. Ibid., 263.

44. Thomas Edison, *The North American Review* (June 1878), quoted in Marshall McLuhan, *Understanding Media: The Extensions of Man*, 276.

45. Marshall McLuhan, *The Gutenberg Galaxy: The Making of Typographic Man*, 4.

46. Marshall McLuhan, *Understanding Media: The Extensions of Man*, 267.

47. Kathy Gannon, *I is for Infidel . . . J is for Jihad, K is for Kalashnikov*, 96.

48. Marshall McLuhan, *Understanding Media: The Extensions of Man*, 169.

49. Carl Dair, *Design with Type*, 92.

50. Marshall McLuhan, *The Gutenberg Galaxy: The Making of Typographic Man*, 105.

51. Ibid., 161.

52. Marshall McLuhan, *Understanding Media: The Extensions of Man*, 189.

53. W. H. F. Talbot, "Brief Historical Sketch of the Invention of the Art," *The Pencil of Nature*, London: Longman, Brown, Green & Longmans, June 1844, Part I. Quoted in Marshall McLuhan, *Understanding Media: The Extensions of Man*, 192.

54. Marshall McLuhan, *Understanding Media: The Extensions of Man*, 41.

55. Marshall McLuhan and Quentin Fiore, *The Medium is the Massage: An Inventory of Effects*, 50.

56. Marshall McLuhan, *The Gutenberg Galaxy: The Making of Typographic Man*, 48.

57. Marshall McLuhan, *Understanding Media: The Extensions of Man*, 83.

58. Steven Roger Fischer, *A History of Writing*, 83.

59. David Crystal, *Spell it out: The singular story of English spelling*, 260.

60. For a thorough study, see "Collapsed Consonant and Vowel Models: New Approaches for English-Persian Transliteration and Back-Transliteration" by Sarvnaz Karimi, Falk Scholer, and Andrew Turpin, School of Computer Science and Information Technology, RMIT University, Australia, 2007.

61. Chapter 3, "Reversal of the Overheated Medium," in Marshall McLuhan, *Understanding Media: The Extensions of Man*.

62. These charts are general renditions of what is already a highly inexact science. Any errors are mine alone. For more accurate histories, I refer you to the principal sources I used to create these charts.

    62A. The principal sources for the Alphabet Chart are: Steven Roger Fischer, *A History of Writing*, 88–89; David Sacks, *Letter Perfect: The Marvelous History of Our Alphabet from A to Z*, pages xiv to xv; and Gordon J. Hamilton, *The Origins of the West Semitic Alphabet in Egyptian Scripts.*

    62B. Language Chart: for the Indo European language branch: Louis Dupree, *Afghanistan*, page 69; Steven Roger Fischer, *A History of Language*, 82–83. For the West Semitic branch: Gordon J. Hamilton, *The Origins of the West Semitic Alphabet in Egyptian Scripts*; and Roger D. Woodard, *The Ancient Languages of Syria-Palestine and Arabia*.

63. David Crystal, *Spell it out: The singular story of English spelling*, 260.

64. Steven Roger Fischer, *A History of Writing*, 69.

65. Gordon J. Hamilton, *The Origins of the West Semitic Alphabet in Egyptian Scripts*, 7.

66. Ibid., 10.

67. David Sacks, *Letter Perfect: The Marvelous History of Our Alphabet from A to Z*, 32–34.

68. Ibid., xiv.

69. Gordon J. Hamilton, *The Origins of the West Semitic Alphabet in Egyptian Scripts*, 5.

70. Steven Roger Fischer, *A History of Writing*, 314.

71. Marshall McLuhan, *Understanding Media: The Extensions of Man*, 260.

72. Steven Roger Fischer, *A History of Writing*, 316.

73. Marshall McLuhan, *Understanding Media: The Extensions of Man*, 341.

74. I buy my body armour from an outfitter in Austin Texas, www.bulletproofme.com

75. http://www.veterans.gc.ca'eng/rates

76. http://www.marines.mil

77. PDF of full text of "Counterinsurgency (COIN) Guidance"—Headquarters, ISAF, COMISAF/CDR USFOR-A, August 2010 available at http://graphics8.nytimes.com/packages/pdf/world/2010/COMISAF-MEMO.pdf

78. Marshall McLuhan and Quentin Fiore, *The Medium is the Massage: An Inventory of Effects*, 68.

79. Marshall McLuhan and Quentin Fiore, *War and Peace in the Global Village*, 5.

80. There are many excellent books on the subject. I have found the following two books particularly helpful: Kathy Gannon's *I is for Infidel . . . J is for Jihad, K is for Kalashnikov* and Ahmed Rashid's *Taliban: Militant Islam, Oil and Fundamentalism in Central Asia*.

81. It is ironic that a mostly illiterate and openly anti-education movement call itself "the students."

82. Stuart Webb, "In the Line of Fire: Afghanistan's IED Experts," *The Telegram*, February 17th, 2012.

83. Ibid., citing "a recent U.N. report."

84. John Foster, "A Pipeline Through a Troubled Land," Canadian Centre for Policy Alternatives, June 19th, 2008.

85. Gretchen Peters, *Seeds of Terror: How Drugs, Thugs, and Crime are Reshaping the Afghan War*, 131.

86. Roxana Tiron, "$400 Per Gallon Gas to Drive Debate Over Cost of War in Afghanistan," The Hill, October 15th, 2010.

87. Ahmed Rashid, *Taliban: Militant Islam, Oil and Fundamentalism in Central Asia*.

88. Map usage courtesy of the Canadian Centre for Policy Alternatives. See http://www.policyalternatives.ca/

89. PDF of full text of "Counterinsurgency (COIN) Guidance"—Headquarters, ISAF, COMISAF/CDR USFOR-A, August 2010 available at http://graphics8.nytimes.com/packages/pdf/world/2010/COMISAF-MEMO.pdf

90. Charles M. Sennot, "Nancy Dupree's Love Affair with Kabul," *Global Post*, June 15th, 2009.

91. Louis Dupree, *Afghanistan*, 95.

92. Ibid., 104–108.

93. Ibid., 109

94. Nicholas Ostler, *Empires of the World: A Language History of the World*, 94.

95. Joshua Paltrow and Habib Zahori, "Afghan Imams Wage Political Battle Against U.S.," *Washington Post*, February 17th, 2011.

96. Jon Krakauer, *Under the Banner of Heaven*, 57–64. Krakauer is one of my favourite writers, and I recommend everything he has written.

97. Ibid., 82.

98. Ibid., 63.

99. Marshall McLuhan, *Understanding Media: The Extensions of Man*, 33.

100. Gretchen Peters, *Seeds of Terror: How Drugs, Thugs, and Crime are Reshaping the Afghan War*, 134.

101. Marshall McLuhan, *Understanding Media: The Extensions of Man*, 339.

102. Gretchen Peters, *Seeds of Terror: How Drugs, Thugs, and Crime are Reshaping the Afghan War*, 134.

103. Alex Sundby, "Afghan Cell Carriers Follow Taliban Rules," *The Wall Street Journal*, March 24th, 2010.

104. Mary Ann Weaver, "Lost in Tora Bora," *The New Yorker*, September 11th, 2005, quoted in Gretchen Peters, *Seeds of Terror: How Drugs, Thugs, and Crime are Reshaping the Afghan War*, 110.

105. These statistics come from a 2010 report by Sheldon Himelfarb for the United States Institute of Peace, "Can You Help Me Now? Mobile Phones and Peacebuilding in Afghanistan," November 2010.

106. Marshall McLuhan and Quentin Fiore, *The Medium is the Massage: An Inventory of Effects*, 48.

107. Marshall McLuhan, *Understanding Media: The Extensions of Man*, 81.

108. Louis Dupree, *Afghanistan*, 70.

109. Marshall McLuhan and Eric McLuhan, *Laws of Media: The New Science*, 226.

110. Nicholas Ostler, *Empires of the World: A Language History of the World*, 110.

111. Ibid., 108.

112. See charts in iProbe 02 _Phone Texting: note 62A (116–117) and note 62B (118–119)

113. Nicholas Ostler, *Empires of the World: A Language History of the World*, 108.

114. Marshall McLuhan, *Understanding Media: The Extensions of Man*, 83.

115. Ibid., pages 82 to 84 and Marshall McLuhan, *The Gutenberg Galaxy: The Making of Typographic Man*, 25.

116. Marshall McLuhan, *Understanding Media: The Extensions of Man*, 82–83.

117. Ibid., 83.

118. David Sacks, *Letter Perfect: The Marvelous History of Our Alphabet from A to Z*, 34.

119. Steven Roger Fischer, *A History of Writing*, 84.

120. From John Coleman Darnell, F. W. Dobbs-Allsopp, Marilyn J. Lundberg, P. Kyle McCarter and Bruce Zuckerman with the assistance of Colleen Manassa. "Two Early Alphabetic Inscriptions from the Wadi-el-Hôl: New Evidence for the Origin of the Alphabet from the Western Desert of Egypt," *The Annual of the American Schools of Oriental Research*, Volume 59, 75 and 83.

121. "Behind the Technology of Predator Drones"—This is a pro-drone video, created for young audiences by the Christian, Texas-based KTLT News, 2006. See: www.youtube.com/watch?v=nMh8Cjnzen8

122. Taylor Owen, "Drones don't just kill," published in *The Globe and Mail*, March 14th, 2013, in partnership with The Canadian International Council.

123. First reported by Jason Evans on the website www.easley.patch.com, February 21st, 2013; cited by Taylor Owen, "Drones don't just kill," published in the *Globe and Mail*, March 14th, 2013, in partnership with the Canadian International Council.

124. Kathy Gannon, *I is for Infidel . . . J is for Jihad, K is for Kalashnikov*, 138.

125. Ibid., 137–142.

126. Taylor Owen, "Drones don't just kill," published in the *Globe and Mail*, March 14th, 2013, in partnership with the Canadian International Council.

127. Ibid.

128. Ibid.

129. "Behind the Technology of Predator Drones"—This is a pro-drone video, created for young audiences by the Christian, Texas-based KTLT News, 2006. See: www.youtube.com/watch?v=nMh8Cjnzen8

130. Marshall McLuhan and Eric McLuhan, *Laws of Media: The New Science*, 96.

131. Ibid., 96.

132. P.W. Singer, *Wired for War: The Robotics Revolution and Conflict in the 21st Century*, 309–310.

133. Marshall McLuhan and Eric McLuhan, *Laws of Media: The New Science*, 97.

134. James Dao, "Drone Pilots Found to Get Stress Disorders Much as Those in Combat Do," *New York Times*, February 22nd, 2013.

135. Ibid.

136. Ibid.

137. Marshall McLuhan and Eric McLuhan, *Laws of Media: The New Science*, 128.

Bibliography

McLuhan, Marshall. *The Gutenberg Galaxy: The Making of Typographic Man*. Toronto: University of Toronto Press, 1962.

McLuhan, Marshall. *Understanding Media: The Extensions of Man*. Cambridge: MIT Press, 1994 (1964).

McLuhan, Marshall with Eric McLuhan. *Laws of Media: The New Science*. Toronto: University of Toronto Press, 1988.

McLuhan, Marshall and Quentin Fiore; produced by Jerome Agel. *The Medium is the Massage: An Inventory of Effects*. Toronto: Bantam Books, 1967.

McLuhan, Marshall and Quentin Fiore; produced by Jerome Agel. *War and Peace in the Global Village*. Corte Madera CA: Gingko Press, 1968.

Not by McLuhan:

Crystal, David. *Spell it out: The singular story of English spelling*. London: Profile Books, 2012.

Dair, Carl. *Design with Type*. Toronto: University of Toronto Press, 1967 (1952).

Darnell, John Coleman, F. W. Dobbs-Allsopp, Marilyn J. Lundberg, P. Kyle McCarter and Bruce Zuckerman with the assistance of Colleen Manassa."Two Early Alphabetic Inscriptions from the Wadi el-Hôl: New Evidence for the Origin of the Alphabet from the Western Desert of Egypt," in *The Annual of the American Schools of Oriental Research*, Vol. 59. Boston: American Schools of Oriental Research, 2005.

Dupree, Louis. *Afghanistan*. Princeton: Princeton University Press, 1980.

Eco, Umberto. *Travels in Hyperreality*. New York: Harcourt, Inc., 1986.

Fischer, Steven Roger. *A History of Language*. London: Reaktion Books, Ltd., 1999.

Fischer, Steven Roger. *A History of Writing*. London: Reaktion Books, Ltd., 2001.

Gannon, Kathy. *I is for Infidel . . . J is for Jihad, K is for Kalashnikov*. New York: Public Affairs, 2005.

Gordon, Terrence W. *Marshall McLuhan: Escape into Understanding A Biography*. Toronto: Stoddart Publishing Co. Limited, 1997.

Hamilton, Gordon J. *The Origins of the West Semitic Alphabet in Egyptian Scripts*. Washington, DC: Catholic Biblical Association of America, 2006.

Krakauer, Jon. *Under the Banner of Heaven*. New York: Anchor Books, a division of Random House, Inc., 2003.

Ostler, Nicholas. *Empires of the World: A Language History of the World*. New York: Harper Perennial, 2005.

Peters, Gretchen. *Seeds of Terror: How Drugs, Thugs, and Crime are Reshaping the Afghan War*. New York: Picador, 2009.

Rashid, Ahmed. *Taliban: Militant Islam, Oil and Fundamentalism in Central Asia, 2nd edition*. New Haven: Yale University Press, 2010.

Sacks, David. *Letter Perfect: The Marvelous History of Our Alphabet from A to Z*. New York: Broadway Books, 2003.

Schnapp, Jeffrey T. and Adam Michaels. *The Electric Information Age Book*. New York: Princeton Architectural Books, 2012.

Singer, P. W. *Wired for War: The Robotics Revolution and Conflict in the 21st Century*. New York: Penguin Books, 2009.

Woodard, Roger D. (ed.). *The Ancient Languages of Syria-Palestine and Arabia*. Cambridge: CUP, 2008.

Helvetica

"I don't think there's been such a hot thing since, as the figure-ground relationship properly executed."

(TYPOGRAPHER MIKE PARKER ON THE INVENTION OF THE HELVETICA TYPEFACE, IN *HELVETICA*)

A list of the nine fonts used in *Looking for Marshall McLuhan in Afghanistan*:

Neue Helvetic Pro 45 Light

Neue Helvetic Pro 45 Light Italic

Neue Helvetic Pro 55 Roman

Neue Helvetic Pro 56 Italic

Neue Helvetic Pro 65 Medium

Neue Helvetic Pro 66 Medium Italic

Neue Helvetic Pro 75 Bold

Neue Helvetic Pro 78 Bold Italic

Colvert Arabic ا ب ج ذ ت ه

Helvetica has been called a "social typeface, because it's available all over."

(PUBLISHER LARS MÜLLER, IN *HELVETICA*).

For the same reason it's also been called "the font of the corporate war establishment."

(GRAPHIC DESIGNER PAULA SCHER, IN *HELVETICA*).

Neue Helvetica is also the font used as the system interface font of the iPhone 4, the version I used to take the photographs in this book.

Acknowledgments

"It's inevitable that the whirl-pool of electronic information movement will toss us all about like corks on a stormy sea, but if we keep our cool during the descent into the maelstrom, studying the process as it happens … we can get through."

(MARSHALL MCLUHAN, FROM "THE PLAYBOY INTERVIEW: MARSHALL MCLUHAN," *PLAYBOY MAGAZINE*, MARCH 1969)

I never expected those five weeks in Afghanistan to provide the material and basis for what would be my first sole-authored book. I always thought my "first book" would be something else—which just goes to show that sometimes books, like life, find us. We need only be open to it. For helping this book to find me, I owe debts to many friends, colleagues and even foes along the way. I have always believed that there is far more kindness in the world than its opposite, and have yet to be proven wrong. Afghanistan was no exception, and I am humbled and grateful for the kindness I was shown by the Afghans I met, especially Habib Zahori, journalist par excellence, who has had a hand in much of the best journalistic work coming out of the country. Shortly after I worked with Habib in Afghanistan, he was turned down a scholarship to study in Canada, which was a loss to Canada.

I would never have written this kind of book if it weren't for the two years I spent from 1988 to 1990 at the Centre for Comparative Literature at the University of Toronto. My professors, colleagues and friends there—all great literary minds—helped set me on a course of literary and semiotic exploration that would influence everything I did thereafter: Ted Chamberlin, Lubomír Doložel, Linda Hutcheon, Peter Nesselroth, Ricardo Sternberg, François Lachance, Diana Kuprel, Calin Mihalescu and Walid Hamarneh; as well as Charles Lock, who first gave me the idea to pursue graduate studies in comparative literature. I hope this book in part answers the question: "What to do with your degree in comparative literature."

This book also would not have happened if Teru Kuwayama hadn't invited me to join his Basetrack team embed in Afghanistan. Thanks to the Knight Foundation for sponsoring Basetrack, and to the other members of the team, all of to whom some credit for this book belongs: Monica Campbell, Tivadar Domaniscky, Matt Farwell, Balazs Gardi, Peter Gardi, David Gurman, Sadika Hameed, Joshua Levy, Sundev Lohr, Laszlo Malahovszky, Omar Mullick, Amy Pereira and Habib Zahori.

We all owe a debt of gratitude to the Marines of the United States Marine Corps, 1st Battalion, 8th Marines (1–8), their translators, the Afghan National Army Soldiers and the Female Engagement Team attached to 1–8 for their service, and for allowing us in their midst during their 2010–11 deployment.

I am especially grateful to Omar Mullick for conversations in Erin Cunningham's garden at the house on Qalai Musa Street in Kabul. Thanks to Erin for providing us with a roof over our heads and warmth in the cold winter in Kabul. Thanks to Una Moore for reminding me of the great possibilities of optimism, youth and outrage; and to Papi Jann for keeping the Internet up and running.

I can't imagine being in Afghanistan without the friendship and wisdom of journalist Monica Campbell, who I first met at the Musa Qala base in Helmand and who knows more than anyone what this book is about. Monica also introduced me to Aaron Schachter and Stephen Snyder at PRI's The World, for whom I wrote my first think-piece tying McLuhan to smartphones and Afghanistan.

Diana Kuprel, who I met in grad school, and who has been a part of my creative, professional and social endeavours on and off for nearly thirty years, asked me to produce a visual essay of my time with Basetrack for the *Literary Review of Canada (LRC)* long before I knew how much I was going to have to say on the subject. I am grateful to Diana and to Alastair Cheng, the managing editor at the *LRC*, for editing this early work, and for sticking by me when a proposed short photo-essay for their new website turned into a ten thousand-word, twelve-part series.

To my beloved book club, who agreed to read *The Art of War* while I was in Afghanistan, and *War and Peace* when I got back: Katie Addleman, Hank Bulmash, Brendan DeCaires, Diana Kuprel,

Jennifer Lanthier, Kelly Rankin, Bruce Walsh and Kendra Ward. They have no idea how much I would miss them if we ever broke up.

Canadian Afghan scholar Rahi Kahn introduced me to the anonymous translator of the "Proceed at Your Own Risk" sign. Afraid to be identified with the project for fear of retaliation from Taliban sympathizers, she asked only to express her wishes for peace in Afghanistan, and that she hoped her work would in some way contribute to that purpose.

Jenny Armour, a genius of graphic design and typography and one of my oldest friends, worked with me for nearly two years on the book's design, and in the final days of tweaking, kerned text until it made her seasick. Jason Logan, too, is a genius. Their contributions to this book have made me speechlessly happy.

Thanks to Sophie Barry for making Phnom Penh and Kabul feel like the greatest places to be on earth; Dr. Anthony Feinstein for talking to me about this book and giving me the expression "prophylactive therapy"; Kathy Gannon for being one of the kindest people a person could want to meet in the field despite also being one of the smartest and bravest; to my constant three: Danny Allman, Guntar Kravis and Daniel MacIvor; to my friend Gilbert Li for generously giving his time for design consultations; Michael Shaw and Meg Handler at *BagNewsNotes* allowed me to riff on the book in their Blog *BagNewsOriginals*; Gretchen Peters for signing her book *Seeds of Terror* (New York: Picador, 2009) for me and writing in it: "I hope this inspires you to go to Afghanistan" (it did); my dear, beautiful nephew Stefan Lavoie inspired me to move ahead with the work when I realized it could speak to a bright young person like him; Lin Stranberg for her invaluable friendship and compassionate ear and for answering last minute calls for editing and proofreading help; and to my friends Caroline Gillis, Bruce MacNeil, Dale McMurchy, Ian Taylor, Darren Whiteside and Melissa Williams.

Steve Simon, author of *The Passionate Photographer* (Berkeley: New Riders, 2012) and many other passionate books of photography, was one of my first friends in New York and has continued to inspire me since. Steve helped me edit hundreds of photographs from Iraq and would have been in the acknowledgements of *Unembedded: Four Independent Photojournalists on the War in Iraq* (Vermont: Chelsea Green, 2005) but for an oversight that I am setting straight here.

Other friends and colleagues in New York have given support and advice, identified with my stories, helped keep things in perspective and contributed to my general happiness and sanity quotient: especially Topaz Adizes, Katja Heinemann, Mike Kamber, John Trotter, Jake Price, James B. Wellford and Melissa Winkler.

I am incredibly fortunate to have a large and supportive family who are the backbone of my well-being: especially my mother Donna, my father Volkmar (Henry), my stepmother Joan, my sister Linda and her husband Daniel, my cousin Martin and his wife Raja, my niece Melanie and my nephew Stefan. They are the goodness in me.

My publisher Masoud Yazdani, founder of Intellect, from the moment we met wasted no time in suggesting we make a book, and then gave me absolute creative freedom to design it exactly as I envisioned. Thanks to everyone at Intellect for bearing with me during this exacting process, especially May Yao and Holly Rose at the head office in Bristol; and Emma Rhys for her lovely perfectionism and keen eye for detail in the final line edit.

I'd also like to acknowledge the Cavalry soldiers and Commanders, especially Major Brett Bair, of "Crazy Horse," C-Troop, 7th US Cavalry, 3rd Infantry Division who welcomed me among them in Iraq from May to August 2003. They gave me high expectations of what to expect from soldiers, and will always be my first military family.

While in the final hours of working on this book, I got word that a Crazy Horse soldier, Sergeant Jared Kennedy, had killed himself after losing his battle with Post Traumatic Stress Disorder (PTSD), ever reminding us that PTSD is a killer, and reaffirming one of the main reasons I wrote this book. My heart goes out to all sufferers of PTSD—and we have no way of knowing how many there are—among all the survivors of war: military, civilian and media.

About the author

Rita Leistner is an award-winning independent documentarian and photojournalist who has photographed and written stories of conflict and post-conflict in war-torn countries from Iraq to Afghanistan and Lebanon to Israel; from post-Khmer Rouge Cambodia, to the ongoing struggle of First Nations People in North America. Her work has been exhibited and published widely. She is a co-author with Ghaith Abdul Ahad, Thorne Anderson and Kael Alford of *Unembedded: Four Independent Photojournalists on the War in Iraq* (Vermont: Chelsea Green, 2005), and with Marie Clements of *The Edward Curtis Project* (Vancouver: Talon Books, 2010). In 2013, as well as publishing *Looking for Marshall McLuhan in Afghanistan*, Rita releases her first short documentary film, *Miklat: The Bomb Shelter Project*, as part of her ongoing trilogy *Portraitscapes of War in the Levant: Landscape, Language and Identity in the Lands of the Bible*. She was honoured to contribute essays to two new notable books on war and photography, Michael Kamber's *Photojournalists on War: The Untold Stories from Iraq* (Austin: University of Texas Press, 2013) and Julian Stallabrass's *Memories of Fire: Images of War and The War of Images* (London: Photoworks, 2013). In addition to writing and photography, Rita teaches courses on the history of photojournalism and documentary photography at Victoria University in the University of Toronto where she holds an MA in comparative literature. Rita worked in lighting and camera support in the film industry in Toronto in the 1990s before moving to Cambodia in 1997 to work as a freelance photojournalist and later to New York where she studied at the International Centre for Photography. She was born in Toronto, Canada.

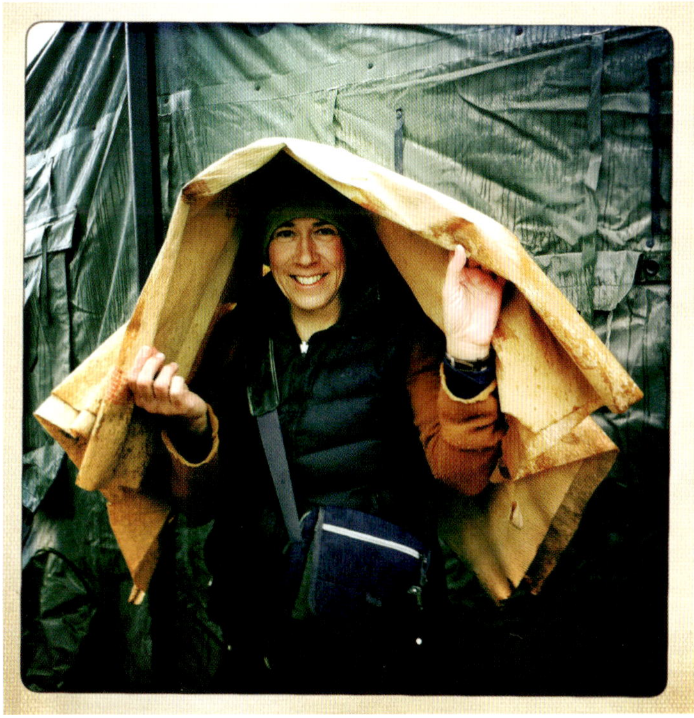

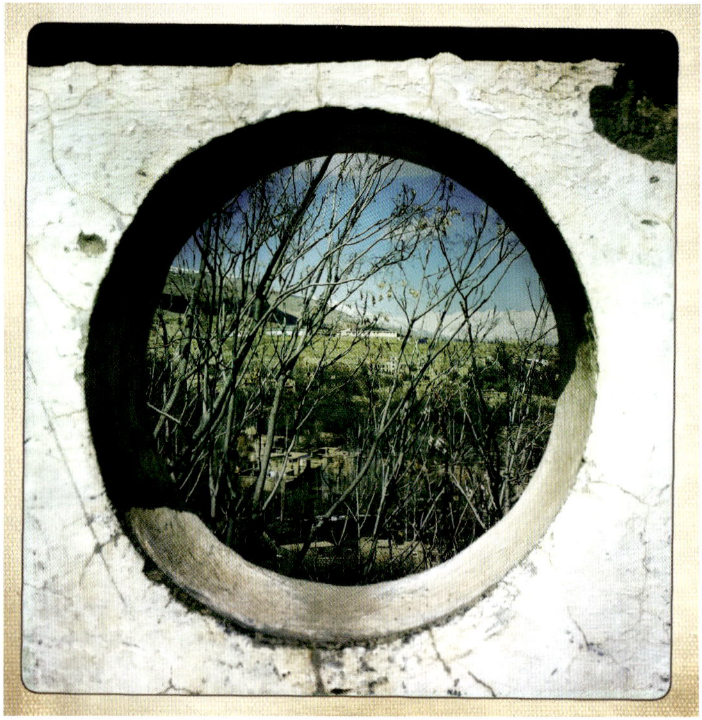

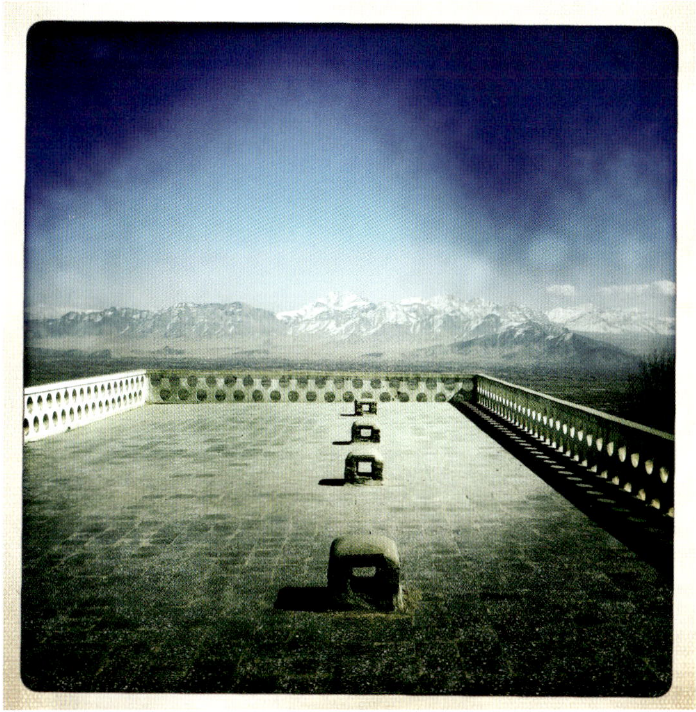

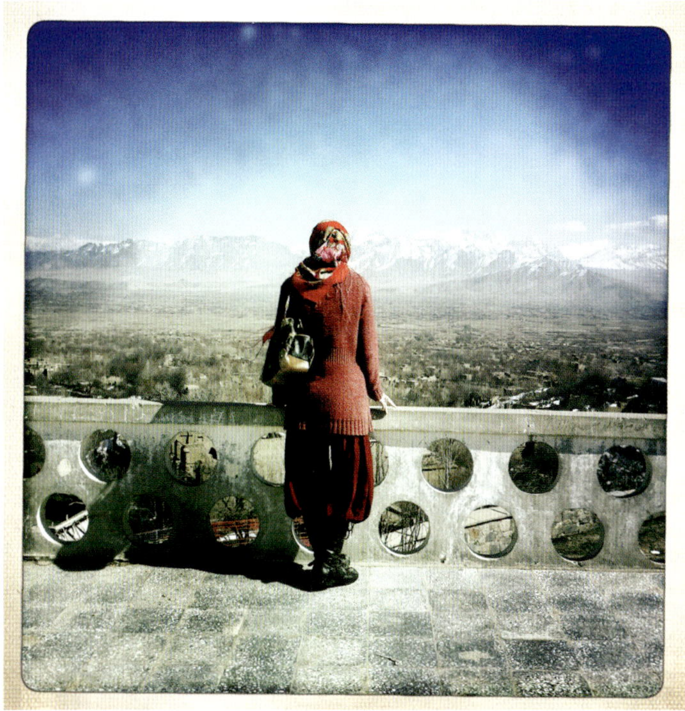

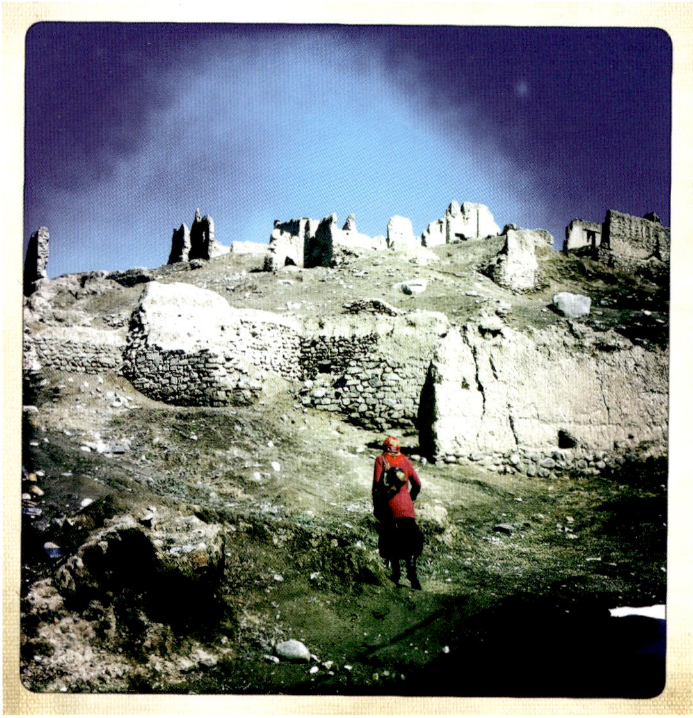